CHANGING TIMES

Toward an Integrated Approach to Reading

Lewis Levine
Lucinda S. Hughey
Hostos Community College

REGENTS/PRENTICE HALL, Englewood Cliffs, New Jersey 07632

Library of Congress Cataloging in Publication Data

LEVINE, LEWIS.
Changing times.

Includes bibliographical references.
1. College readers. I. Hughey, Lucinda S. II. Title.
PE1122.L397 1985 428.6 84-9904
ISBN 0-13-128182-8

For Bernard Levine
and
Leah S. Hughey

Editorial/production supervision and
interior design: Patricia V. Amoroso
Cover design: Joe Curcio
Manufacturing buyer: Harry P. Baisley

Printed in the United States of America

10

ISBN 0-13-128182-8

Prentice-Hall International (UK) Limited, *London*
Prentice-Hall of Australia Pty. Limited, *Sydney*
Prentice-Hall Canada Inc., *Toronto*
Prentice-Hall Hispanoamericana, S.A., *Mexico*
Prentice-Hall of India Private Limited, *New Delhi*
Prentice-Hall of Japan, Inc., *Tokyo*
Simon & Schuster Asia Pte. Ltd., *Singapore*
Editora Prentice-Hall do Brasil, Ltda., *Rio de Janeiro*

CONTENTS

2 Sex Is Not a Four-Letter Word *25*

3 Reading into It: The Medium and the Message *47*

4 Conflict in Black and White *68*

5 "I Have a Dream" *90*

6 A Partnership of Miracles *109*

7 Anatomy of a Movement *123*

INTRODUCTION

Changing Times is a reading text designed to help students acquire the basic reading and study skills necessary for success in college-level work. The book introduces selected skills through a carefully sequenced approach; each chapter builds on, and reinforces skills and vocabulary taught in, preceding chapters. The various skills presented within each chapter also complement each other.

READING SELECTIONS

The reading selections (referred to as "articles" in the text) provide students with a historical, social, and cultural context with which they can view and better understand their place within a changing society. The readings are intended to provoke active class discussion while at the same time exposing students to the kinds of themes they will encounter in college-level courses (for instance, history, sociology, psychology, science). As students gain confidence and proficiency, they are asked to deal with readings of more ample length. Most chapters contain a supplementary reading, usually in the form of a short story, a poem, or a song lyric. The supplementary readings highlight various themes and concepts introduced in the main reading selection and help students discover some of the techniques used in different styles of writing.

EXERCISES

A variety of exercises follows each main reading selection. The exercises are designed to develop and reinforce understanding of the material. Although certain types of skills are dealt with in most chapters, the exercises are presented in a varied format so that students are both challenged and given the opportunity to approach similar skills in different ways. Every class has its own set of special needs and interests. Consequently, the amount of time dedicated to each exercise will vary accordingly. Many of the exercises are designed to be introduced in class and then assigned for homework. In addition, the exercises lend themselves to use in a variety of ways: individually, in pairs, in small groups, and in a whole class.

READING COMPREHENSION

The text offers students a variety of activities and strategies to improve reading comprehension and critical thinking.

1. ***Comprehension questions:*** Each reading is followed by a set of comprehension questions which allows students to focus on the important ideas and concepts presented in the reading. The questions may be used to give students practice in writing or as the basis for class discussion.
2. ***Paragraph analysis:*** Exercises are provided to help students understand the organization and development of a writer's ideas. They stress identification of paragraph topics, stated and unstated main ideas, significant details, and determining sequence.
3. ***Seeing relationships:*** There is particular emphasis on various kinds of writing patterns and techniques commonly found in academic prose. These include
   a. Comparison/contrast
   b. Cause and effect
   c. Examples and illustrations
   d. Explanations
   e. Extended definitions
   f. Distinguishing of fact, opinion, and interpretation
   g. Analogies and figurative language
4. ***Outlining:*** Students have extensive opportunity to extract the essential information contained in each article. These outlining activities are designed to improve students' ability to classify, categorize, and paraphrase what they've read.

VOCABULARY DEVELOPMENT

The variety of strategies for developing students' vocabulary is one of the important features of the text.

1. ***Context clues:*** Students are encouraged to try to understand the meaning of unfamiliar vocabulary by analyzing the way words are used in a sentence or paragraph. Exercises for understanding vocabulary in context begin each main article, giving students practice in a particular skill and highlighting the vocabulary used in each article. A section entitled "The Reader as Detective" presents some of the types of context clues that authors use in their writing. It is suggested that this section be reviewed by students with their teacher during class time before they begin the first lesson.
2. ***Word forms:*** Students also experience how to build their vocabulary by learning to recognize and analyze the various parts of words by means of prefixes, roots, and suffixes.
3. ***Dictionary usage:*** Exercises devoted to use of an all-English dictionary appear in many of the chapters, highlighting the multiple meanings of words.

As is the case with most of the skill exercises, the vocabulary development exercises that follow each reading have a varied format. The vocabulary puzzles which appear in several of the chapters are intended to be both challenging and fun.

TOPICS FOR DISCUSSION AND COMPOSITION

Each chapter contains a series of topics that may be used as a springboard for both discussion and composition. It is hoped that these topics will provoke interest, debate, and disagreement as well as providing an opportunity for students to express and support their own views and opinions.

A NOTE OF APPRECIATION

We wish to thank our families, friends, and colleagues who gave us so much support and encouragement at so many times during the preparation of this book. Our thanks to Maria Bennett, Diana Diaz, Kathleen Kane, Cynthia Moore, Aida Ortiz-Ruiz, Phil Ross, and Fran Webb for their suggestions and advice. Special thanks to Tere Justicia, who not only recommended many of the supplementary readings that appear in this book, but who was a constant source of support and friendship. Many thanks to Kent Smith for his generous and wise counsel, to John Scarry and Lee Kirby for their advice on the publishing world, and to Pat Parzych for her special party that helped launch this project.

We also thank Terry Rodriguez, Carmen Vasquez, Phyllis Harris, and Anne Kepple, especially, for helping us prepare the manuscript. Our thanks to Earl Martin, Kathy McDowell, and Diane Beckett for putting up with us, and for helping us assemble the manuscript for use with our students.

We also wish to express our appreciation to Jon Nissenblatt, who helped get the project going, to our editor, Marianne Russell, for her continual support and patience, and to those anonymous reviewers, for all their constructive criticism.

And to our students at Hostos Community College, we thank you for your enthusiasm, your love, and your sense of urgency to learn and to grow, all of which inspired our dream and helped turn it into a reality.

CREDITS

Throughout *Changing Times* we have quoted from copyrighted material, and we are grateful to the copyright holders acknowledged below for their permission.

Woody Allen, "Examining Psychic Phenomena." Copyright © 1972 by Woody Allen. Reprinted from *Without Feathers,* by Woody Allen, by permission of Random House, Inc.

Isaac Asimov, "The Immortal Bard" copyright © 1953 by Palmer Publications, Inc. from *Earth Is Room Enough* by Isaac Asimov. Reprinted by permission of Doubleday & Company, Inc.

Russell Baker, "Back to the Dump" copyright © 1983 by The New York Times Company. Reprinted by permission.

John Collier, "The Chaser," copyright © 1940, © renewed 1967 by John Collier. Reprinted by permission of the Harold Matson Company, Inc.

Robert Frost, "The Road Not Taken," from *The Poetry of Robert Frost,* edited by Edward Connery Lathem. Copyright © 1916, © 1969 by Holt, Rinehart and Winston. Copyright © 1944 by Robert Frost. Reprinted by permission of Holt, Rinehart and Winston, Publishers.

Nikki Giovanni, last 7 lines of "Nikki-Rosa" (". . . I really hope . . . I was quite happy.") in *Black Feeling, Black Talk, Black Judgement,* by Nikki Giovanni. Copyright © 1968, 1970 by Nikki Giovanni. By permission of William Morrow & Company.

Nikki Giovanni, last stanza of "When I Die" (". . . and if ever . . . true/revolution") in *My House* by Nikki Giovanni. Copyright © 1972 by Nikki Giovanni. By permission of William Morrow & Company.

Grace Halsell, "Living as a Navajo," originally published in *The Washington Post,* July 29, 1975, p. A16. Reprinted by permission of the author.

S. Ralph Harlow, "The Mystery of Dreams" from *A Life After Death* by S. Ralph Harlow. Copyright © 1961 by S.R. Harlow and Evan Hill. Reprinted by permission of Doubleday & Company, Inc.

Langston Hughes, "Dream Deferred." Copyright © 1951 by Langston Hughes. Reprinted from *The Panther and the Lash,* by Langston Hughes, by permission of Alfred A. Knopf, Inc.

John Lennon and Paul McCartney, "When I'm Sixty-Four" copyright © 1967 by Northern Songs Limited. All rights for the U.S.A., Mexico, and the Philippines controlled by Maclen Music, Inc. c/o ATV Music Corp. Used by permission. All rights reserved.

W. Somerset Maugham, "Mr. Know-All" copyright © 1924 by W. Somerset Maugham from *The Complete Short Stories of W. Somerset Maugham.* Reprinted by permission of Doubleday & Company, Inc.

Paul Simon, "Old Friends." Copyright © 1968 by Paul Simon. Used by permission.

The authors also wish to thank the following publishers for their permission to quote from the sources listed below.

Harcourt Brace Jovanovich, Inc. for the quote from pages 187–88 of *Orlando* by Virginia Woolf.

Alfred A. Knopf for the quote from *Changing* by Liv Ullmann, copyright © 1977 by Alfred A. Knopf, Inc.

Newmarket Press for the quote from *The Words of Gandhi.*

W. W. Norton and Company, Inc. for the quote from *The Feminine Mystique* by Betty Friedan, copyright © 1963 by W. W. Norton and Company, Inc.

Simon and Shuster for the quotes from *2081,* by Gerard K. O'Neill, copyright © 1981 by Gerard K. O'Neill.

THE READER AS DETECTIVE

A reader is very much like a detective. The job of a detective is to find the solution to a problem or mystery. A good detective knows what to look for. A good detective is sensitive to the things around him or her and is able to ask intelligent and probing questions. He or she knows which clues and information in a case are important and which are not. A detective knows how to use and interpret these important clues to find a solution.

A reader has a similar job to do. A reader is also presented with information, much of it new and unfamiliar, and is expected to understand and interpret what is read. A good reader, like a good detective, knows what to look for. A good reader is able to ask intelligent, thoughtful questions before actually beginning to read. A good reader uses the title and subtitle of an article to form questions which he or she then tries to answer while reading. A good reader can tell the important ideas from the less important ones and is able to see the relationship between them.

To understand an author's ideas, the reader must also be able to understand the vocabulary an author uses. A reader will often encounter unfamiliar words while reading. Here again, the good reader learns to identify which words are essential to understanding the writer's ideas and which words are not. The good reader also knows different ways to solve the mystery of an unfamiliar word.

There are three basic ways that a reader can use to understand the meaning of an unfamiliar word. One way is to identify the structure of a word; that is, to analyze the different parts of the word (its prefix, suffix, and root). A second way is to look the word up in a dictionary. A third way, and perhaps the most important and most useful one of all, is to use the *context* of a word to understand its meaning. *Context* is the sentence or paragraph in which a word appears. Many times, the sentence or sentences around the unfamiliar word will offer an indication of, or clue to, the word's meaning. These indications or clues are referred to as *context clues.*

The following list shows some of the different kinds of context clues authors provide in their writing. After each kind of clue you will find a brief explanation and some examples.

WHAT KINDS OF CONTEXT CLUES TO LOOK FOR

1. ***Synonym or restatement clues***: Authors sometimes use another word in the same sentence or a neighboring sentence that has the *same meaning* as the unfamiliar word.

Do you know the meaning of these words: **plight, emulate, cocksure?**

Read each sentence in the following list. Try to find another word or words with the *same meaning* as the boldface word.

a. The woman found herself in a difficult situation. In fact, her **plight** was so serious that she decided to get help.
b. Children often try to **emulate** or copy the behavior that they see on television.
c. Mr. Kelada was incredibly **cocksure.** It was this excessive self-confidence that made you want to prove him wrong whenever he gave an opinion.

2. ***Comparison/contrast clues***: A sentence may contain a word that has the *opposite meaning* from the unfamiliar word. Authors sometimes use words such as *on the other hand, however, although, unlike, yet,* and *but* to alert the reader to the fact that a word with an opposite meaning is being used.

Do you know the meaning of these words: **stroll, slip, deprecating?**

Read each sentence in the next list. Try to find a word or words with an *opposite meaning* from the boldface word. What word is used to indicate an opposite meaning?

a. Some people like to walk quickly home after work, but I prefer to **stroll** home and look at the store windows along the way.
b. Although the doctor usually performed the operation perfectly, the nurse knew he had **slipped** when she saw the patient's blood pressure suddenly rise.
c. When I was a child my mother seemed to approve of almost everything I wanted to do. My father, however, always seemed to have a **deprecating** reaction to whatever I did.

3. ***Example clues:*** Authors sometimes provide specific examples to *illustrate* or explain the meaning of a word.

Do you know the meaning of these words: **detachment, demeanor, loquacious?**

Use the *examples* in each sentence to identify the meaning of the boldface word.

a. There was a kind of **detachment** about the old man's behavior. It appeared as if he didn't care what you were saying to him, as if what you were saying were of no interest to him.
b. In a battle situation he always appeared calm and relaxed. It was this calm **demeanor** that earned him the respect and admiration of the other soldiers.
c. Mr. Kelada was the most **loquacious** man I'd ever met. He talked with everyone on the ship, and he always had something to say, no matter what the topic.

4. ***Direct explanation clues***: Sometimes a writer may directly explain the meaning of a word. The author may indicate a direct explanation by using commas or parentheses. A third way may simply be to use a phrase that explain's a word's meaning.

Do you know the meaning of these words: **imperceptible, phial, siren?**

Try to find the explanation for each boldface word in the following list:

a. The powerful poison was **imperceptible** when mixed in liquid; that is, it could not be tasted, seen, or smelled.
b. From the shelf above him, the old man took down a **phial,** a small glass bottle used to keep liquids, and he placed it on the table in front of him.
c. According to ancient mythology many sailors met their deaths at sea at the hands of **sirens,** beautiful creatures who were part woman and part bird and who were able to seduce men with their singing.

5. ***Experience or situation clues***: Some words can be understood simply by the *circumstance* or *situation* in which they are used. The reader may be able to understand a word's meaning because the situation described is similar to the reader's own experience.

Do you know the meaning of these words: **creak, apprehensive, berth?**

Use the situation described in each sentence to identify the meaning of the boldface word.

a. Alan found himself on the first floor of an old, seemingly abandoned building. As he walked up to the second floor he could hear the old wooden stairs **creak** with each step he took.
b. It was the first time Nancy had been in a big city. She felt a little **apprehensive** as she walked out onto the street, with so many strange faces staring at her.
c. It was our first night on the ship. Feeling tired after a long, uneventful day at sea, I returned to my cabin, lay down on my **berth,** and quickly fell asleep.

Take a moment to review the different kinds of context clues. Learn to recognize context clues when you read. Don't be afraid to use them to help you guess the meaning of unfamiliar vocabulary. Become a good word detective. Use context clues to solve the mystery of new words.

1

MASCULINE/FEMININE: THE WAY WE WERE

Photograph by Ken Karp

Understanding Vocabulary in Context

Directions: *Read each group of sentences carefully. Then circle the one word on the left that has the same meaning as the boldface word. The first one has been done for you as an example. The boldface word in each sentence appears in the reading selection that follows this exercise.*

-opinionated -curious -passive -aggressive	1. Richard is usually very **unassertive** in class. His friend Sally, on the other hand, is totally different. She has strong opinions about almost every subject and often tries to impose her ideas on the rest of the class.
-things feared -things studied -things hoped for or anticipated	2. His parents always hoped he would be a successful doctor or lawyer after he graduated from college, but when he never finished high school, they were forced to change their **expectations.**
-conduct, actions -ideas, thoughts -needs, longings -desires, wants	3. Janet seemed so sincere when she told me she would come to visit me last weekend. However, when she never came, I realized once again how people's **behavior** does not always correspond to their good intentions.
-husband, spouse -feeling, opinion -information, news -function, use	4. They're a strange couple. Unlike her husband, who always has very positive feelings about doing new things, she has a rather negative **attitude** when it comes to trying something different.
-rules -hopes -requirements -dangers	5. Compared to the peace and quiet of the country, city life can be very hazardous. Pollution, crime, and constant traffic all pose **threats** to human health and safety.
-unfortunate, unlucky -necessary, mandatory -difficult, hard -enjoyable, pleasant	6. In most universities students are required to take a certain number of courses in specific areas of study. In some colleges it is also **compulsory** to study a foreign language for at least one year.
-unusual -uncomfortable -inescapable -unimportant	7. Most nations try to find a peaceful solution to their disputes and differences. In some cases, however, one country refuses to consider or respect the other's position, and war and violent conflict become **unavoidable.**
-vacation -salary -boss -position	8. The company gave her a new **role** in the office. She's now the office manager instead of a secretary. She supervises several other people, not just herself.
-friendly, warm -sick, ill -loyal, devoted -unhappy, sad	9. What a **faithful** husband he was! During the year before his wife's tragic death he went to visit her in the hospital virtually every day.
-exciting -interesting -helpful -incorrect, wrong	10. Tourists usually depend on a map and good directions from other people to find their way around a strange city. But sometimes they get lost when other people give them **misleading** information.
-laugh -move -cry -watch	11. As the boy watched his father's body being lowered into the ground, he suddenly realized that he would never see his father again. At first, the tears came slowly to his eyes. Then he began to **weep** uncontrollably.

Directions: *For the following sentences, write a short definition of each boldface word in the space provided.*

1. During the nineteenth century in the United States, most wealthy women who attended universities also learned **embroidery**, the art of decorating fabrics and clothes with needlework.

   Definition: ______________________________

2. In most Western countries, the adult male of the family has usually been the **breadwinner**, that is, the provider of material goods necessary for survival.

   ____

Masculine/Feminine: The Way We Were

(1) What do you think of when you hear the word *masculine*? If you are like most people, you probably see someone who is strong, tough, aggressive, competitive, competent, and self-confident. Or maybe other qualities come to mind such as logical, rational, self-controlled, experienced, serious. If you were to try to write the opposite for all these words you might make a list like this: weak, delicate, passive, unassertive, helpless, illogical, irrational, unstable, innocent, flighty. Add to this list of opposites the following words: beautiful, soft, gentle, loving, tender, faithful. What name would you give your list? Remember, your list of words is the opposite of all those masculine qualities. The opposite of masculine is. . . . That's right. Your list of opposites could easily be a traditional description of the word "feminine."

(2) Take a moment to reexamine those qualities associated with "masculinity." Compare them with the list of opposite words—those so-called "feminine" qualities. What would you prefer to be: strong or weak, competent or helpless, logical or illogical, rational or irrational? Which qualities seem positive to you? Which ones negative? Which qualities do you consider superior? Which ones inferior? Most likely, the "masculine" qualities seem positive and superior, the "feminine" qualities negative and inferior. Yet these have been the ideas that many people have associated with masculinity and femininity.

(3) These traditional attitudes of what is "masculine" and what is "feminine" have strongly influenced the behavior of both men and women. Because women have had less physical strength than men, women were thought of as "the weaker sex." It was also considered "weak" to openly express emotions such as suffering, fear, or anxiety. Consequently, it was acceptable for women, "the weaker sex," to show their emotions freely and openly in much the same way as children do. They were free to cry whenever a sad or tragic event occurred. It was considered perfectly normal for them to weep at the end of a sad movie. They were able to openly admit that they were nervous or afraid. For men, however, this was not the case. If a man wanted to appear "strong" and "masculine," he could not show fear or sorrow; that would have been a sign of weakness or vulnerability.

(4) There are numerous other examples of how these conventional attitudes about the two sexes have helped determine our actions. Take relationships, for instance. It was usually a man who initiated a relationship with a woman. He was the aggressor. He was invariably the one who asked a woman

to go out on a date. It would not have been proper for a woman to invite a man. Instead, she was supposed to wait until a man invited her. It would not have been very "ladylike" to do otherwise. Even in conversation, men and women were expected to behave differently. It was perfectly acceptable for a man to assert his opinion when in mixed company. A woman, on the other hand, was expected to assume a quiet, more passive role in the conversation. Like children in adult company, women were expected "to be seen, not heard."

"A WOMAN'S PLACE IS IN THE HOME"

(5) These differences in attitudes and behavior have existed for so long that we cannot know when they actually originated. In order to preserve and perpetuate the human race, men and women have had specific yet different functions in society. These different roles of men and women, commonly referred to as *sexual division of labor,* have had a strong impact and influence on family life. In most Western countries the male has been responsible for the support and protection of the family. He was expected to earn the money to buy food, clothing, and shelter for his family. He was the "breadwinner," the provider of the material goods necessary for survival. The woman, meanwhile, remained at home to raise the children. She was expected to prepare the food, clean the house, wash the clothes, and maintain harmony in the home. When her husband returned from a hard day at his job, she was supposed to be there waiting to comfort him and take care of his needs. That too was part of her "job."

(6) Different attitudes and expectations also existed regarding education for males and females. Even as public education became compulsory for all children in the United States, people continued to think of education for women as "unnecessary" or "frivolous." In the nineteenth century, for instance, a college education was generally available only to women from rich families. But even those wealthy, privileged women received instruction only in certain areas such as music, foreign languages, and embroidery. In fact, many people didn't want women to receive any formal education at all. Some even believed that if a woman were too well educated she might actually lose the biological ability to bear children. Women with a high level of education were sometimes referred to as "enemies" of humanity and were considered a threat to the future existence of the human species. Even in more recent times, parents and teachers have had different expectations for boys than for girls. It was "unfeminine" for girls to be too intellectual or competitive in school. As a result, many girls deliberately tried *not* to do well in their schoolwork for fear of appearing too "masculine." Moreover, many parents did not encourage their daughters to continue their education past high school. After all, parents thought, why waste so much time and money on a college education; women are only going to be housewives anyway.

(7) Of course it would be misleading to say that all women remained at home. Some did hold other jobs. Prior to the 1960s, most of these women worked as nurses, nursery and elementary school teachers, waitresses, and secretaries. It's not difficult to understand why if you examine the characteristics of these jobs; all involve the care of people in some way. The nurse takes care of the sick and assists the doctor, usually a man. The secretary assists her boss, also a man in most cases. The nursery and elementary school teacher takes care of children. The waitress serves people food. The conclusion seems unavoidable: The salaried jobs that most women did in the past were merely extensions of the work that they were expected to perform at home. Thus, even for women who worked outside the home, the old expression "A woman's place is in the home" still rang true.

Comprehension Questions

1. Why were women considered the "weaker sex"?
2. In what way did society permit women to behave like children?
3. If a man publicy expressed feelings of fear or sorrow, what did that signify to most people?
4. What were people's reactions if a woman invited a man to go out on a date?
5. Explain in your own words the following expressions:

   a. " 'Women were expected to be seen, not heard.' "
   b. "sexual division of labor"
6. In the nineteenth century, how were wealthy women different from most other women? How were they different from well-educated men of that time?
7. During the nineteenth century, why did some people consider well-educated women to be " 'enemies' of humanity" and "a threat to the future existence of the human species"?
8. Why were many girls *not* encouraged to continue their education after they completed high school?
9. What conclusion does the article make about women's work *in* and *out* of the home?
10. What examples are given to support this conclusion?

Topics for Discussion and Composition

1. Do you agree with the information presented in the article? Give reasons for your answer.
2. Man for the field and woman for the hearth
   Man for the sword and for the needle she
   Man with the head and woman with the heart
   Man to command and woman to obey;
   All else confusion.

   —ALFRED, LORD TENNYSON, nineteenth-century English poet, from *The Princess* [1847], song, *O Swallow.*

   How does Tennyson see the roles of men and women? Do you agree with him?
3. To be a woman is to have the same needs and longings as a man. We need love and we wish to give it. If only we could all accept that there is no difference between us where human values are concerned. Whatever sex. Whatever the life we have chosen to live.

   —LIV ULLMANN, actress, author of *Changing*

   What is Ullman saying about the roles of men and women? Do you agree with her?

4. A girl should not expect special privileges because of her sex, but neither should she "adjust" to prejudice and discrimination. She must learn to compete . . . not as a woman, but as a human being.
   —BETTY FRIEDAN, *The Feminine Mystique,* 1963

   What would Ms. Friedan say about Tennyson's ideas? About Ullmann's ideas?

5. Do you agree with the idea that women are the "weaker" sex?

6. How do you know if a man is strong? How do you know if a woman is strong? What differences, if any, are there between a strong man and a strong woman?

7. Do you think that a woman should invite a man to go out on a date with her? Why or why not? When is it acceptable for a woman to invite a man?

8. Who should pay when a man and woman go out on a date for the first time?

9. "A woman without a man cannot meet a man, any man, of any age, without thinking, even if it's for a half-second, "Perhaps this is *the* man."—DORIS LESSING, *The Golden Notebook*

   What do you think of Lessing's statement? Do you think men also feel this way in the same situation? What do you think about when you meet a man or woman?

10. In your family, what kind of division of labor exists? What role does each person have? Is each person's role based on his or her sex? Explain.

11. Do you consider the work of a housewife a "real" job? Why or why not?

12. Should women receive a salary for their work in the home? If yes, who should pay it?

Paragraph Analysis: Identifying Paragraph Topics

Every well-written paragraph has a topic. The topic tells what the entire paragraph is about. Usually the topic is only a phrase, not a complete sentence. The phrase can be long or short. The important thing is that the phrase include the principal subjects of the entire paragraph. These principal subjects form the topic of the paragraph. Is the paragraph about "Problems," "Television Movies," "Places to Visit in Your Community"? The topic gives you a *general* answer to these kinds of questions.

Directions: *Identify the topic of each paragraph at the beginning of chapter 1. Remember the topic should contain the important subjects of the entire paragraph, not just part of it. You will probably need to reread the paragraphs. Put a check (✓) next to the phrase that you think is the best choice for the topic of each paragraph. The first one has been done for you as an example.*

Paragraph 1.

_____ The Importance of Being Strong, Competent, and Self-Confident
__✓__ Traditional Qualities for the Words *Masculine* and *Feminine*
_____ Why Masculine Qualities Are Better than Feminine Qualities

Paragraph 2.
_____ How to Make a List of Feminine Qualities
_____ People's Associations with Masculine and Feminine Qualities
_____ Negative Associations with Masculinity

Paragraph 3.
_____ Tragic Events in Life
_____ Influence of Traditional Attitudes on Behavior
_____ Why Men Don't Cry in Public
_____ Why Women Can Show Fear and Sorrow

Paragraph 4.
_____ Opinions of Men and Women in Conversation
_____ The Passive Role of Women in Relationships
_____ How Attitudes Influence Behavior
_____ Aggressive Men

Paragraph 5.
_____ Women's Work in the Home
_____ What All People Need for Survival
_____ Sexual Division of Labor

Paragraph 6.
_____ The Importance of a College Education in the Nineteenth Century
_____ Why Wealthy Women Studied Music and Language
_____ The Relationship between Sex and Levels of Education

Paragraph 7.
_____ Why Women Have Not Remained at Home
_____ Elementary School Teachers
_____ What Nurses Do to Help Doctors and Patients
_____ Similarities between Work of Women in and out of the Home

Seeing Relationships: Comparison/Contrast

Comparatively Speaking: Many times an idea is best understood when it is compared with something else. Often authors will intentionally compare one idea with another in order to clarify or emphasize a particular idea or point of view. Authors often use specific words to inform or alert the reader that they are using a *comparison/contrast* relationship. Listed next are some words used to indicate similarities and differences.

Words that Indicate Similarities	Words that Indicate Differences
-similar, same, alike	-different, dissimilar
-both, together	-however, but, yet, unlike
-likewise, similarly	-on the other hand, by contrast
	-although, whereas, while
	-more, less

Directions: *Use the information presented in the article to help you make the following comparisons between the two sexes:*

	Males	Females
Qualities Traditionally Associated with Each Sex	1. ______	1. ______
	2. ______	2. ______
	3. ______	3. ______
	4. ______	4. ______
	5. ______	5. ______
	6. ______	6. ______
	7. ______	7. ______
	8. ______	8. ______
How Each Sex Was Expected to Behave in Public	1. ______	1. ______
	2. ______	2. ______
	3. ______	3. ______
Traditional Role of Each Sex in the Family	1. ______	1. ______
	2. ______	2. ______
Parents' Expectations for Education of Each Sex	1. ______	1. ______
	2. ______	2. ______

Vocabulary Development

Directions: *Match these synonyms and antonyms to the vocabulary on the left of the following list. The first one has been done as an example.*

Synonyms: rational, warm, capable, gentle, pretty, loyal, powerful, rugged, self-assured, ladylike, responsive, worldly

Antonyms: rough, masculine, delicate, insecure, ugly, weak, innocent, helpless, unfaithful, insensitive, illogical, unfriendly.

Vocabulary Word	Synonym	Antonym
1. strong	*powerful*	*weak*
2. logical		
3. tough		
4. experienced		
5. competent		
6. self-confident		
7. faithful		
8. beautiful		

9. tender ______ ______
10. feminine ______ ______
11. friendly ______ ______
12. sensitive ______ ______

Class Activity: *In the space provided, make a list of the qualities you think an ideal man and an ideal woman should have. Use vocabulary words from the exercise you just completed. Add your own words also. Compare your list with those of other members of your class. You may want to do this activity in small groups.*

Ideal Man		**Ideal Woman**	
______	______	______	______
______	______	______	______
______	______	______	______
______	______	______	______
______	______	______	______
______	______	______	______
______	______	______	______

For Discussion: Do you think such a person actually exists?

Denotations and Connotations

Although many words have synonyms (other words with similar meanings), no two words are exactly the same. It's true that dictionaries give us the specific meanings of words. For example, the word *woman* means a *person of the female sex.* This definition is referred to as the *denotation* of the word, that is, what the word means literally.

However, words can also evoke or produce emotions in people. Take the word *doctor,* for instance. One person may immediately associate the word with feelings of pain and anxiety, remembering an unpleasant visit to a doctor's office or hospital. Another person may have very positive associations with the word *doctor.* For that person, a doctor may be someone who is gentle and supportive or someone who once helped save a life or alleviated pain. Thus, how we react to a word depends on our own previous experience with the word. The feeling associated with a word is called the word's *connotation.* A connotation is *not* what the word means literally, but rather the emotion or image that the word produces in us. Some words evoke the same feelings in almost everyone who hears them, for example, dentist, weak, warm.

Let's return to the word *woman,* which has several synonyms: female, lady, dame. Each synonym, although similar, is *not* exactly the same as *woman.* In the United States, the word *dame* refers to a woman, but it's a word that indicates little respect. In Great Britain, on the other hand, *dame* can also be the title given to a woman to recognize or honor her talent and achievement. Compare the use of the word *dame* in these two sentences:

1. **Dame** Joan Sutherland is one of the most respected and admired opera singers in the world.
2. When my friend spotted a pretty **dame** walking in the street he called to her, "Hey baby, why don't you come over here and give me a kiss?"

Directions: *In these sentences, pay special attention to the boldface words. What are the connotations of each word? Some words may seem positive, negative, or neutral; others formal or informal. What associations or feelings does each word have for you?*

1. I met an **old man** in the park. I met an **old guy** in the park.
   I met an **elderly gentleman** in the park.
2. Margaret has been our **housekeeper** for ten years.
   Margaret has been our **servant** for ten years.
3. **Make a list** of the words you don't know.
   Maintain a record of the words you don't know.
4. She was **shocked** by the news. She was **surprised** by the news.
5. He spoke to his wife in an **assertive** way. He spoke to his wife in an **aggressive** way.
6. Compare these two newspaper headlines about the same event. How does each headline make you feel about the event?
   "Diet Doc's Maid Kept Secret List of Lovers"
   "Doctor's Housekeeper Kept Record of House Guests"

Vocabulary Development

Directions: *Use each of these words to complete the sentences that follow.*

wealthy	impact	unavoidable	arrangement
compulsory	instead	sorrow	behavior
proper	shelter	otherwise	threat

1. The teacher told the child's parents she wasn't happy with his ____________________ in class.
2. I don't want any coffee, but I would like a glass of milk ____________________ .
3. We were walking in the park when suddenly it began to rain quite hard. Luckily, we didn't get wet. We were able to find ____________________ nearby.
4. The attitudes of people usually have a strong influence or ____________________ on their behavior.
5. The bank refused to cash her check because she didn't have ____________________ identification.
6. There's an expression that says that only two things in life are ____________________: death and taxes.
7. On the first day of class our teacher said that he expected us to complete all assignments on time and that class attendance was also ____________________ .
8. Although his parents were very poor, he's a ____________________ man, having earned a fortune in the construction business.
9. Nuclear war is perhaps the single greatest ____________________ to our survival on this planet.
10. After his wife died, he was filled with a feeling of great ____________________ .
11. My friend offered to help me learn Spanish if I would help her learn English. That sounds like a fair ____________________ .
12. She needs to practice more. ____________________, she'll never learn how to speak English properly.

Directions: *Use each verb listed to complete the sentences that follow.*

earn	provide
raise	weep
remain	waste
perform	admit

1. Children depend on their parents to ____________________ them with food, clothing, and shelter.

2. He needs to ______________________ a higher salary if he expects to get enough money to buy a new car.

3. Single parents find themselves in the difficult situation of having to ______________________ their children alone.

4. She always feels the need to be doing something. She claims that it's because she doesn't like to ______________________ time.

5. You can leave if you want, but I prefer to ______________________ here for awhile.

6. Although I don't really like her, I must ______________________ that she's very intelligent and competent.

7. The supervisor threatened to fire all the employees if they didn't ______________________ their work properly.

8. He began to ______________________ uncontrollably when he learned that his father had died.

Directions: *Complete this list of sentences using the following expressions. Change the form of the verb where necessary.*

to take care of	to come to mind	division of labor
to be likely to	to have a choice	to assert an opinion

1. The radio report predicted terrible weather for today. They said that it ______________________ rain sometime this afternoon.

2. Our family ______________________ to make. For our summer vacation we can either remain in the city or go on a camping trip.

3. We're trying to think of an answer to the problem but no solution ______________________ .

4. My brother-in-law ______________________ even when he knows nothing about the subject being discussed.

5. Their family has an interesting arrangement. The mother works in an office while the father remains home and ______________________ the children.

6. A father who cooks and a mother who washes the dishes is a simple example of ______________________ .

Word Forms

The Prefix: A prefix is a group of letters that comes *before* a root word and changes the meaning of the word. The following prefixes can all be used to form the negative of each root word:

Prefix		Root Word		New Word	Meaning
un	+	stable	=	unstable	not stable
il	+	legal	=	illegal	not legal
ir	+	rational	=	irrational	not rational
in	+	justice	=	injustice	no justice
im	+	possible	=	impossible	not possible
dis	+	agree	=	disagree	not agree
non	+	essential	=	nonessential	not essential

Spelling Note: It is sometimes necessary to use the dictionary to determine which prefix to use before a word. However, there are some general rules you can follow.

1. The prefix "im" usually comes before words beginning with the letters "b," "m," and "p."
   (Examples: imbalance, immodest, imperfect)
2. The prefix "il" is only used before a word beginning with the letter "l."
   (Examples: illegal, illogical.)
3. The prefix "ir" is only used before a word beginning with the letter "r."
   (Examples: irrational, irresponsible.)

   However, other prefixes can sometimes be used before words beginning with the letters "l" and "r," depending on the words.
   (Examples: disloyal, unreasonable.)
   You *cannot* say *illoyal* or *irreasonable*.

Directions: *Change the following words to the negative by using a prefix. Use a dictionary to check your spelling.*

1. moral IMMORAL
2. competent INCOMPETENT
3. logical ILLOGICAL
4. employment UNEMPLOYMENT
5. prepared UNPREPARED
6. advantage DISADVANTAGE
7. regular IRREGULAR
8. human INHUMAN
9. patient IMPATIENT
10. respectful DISRESPECTFUL
11. proper IMPROPER
12. equality INEQUALITY
13. perfect IMPERFECT
14. assertive UNASSERTIVE
15. usual UNUSUAL

Directions: *Use these prefixes to complete the words in the following sentences.*

un **il** **ir** **in** **im** **dis** **non**

Example: You did not obey the law. Your actions were __il__ legal.

1. She is not very warm with other people. In fact, she is rather ______ friendly.

2. You never know if he's going to come on time. He's such an ______ responsible person.

3. In India, many people can neither read nor write. They are ______ literate.

4. He's not loyal to his wife. He's an ______ faithful husband.

5. Because of her ______ experience, she had a difficult time finding a job.

6. Some adults act more like children than grown-ups. They are very ______ mature.

7. He never listens to his parents. He ______ obeys them all the time.

8. She doesn't care about the feelings of other people. She's an ______ sensitive person.

9. They ______ like staying out when they have to get up early for work the next day.

10. They are ______ able to go to the movies because they have to study for an exam.

11. The demonstration was peaceful. People protested in a ______ violent way.

12. He was fired from his job because of his poor performance and ______ proper conduct.

Directions: *Complete each of the following groups of sentences by using the correct form of each word given in the word form list. Be sure that the number of each word form corresponds to the number of the sentence. Change the form of the verb when necessary. The first item has been done as an example.*

Noun	Verb	Adjective	Adverb
1. strength	strengthen	strong	strongly
2. weakness	weaken	weak	weakly
3. sadness	sadden	sad	sadly
4. threat	threaten	threatening	threateningly
5. protection	protect	protective	protectively
6. expression	express	expressive	expressively
7. action	act	active	actively
8. support	support	supportive	supportively
9. comfort	comfort	comfortable	comfortably
10. love	love	loving	lovingly

1. Although most women still have less physical ______ *strength* ______ than men, that doesn't prevent them from having ______ *strong* ______ opinions on a subject.

2. It was tragic to see how ____________ the man had become. It was clear that his illness had ____________ him greatly.

3. The old woman spoke so ____________ about her life that I too began to feel ____________ .

4. Even though the young man made a ____________ gesture with his knife, I knew that his ____________ to kill me came more out of fear than any real intent.

5. Birth control ____________ women from getting pregnant. Of course not everyone believes that this kind of ____________ should be used.

6. The ____________ of emotions was expected to be different for men and women. Women were allowed to ____________ their feelings more openly.

7. Although my friend is ____________ looking for a job, she ____________ as if she doesn't even care if she finds one.

8. There are different kinds of ____________ that people can give. Economic ____________ involves giving money to assist another person. Emotional ____________ usually

means that one person ____________ another by giving encouragement and hope.

9. It's a __Comfort__ for him to know that his retired parents are living __comfortly__ in Florida.

10. __Love__ parents try to give their children as much __Love__, comfort and support as possible.

MAKING GENERALIZATIONS ABOUT WORD FORMS

Directions: *Refer back to the part of the word form list indicated in the directions that follow. Try to identify how the indicated group of words is similar. Then complete the statements that follow. The first one has been done as an example.*

1. Refer to the verbs in items 1–4. These four verbs all end in the suffix ___*en*___. The suffix *en* indicates that a word is a ___*verb*___. To form the verb the suffix *en* is sometimes added to either a ___*noun*___ or an ___*adjective*___.

2. Refer to the nouns in items 5–7. These three nouns end in the suffix ____________. The suffix *ion* indicates that a word is a ____________. To form the noun, the suffix ____________ is added to a ____________.

3. Refer to the adjectives in items 5–8. These four adjectives end in the suffix ____________. The suffix ____________ indicates that a word is an ____________. To form an adjective, the suffix ____________ is added to a ____________.

4. Refer to the verbs and the nouns in items 8–10. In these cases, both the verbs and the nouns have the same ____________.

5. Refer to the adjectives and adverbs in items 1–10. In every case except one, the adverb is formed by adding the suffix ____________ to the adjectival form of the word.

Dictionary Skills: Multiple Definitions

Directions: *Many words in English have more than one meaning. The meaning of a word depends on how it's used in a sentence. First, look carefully at the different definitions of each of the words listed in this exercise. Second, read the sentences that follow. Then write the correct dictionary definition of the boldface word in the space provided. The first item has been done as an example.*

bear (bâr) *v.* **bore, borne,** or **born, bearing.** 1. To carry; support. 2. To endure: tolerate. 3. To have; show; exhibit. 4. To give birth to. 5. To produce; yield. 6. To proceed in a specified direction, (*bear* right).

1. During the nineteenth century some people actually believed that too much education would interfere with a woman's biological ability to **bear** children.
   4. to give birth to
2. The company claims that it doesn't **bear** any responsibility for any items lost or stolen on its premises.
   ____
3. He avoids going to hospitals because he can't **bear** to see people suffering.
   ____

call (kôl) *v.* 1. To say in a loud tone; shout; announce. 2. To summon; to ask to come. 3. To name; to give a name to. 4. To telephone. 5. To consider; evaluate. 6. To stop; cancel.

4. At the doctor's office a nurse usually **calls** the patients when the doctor is ready to see them.
   ____
5. The teams **called** the game because of the heavy rains.
   ____
6. On his birth certificate his name is Robert, but all his friends **call** him "Bob."
   ____
7. Richard **called** to his friends who were walking down the street, but they were too far away to hear.
   ____
8. The baseball manager **called** the young player the best pitcher he had seen in the last ten years.
   ____
9. Since my sister moved to Texas I don't get to see her very often. I like to **call** her every few weeks to see how she's doing.
   ____

care (kâr) *n.* 1. Worry, anxiety; mental distress. 2. Close attention; caution; watchfulness. 3. Supervision; charge; custody.

10. The artist painted with great **care**, making sure to reproduce each line exactly as it appeared.

____

11. The man finished all his work and was now ready to enjoy his vacation. He felt as if he didn't have a **care** in the world.

____

12. The child will need an operation to correct her sight. Fortunately, she is in the **care** of an excellent doctor.

____

extension (ĕk-stĕn′ shən) ***n.*** (*extensio* past participle of *extendere*) **1.** An extending or being extended. **2.** An extended part; continuation; addition: as in *an extension to a factory.* **3.** A branch of a university for students who cannot attend the main part of the university. **4.** An extra telephone connected to the same line as the main telephone. **5.** An extra period of time.

13. My neighbors needed more space, so they built an **extension** onto their house.

____

14. The professor gave the students an **extension** because everyone complained that the assignment was too difficult.

____

15. Most big companies have an **extension** in every office.

____

16. Some urban colleges are trying to establish **extensions** in the suburbs.

____

17. The salaried jobs most women did in the past were merely **extensions** of the jobs they performed in the home.

____

support *v.* **1.** To bear the weight of, especially from below. **2.** To provide for or maintain by providing money. **3.** To corroborate or substantiate; to prove. **4.** To help the cause of by approving, favoring, or advocating. **5.** To endure; to tolerate; to put up with.

18. Whenever you express your personal point of view in a composition, it's important to give specific information that **supports** your opnion.

____

19. He's been working at two different jobs in order to **support** his family.

____

20. Long steel cables serve to **support** famous suspension bridges such as San Francisco's Golden Gate.

____

21. It's obvious she **supports** the president since she's always saying positive things about his policies.

____

Classifying and Categorizing Information

Exercise A: *Arrange the following activities in the appropriate categories:*

watch television	write a composition	pass exams
buy food	attend classes	wash dishes
complete homework	go to the movies	clean the bedroom
wash clothes	attend a concert	play in the park

Domestic Activities	School Activities	Recreational Activities
1. ____________	1. ____________	1. ____________
2. ____________	2. ____________	2. ____________
3. ____________	3. ____________	3. ____________
4. ____________	4. ____________	4. ____________

Exercise B: *In the following series of words, circle the one word that does not belong with the other words in the same group. In the space provided, write a title that explains why the other three words belong together. The first item has been done for you. Note: There is more than one correct answer to some of these items. It depends on the title you choose to give each group.*

1. family members
   father
   doctor (circled)
   mother
   sister

2. ____________
   meat
   potatoes
   rice
   table

3. ____________
   red
   large
   small
   tall

4. ____________
   rain
   sun
   mountain
   wind

5. ____________
   Bolivia
   France
   Ecuador
   Colombia

6. ____________
   Washington
   Lincoln
   Hitler
   Kennedy

7. ____________
   Jefferson
   Roosevelt
   Nixon
   Kennedy

8. ____________
   food
   television
   shelter
   clothing

9. ____________
   cook food
   wash clothes
   go to movies
   clean house

10. ____________
    swimming
    music
    football
    volleyball

11. ____________
    baseball
    basketball
    boxing
    tennis

12. ____________
    schoolteacher
    nurse
    waitress
    engineer

13. ____________
    illegal
    impossible
    happy
    insensitive

14. ____________
    elect
    extension
    protection
    expression

15. ____________
    table of contents
    index
    title page
    introduction

How the Ethiopian Woman Tamed Her Husband

MURAD KAMEL

Once there was a woman who was greatly troubled by her husband. He no longer loved her. He neglected her and seemed to care little whether she was happy or sad.

So the woman took her troubles to the local witchdoctor. She told him her story, full of pity for herself and her sad plight. "Can you give me a charm to make him love me again?" she asked anxiously.

The witchdoctor thought for a moment and replied, "I will help you, but first you must bring to me three hairs from the mane of a living lion. These I must have before I can make the charm for you."

The woman thanked the witchdoctor and went away. When she came near to her home she sat down on a rock and began to think, "How shall I do this thing? There is a lion who comes often near to my village, it is true. But he is fierce and roars fearfully." Then she thought again and at last she knew what she would do.

And so, rising early next morning she took a young lamb and went to the place where the lion was accustomed to stroll about. She waited anxiously. At last she saw the lion approaching. Now was the time. Quickly she rose and, leaving the lamb in the path of the lion, she went home. And so it was that every day early in the morning the woman would arise and take a young lamb to the lion. Soon the lion came to know the woman, for she was always in the same place at the same time every day with a young and tender lamb, which she brought for his pleasure. She was indeed a kind and attentive woman.

It was not long before the lion began to wag his tail each time he saw her and coming close to her he would let her stroke his head and soothe his back. And each day the woman would stay quietly stroking the lion, gently and lovingly. Then one day when she knew that the lion trusted her she carefully pulled three hairs from his mane and happily set out for the witchdoctor's dwelling.

"See," she said triumphantly as she entered, "here they are!" And she gave him the three hairs from the lion's mane.

"How is it you have been so clever?" asked the witchdoctor in amazement.

And so the woman told him the story of how she had patiently won the hairs from the lion.

A smile spread over the face of the witchdoctor and, leaning forward, he said, "In the same way that you have tamed the lion, so may you tame your husband."

QUESTIONS

1. Why did the woman go to the witch doctor?
2. What did the witch doctor tell her to do? Why do you think he asked her to do this instead of simply advising her to deal directly with her husband?
3. How did the woman accomplish the assignment? What kind of person do you think the woman was?
4. What do you think the lamb represents? The lion? What qualities are associated with each of these animals?

5. What do you think the message of this story is? What lesson is being communicated?
6. Compare the message of this story to the ideas presented in the article at the beginning of this chapter. What similarities and differences do you see between the two?
7. The story "How the Ethiopian Woman Tamed Her Husband" is an example of a folktale. What elements does a folktale have that make it different from other kinds of stories?
8. How do folktales influence people?

Directions: *In the space provided, write the one word or phrase from the right-hand column that has the same meaning as the word on the left. Do not use a dictionary; refer to the story.*

1. mane	____________	not pay attention to
2. fierce	____________	answer
3. neglect	____________	residence
4. troubles	____________	move back and forth
5. plight	____________	great surprise
6. approach	____________	go in the direction of
7. wag	____________	problems
8. stroke	____________	wild
9. set out for	____________	intelligent
10. dwelling	____________	come near
11. amazement	____________	situation
12. clever	____________	caress
13. reply	____________	long hair located on the neck of an animal

2

SEX IS NOT A FOUR-LETTER WORD

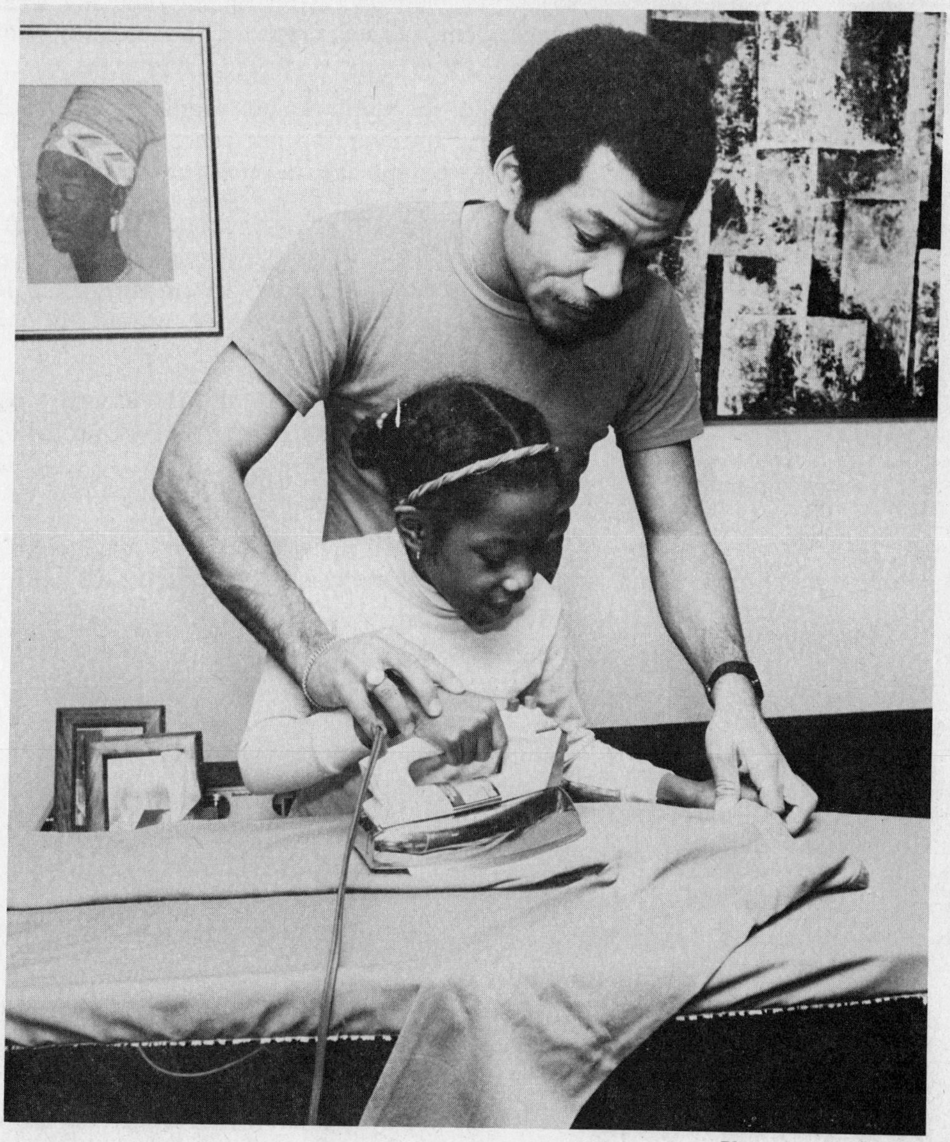

Photograph by Ken Karp

Understanding Vocabulary in Context

Directions: *Read each group of sentences carefully. Then circle the one word on the left that has the same meaning as the boldface word. The boldface word in each sentence appears in the reading section that follows this exercise.*

—obvious
—wonderful
—unimaginable
—easy

1. All my life I had always assumed that my aunt and uncle had a happy, loving relationship. When I learned that they were actually getting divorced, it seemed **inconceivable** to me.

—conscious of
—ignorant of
—confused about
—angry about

2. Television, magazines, and other forms of mass media have done much to increase people's understanding of health care. One consequence of the mass media's influence is that people today are more **aware of** of the importance of proper diet and nutrition.

—very angry
—very interested
—very curious
—very surprised

3. Our professor rarely gets upset or angry in class. That's why we were all so surprised and shocked when she suddenly became **outraged** just because one student had not prepared the lesson.

—threat
—possible ability
—excuse
—solution

4. As a child, the world-famous pianist demonstrated incredible talent as a musician. However, it took years of dedication and practice for him to realize his **potential** as a musician.

—cooperation
—satisfaction
—confusion
—unhappiness

5. As a little girl growing up in the mountains of Appalachia, she had always dreamed of becoming a lawyer someday. Thus, it was with a great feeling of pride and **fulfillment** that she entered the courtroom to argue her first case.

—equality
—prevention
—university
—status

6. It's often believed that people who attend famous universities, such as Harvard and Princeton, have a better chance of getting a job with a good salary and high **prestige**.

something that is
—hard to do
—easy to do
—dangerous

7. In 1945, the war-torn nations of the world faced a great **challenge**: to rebuild their countries and restore people's confidence in both themselves and the future.

—happy period
—unpopular war
—new information
—violent change

8. For many Americans, the 1960s will be remembered as a time of great **upheaval**. As an unpopular war raged in Southeast Asia, the youth of the country demonstrated to end the war and experimented with drugs and alternate life-styles.

feeling of
—hate
—distrust
—respect
—doubt

9. Many psycholgists claim that self-**esteem**, a person's feeling of respect toward himself, is one of the most important qualities that a person can possess.

—follow
—avoid
—dislike
—eliminate

10. Although he had a high-paying position with a great deal of status, he suddenly decided to quit his job in order to **pursue** a career in a completely different field.

11. In recent years there have been several major **trends** in education. One **trend** is toward increased emphasis on mastering the basic skills such as reading, writing, and math. Another **trend** is toward offering courses in computer technology in more schools.

—tendency
—university
—truth
—topic

12. Traditions in some countries have remained the same for many centuries, while in other nations local customs seem to **alter** constantly, so that a visitor never knows what to expect.

—stay the same
—change
—visit
—expect

13. During the war in Vietnam, the U.S. maintained a military force in that Asian country for more than ten years, but in 1974 the American government **withdrew** its soldiers from that war-torn nation.

—maintained
—destroyed
—paid
—removed

14. Children **rely on** their parents to take care of their physical needs. They also depend on their parents to help them with problems.

—play with
—listen to
—depend on
—observe

15. Children often **take for granted** their parents' efforts to take care of them, that is, they consider their parents' work as something natural and expected.

—dislike
—enjoy
—try to be careful
—think of as natural

Focusing Your Attention

The next chapter is concerned with the *changing role of women in American society.* What do you think the article will talk about? Write down at least five questions related to this topic. Then read the article to see how many of your questions have been answered.

Sex Is Not a Four-Letter Word

I love there being two sexes, don't you?—JAMES THURBER (1894–1961)

(1) In recent years the roles of men and woman have changed dramatically in the United States. In business, education, politics, and sports, women's presence is being felt in ways that would have seemed inconceivable only two or three decades ago. This relatively new and widespread participation by women has often been referred to as the "Women's Liberation Movement." Supporters of "Women's Lib" have tried to show that the traditional attitudes about masculinity and femininity are neither valid nor beneficial to either sex. Men and women, they believe, should have equal opportunities to develop the qualities and skills of each other's traditional domain. For women, this means adequate recognition of their contributions and equal opportunity to work, study, and improve themselves. For men, this means the freedom to express

their feelings more openly, without having to worry about appearing "weak" or "unmasculine." Men are encouraged to share more equally the responsibility of raising children and taking care of the home. "Women's Lib" has caused millions of people to reexamine their attitudes about masculinity and femininity. For millions of others, it has resulted in a whole new consciousness regarding the roles of men and women in society.

(2) Trying to understand the causes of any great social change is never an easy task. The forces of change are usually so varied and complex that they seem to collide together like the great waves of an ocean storm. For many social observers, the "Women's Lib Movement" has its roots in *other* social movements in the United States. As early as the 1950s, organized efforts to improve opportunities for black people in the United States began to spread. By the 1960s these attempts escalated into a widespread movement of social protest (the Civil Rights Movement). Later, in the late 1960s and early 1970s, many people, outraged by the killing of innocent and defenseless people in Vietnam, protested the involvement of United States citizens in another country's civil war (the Peace Movement). Both the Civil Rights Movement and the Peace Movement brought about important social and political changes. In 1964 the United States government changed many of its laws in an effort to ensure better economic and educational opportunities for blacks, which included passing the Civil Rights Act of 1964. In 1974, more than ten years after the first American soldier was sent to Vietnam, the government finally withdrew the last of its military forces from that country.

(3) Many women participated in those efforts to abolish the injustices of racial discrimination and inhuman violence. Women helped in numerous ways: they organized political demonstrations and meetings, they wrote letters to government leaders, they spoke to friends, neighbors, and strangers. Their political protest produced two important results. First, women realized more clearly than ever before that society (dominated by men) discriminated against them in many of the same ways it discriminated against blacks and other minority groups. They saw how society did not offer women equal opportunity and access to many areas of American life. Many women felt that their work in the home went unappreciated and that their husbands took their contributions for granted. Second, women saw the positive effects that organization and unity could produce. Many women began to unite and organize themselves. They formed "consciousness-raising" groups where they discussed their mutual problems and examined possible solutions. Books such as *The Feminine Mystique, The Second Sex,* and *Sisterhood Is Powerful* sold millions of copies and further helped to change people's attitudes. In the spirit of equal opportunity for all, woman demanded equal opportunity for themselves. The participation of women in the Civil Rights and Peace movements brought a new consciousness and unity into the lives of many women. It also increased the awareness of many men.

(4) Although the Civil Rights and Peace movements had a tremendous influence on women's changing role, they are not the only reasons for women's new status. Other important factors have helped bring about change. One reason has to do with recent advances in medical technology. Birth control methods have made it possible for women to decide how many children they want. Birth control also enables women to wait until they have established themselves in a profession before having children. In addition, as satisfactory day-care facilities have become more readily available, it's become easier for many women to work outside the home. Another reason has to do with the high cost of living and the high rate of inflation. In recent years, prices have risen greatly in most countries. Often a husband's income is no longer sufficient to support

a family. Many of today's families must rely on a second income, a wife's earnings, to maintain the same standard of living as before. Moreover, many more men accept the fact that women can work at most jobs as well as they can. As the number of working women increases, social acceptance increases as well.

(5) In a country such as the United States, with its relatively high standard of living, many people are no longer completely satisfied with only material possessions and comfort. More people today, particularly members of the upper and middle classes, place a great deal of importance on trying to "realize their potential." They want their work to contribute in some way to their personal development. They feel that a job should stimulate them to think and should offer them new and interesting experiences. By having fresh challenges, they hope to grow both emotionally and intellectually. More and more people today are asking themselves, "Is my work fulfulling? Is it challenging? Am I growing as a person?" Still other people look for personal fulfillment in other ways. Some prefer a job in which they can help others. Helping other people, they feel, gives a special meaning and purpose to their lives. They get a great deal of satisfaction from feeling that they're doing something to make the world a little better place in which to live. Thus, the desire for self-fulfillment has caused many women to leave their housework to pursue other kinds of work.

TRADITIONS IN TRANSITION

(6) There are many areas that reflect the dramatic changes of the past decades. Education is one clear example. Universities, once the province of men and only later a few wealthy women, have more recently opened their doors to the female sex. Today, women make up one-half of all students in North American universities. More women are receiving training in professional fields with high status such as law, medicine, and engineering. In 1969 only 7 percent of all law school graduates were female. In 1979 more than 31 percent were women. By 1990, the number of women with B.A.s in business is expected to be eight times the number during the 1960s.

(7) With changes in education have come changes in the work world as well. Prior to 1950, most women who worked at jobs outside the home did not have professional careers, except for those in the health and teaching fields. Recent trends reveal a totally different picture. Between 1950 and 1978 the percentage of American women in the work force increased from 34 percent to 50 percent. Even more significant is the increase in women with skilled jobs. Between 1960 and 1970 their number rose a full 80 percent. In business, the number of self-employed women increased 43 percent, an amount five times greater than the increase for men.

(8) The family life of millions of Americans has been greatly altered as a result of these recent trends in education and business. The desire to pursue professional careers has prompted many men and women to delay marriage. Today, in fact, more than one-fifth of all American households are single men and women. For married couples, another kind of life-style has become widespread. The traditional model of wife-at-home and husband-at-work is no longer the general rule. Today both spouses work away from home in almost one-half of all American families. Many women report that their new roles have done much to improve their self-assurance and self-image. Now that they too are "breadwinners," they claim to have a greater feeling of independence, competence, and self-esteem.

(9) Yet despite the improved status of women, inequality and injustice still exist. When there is high unemployment, women are often the first to lose their jobs. In many professions men continue to receive higher salaries than

women, even though both sexes are performing the same work. Hiring practices of some companies tend to favor men over women, especially for promotions and supervisory positions, even though the women may be just as qualified. Women are still kept in positions of low status and prestige or are overlooked at promotion time. While national laws prohibiting this kind of discrimination do exist, the government is not always able (or willing) to enforce them.

THE SEXUAL REVOLUTION

(10) The 1960s is remembered as a period of great upheaval and change, and perhaps one of the most dramatic changes involved people's attitudes about another topic: premarital sex. Prior to the 1960s, American society considered it perfectly "natural" for a single man to engage in premarital sex. Yet for a woman, it was thought to be "wrong" or "immoral" if she were to have sexual relations before marriage. However, as many American women questioned society's traditional attitudes, they became more critical of this "double standard." Many could no longer accept behavior and attitudes that seemed to favor men at women's expense. Today most American women decide for themselves when and with whom they want to become sexually involved. Marriage, which once represented a way for people to fulfill their sexual needs and desires, no longer serves this function so completely in American society.

(11) These more liberal attitudes regarding premarital sex have caused a major change in people's life-styles. Nowadays it is not uncommon to hear that a man and woman are living together but are not legally married. In fact, many Americans are quite casual about living together, and even many members of the older generation have become more tolerant and accepting of the situation. One 1978 United States Government study found that this type of arrangement existed in 1.1. million households, more than double the number of unmarried couples living together in 1970. Experts believe that there are many more unmarried couples than the government study indicates, since many couples prefer not to admit that they are living this way. Living together was once considered a revolutionary or radical way of life. Today it has become just another life-style for many of today's unmarried men and women.

Comprehension Questions

1. How has the role of women changed in the United States during the last decade?
2. What are some of the important changes that the Women's Lib Movement has tried to bring about? How are these changes different for men and women?
3. What was the principal goal and objective of the Civil Rights Movement?
4. What did participants in the Peace Movement try to do?
5. How did these two movements help to produce changes in the role of American women?
6. Give at least two reasons mentioned in the article that help explain why more women have been wanting these changes.
7. What development in medical technology has helped to change women's status in society? Explain.

8. Why are some American men accepting the fact that so many women are working out of the home?
9. In your own words, explain what is meant by the phrase "a desire for self-fulfillment."
10. How have people's attitudes in this country changed regarding premarital sex? What effect or influence have these new ideas had on people's lifestyles?
11. The expression "a four-letter word" can also refer to a "dirty" word or curse word that is generally not found in a dictionary. Refer to the title of the chapter. What double meaning does the title have?

Point/Counterpoint

A CASE IN POINT

"Linda's Home and Garden"

My name is Linda. I'm 28 years old and happily married. Or so I thought, until recently. Ernest and I have been married for five years. Two years ago, we had our first child. You would think that everything would be wonderful. Ernest has a good job with a good future. All I have to do is stay home, keep the house clean, take care of the baby and be there for when Ernest gets home. I guess that's the problem. I don't want to stay home all day long anymore, alone with the baby. I'm going crazy looking at the walls, with no one to talk to. I'm tired of washing clothes, preparing meals and cleaning the house. It's so boring. Every day the same routine. Nothing interesting or new ever happens. My mind feels empty, like there's nothing there. I have nothing interesting to talk about. When Ernest comes home he's filled with stories about the people at work, about what he's doing, what he's planning. He's full of life and energy. And me, I've nothing to tell him. How exciting is cleaning the bathroom or changing a diaper?

I was really beginning to resent Ernest and his enthusiasm about his work. So finally, a couple of months ago, I told him I needed a change. I want to go back to school and prepare for a career. I'm smart. I have a lot to offer. And I'm dying to have some challenges in my life. Something to stimulate me. Something to look forward to when I get up in the morning other than dirty clothes and dishes. Many of my friends are in school or out pursuing careers. I'm losing touch with them because we have so much less in common. It's like we're living in different worlds. And their world is so much more interesting and challenging.

But Ernest doesn't understand. He wants me to be home to take care of the baby and the house. He doesn't want me to leave the baby with a babysitter. I'm beginning to feel like a slave, like I'm in prison. I'm unhappy all the time. Ernest says I have to accept the situation, at least until the children are much older. He refuses to listen to me. But I can't go on this way. It's destroying me and it's destroying our marriage. I will lose all respect for myself if I permit this to continue. I need my own life and my own career. I don't know what I'm going to do.

QUESTIONS FOR CLASS DISCUSSION

1. How does Linda see her life? What problems does she think she has?
2. What do you think Linda should do?
3. In addition to a career, what are some other alternatives Linda could explore?

A CASE IN POINT

"The Importance of Being Ernest"

My name is Ernest. You probably heard Linda tell you about our problem. I can't believe what's happening. Everything used to be so beautiful between us. When we got married five years ago she was working as a secretary in an office. She couldn't wait to leave her job and raise a family with me. She was so excited about that. But now, everything has changed. Lately, she's driving me crazy with her new ideas of returning to school and having her own career.

I don't mind if she has a career. But not now. We have a small baby. She wants to leave the baby in a day care center or with some babysitter. I can't accept that! A young child needs a mother's love and attention. I can't see some stranger raising my children. Linda has changed too much for me. She's always complaining about her situation. She says she's bored. She doesn't feel fulfilled. What's the matter with her? I'm not enough to make her happy? I know a lot of women who are happy to be home taking care of their family.

She's only thinking about herself. What about me? I work hard all day to earn a living so we can live comfortably. Then I have to come home and listen to her complaints. I try to help around the house and with the baby, not like most other husbands. What more can she expect? I know if she goes back to school she will have less time for the baby and me. I feel like she's saying that a career is more important to her than I am. That kills me. Why can't she wait until we have at least another child? When they're older and in school, then she can go back and study. What's wrong with her? She has changed too much. She's not the same woman I married five years ago. She's abandoning me, the baby, our dreams, everything we wanted when we got married. If she continues like this, she's going to ruin everything.

QUESTIONS FOR CLASS DISCUSSION

1. How does Ernest view his life? What are his concerns and problems?
2. Who or what do you think is responsible for the problems that Linda and Ernest are having?
3. How would you finish this story? What do you think will happen to Linda and Ernest?

Topics for Discussion and Composition

1. Do you think there are certain things that *only* men should do? *Only* women should do? Give reasons for your answers.
2. Do you think people should use birth control? Why or why not?
3. What is your opinion about day-care centers? What are the benefits of day care? What are the disadvantages?
4. Some companies prefer to hire women instead of men because the companies are trying to balance the number of men and women they employ. Do you think this is a good idea?
5. What do you think is the best age for a person to get married? Why? How can a person know when he or she is really ready for marriage?
6. Many North Americans choose to live together before getting married. Do you think this is a good idea? Why or why not?
7. It's very common in American society to have sex before marriage. Do you think this is a good situation?
8. Divorce is a widespread problem in the United States and many other countries. Why do you think so many marriages are ending in divorce? What can married couples do to reduce the chance of divorce?
9. There are different reasons why people choose or accept a particular job. If you were offered the following job contract, would you accept it?
   a. *Salary:* One million dollars per year for a minimum of twenty-five years (If you fail to complete the twenty-five years, you must return *all* the money and material possessions acquired during your period of employment.)
   b. *Work Schedule:* Twelve hours per day, six days per week, one week annual vacation
   c. *Job Description:* Security guard for a chemical laboratory. Your job is to observe the lab facilities from a 20-foot tower to make sure no unauthorized personnel enter the company's premises. You must work alone at all times. No visitors or other distractions such as radios, books, or TV are permitted during work hours.

Sign your name on the dotted line if you accept.

Paragraph Analysis: Identifying Topics and Main Ideas

Directions: *Refer to paragraphs 1–5 at the beginning of chapter 2. As you did in chapter 1, put a check next to the one phrase that best expresses the* **topic** *of each paragraph. Then identify which sentence in each paragraph makes a general statement about the paragraph's topic. This one sentence should tell in a general way what the entire paragraph is about. This sentence is called the* **main idea** *or* **topic sentence** *of the paragraph. Copy this main-idea sentence from each paragraph into the space provided.*

Paragraph 1.

_______ Traditional Attitudes about Masculinity and Femininity

_______ Sex Roles and the Women's Lib Movement

_______ Business, Education, and Politics

_______ Adequate Recognition for Women at Work

Main Idea or
Topic Sentence: ____

____

Paragraph 2.

_______ Civil Rights Movement

_______ Defenseless and Innocent People in Vietnam

_______ Vietnam War and the Peace Movement

_______ Roots of the Women's Liberation Movement

Main Idea or
Topic Sentence: ____

____

Paragraph 3.

_______ Effect of Social Protest on Women's Attitudes

_______ Exploitation of Women by Their Husbands

_______ Injustices of Racial Discrimination and Oppression

_______ Government Leaders, Neighbors, and Friends

Main Idea or
Topic Sentence: ____

____

Paragraph 4.

_______ Medical Technology and Birth Control

_______ High Rate of Inflation and Cost of Living

_______ Reasons Why Women's Status Is Changing

_______ Day-Care Facilities in the United States

Main Idea or
Topic Sentence: ____

____

Paragraph 5.

_______ High Standard of Living

_______ Material Possessions and Comfort

_______ Meaning of Life

_______ Need for Self-Fulfillment

Main Idea or
Topic Sentence: ____

____

Seeing Relationships: Cause and Effect

Effectively Speaking: In trying to understand change of any kind, whether the change is personal, social, or historical, it's important to try to identify what is responsible for the change (the causes) and what the results of the change are (the effects). Authors will frequently use a *cause-and-effect* relationship to identify or explain why particular changes occur and what happens as a result. Listed below are some of the words and phrases authors use to alert the reader to the fact that a *cause-and-effect* relationship is being employed.

Words that Indicate a Cause-and-Effect Relationship

to cause	a cause of	because of
to contribute to	a product of	due to
to produce	a reason for	since
to lead to	a consequence	consequently
to be responsible for	an outcome	
to bring about	a result of	
to result in		

Directions: *The role of women in the United States has changed dramatically since the early 1960s. Use the information presented in the article (paragraphs 2,3,4,5) to help you identify some of the different causes for this important social change.*

Factors that Contributed to Women's New Role in Society

1.
2.
3.
4.
5.
6.

Directions: *As a result of the Women's Lib Movement, many different changes have occurred in American society. Use the information contained in the article (paragraphs 1,3,6,7,8,10,11) to list some of the results or effects of women's changed role in society.*

Some Effects of Women's Changed Role in Society

1.
2.
3.
4.
5.

Vocabulary Development

Directions: *Use the following words to complete the paragraph:*

role	fulfillment	standard
decades	rise	movement
birth	remain	factors
remove	availability	

During the last few ____________________, many ideas and attitudes have changed regarding the ____________________ of women in society. The Women's Lib ____________________ has been responsible for many of these changes. Supporters of this movement have tried to ____________________ the traditional divisions between men and women. There are many ____________________ that have contributed to this change. One factor is the greater ____________________ of day-care facilities. A second factor is the use of ____________________ control. Another reason is the desire of families to maintain the same ____________________ of living despite the ____________________ in living costs. Other reasons include women's needs for personal ____________________ and more acceptance by men of the idea that more women no longer want to ____________________ at home as housewives.

Directions: *Complete each word in the following sentences. Use the letters already in the spaces to help you. Only one letter may be used for each blank space. The first item has been done for you as an example.*

1. Many women prefer to p u r s u e professional careers rather than remain home as housewives.
2. During the 1960s, attempts to improve opportunities for blacks developed into a w i d e _ _ _ _ _ _ _ _ movement of social protest.
3. Many people today want their jobs to provide them with fresh c h a l l _ _ _ _ _ _ as well as the money to acquire material comfort.
4. Many families have to r e _ _ on two incomes in order to maintain their standard of living.
5. The decade of the 1960s is remembered in the United States as a period of great u p _ _ _ _ _ _ _ _ and change.
6. Living together without being married has become a more accepted l i f e s t _ _ _ since the "Sexual Revolution" of the 1960s.

7. Earning a salary tends to give people a greater feeling of self-confidence and self e s t _ _ _ _.
8. There are many different factors that have helped to b r i _ _ about dramatic changes in society.
9. In business, women generally still have positions of lower s t a _ _ _ and p r e s _ _ _ _ _ .
10. Birth control and day care help women who want to e s t a _ _ _ _ _ _ themselves in a profession or career.
11. The h i r _ _ _ practices of some companies are sometimes discriminatory.
12. In the United States, the desire to delay or postpone marriage has become a growing t r e _ _ in recent years.

Word Forms

PREFIXES

Directions: *Study this list of prefixes and their meanings. Then use one of the prefixes in combination with the boldface word in each of the sentences to form the new word necessary to complete the sentence. The first sentence has been done for you as an example.*

Prefix	Root Word	New Word	Meaning
mis	conduct	*mis*conduct	*bad* or *wrong* conduct
pre	view	*pre*view	view *before*
re	elect	*re*elect	elect *again*
en	danger	*en*danger	*cause* danger, *make* dangerous

1. Although she didn't want to go out with him when he **invited** her the first time, she finally said yes when he ***reinvited*** her.
2. Many words in English are very difficult to **pronounce**. That's why people learning English often MISPRONOUNCE them.
3. Prior to the 1960s most people recognized that sex was a natural part of **marital** relations, but they felt it was wrong for a woman to have PREMARITAL sex.
4. Although a student may already have a **large** and **rich** vocabulary in English, an understanding of prefixes and suffixes helps to ENLARGE and ENRICH that vocabulary.

5. **Understanding** is an important part of any relationship. When couples don't communicate their feelings to each other, __MISUNDERSTANDING__ is often the result.

6. When faced with a particularly difficult challenge, people need **courage** to continue. People need other people to support and __ENCOURAGE__ them in their efforts.

7. People don't always **examine** their own attitudes and opinions very carefully. Controversy and disagreement often force people to __RE-EXAMINE__ their beliefs and ideas.

8. It's not easy to **interpret** correctly the causes of a complex social movement such as Women's Lib. In fact, it's easy to __MISINTERPRET__ what actually occurred.

9. Since the political party had been well **organized** for the presidential election, it was relatively easy to __REORGANIZED__ the party members to support a common candidate in the mayoral election.

Directions: *Complete the following groups of sentences by using the correct form of each word given in the word form list. Be sure that the number of each word form corresponds to the number of the sentence group. Change the form of the verb when necessary. The first sentence has been done for you as an example.*

Noun	Verb	Adjective
1. drama	dramatize	dramatic
2. recognition	recognize	recognizable
3. standard	standardize	standard
4. development	develop	developed
5. involvement	involve	involved
6. improvement	improve	improved
7. discrimination	discriminate	discriminatory
8. stimulation	stimulate	stimulating
9. meaning	mean	meaningful
10. training	train	trained

1. During the last decades there has been a __***dramatic***__ change in people's life-styles. Today one in four is a single-person household, compared with one in ten in 1955.

   This statistic helps to __DRAMATIZE__ how much society has changed in a relatively short time.

2. Women's involvement in the protest movements of the 1960s helped them to __RECOGNIZE__ the many inequalities of American society. This __RECOGNITION__ on their part served to bring about more demands for equal opportunity.

3. The military has specific __STANDARD__ that it expects its officers and soldiers to follow. While in the service, people are expected to follow a __STANDARD__ code of behavior.

4. Medical science is constantly trying to DEVELOP new and better ways to treat disease. In recent years the DEVELOPMENT of artificial organs has helped people to survive illnesses that in the past resulted automatically in death.
5. On a national level, Americans don't seem to be very INVOLVED in their country's politics, since only a small proportion of citizens actually vote in presidental elections. On the local level, however, there's a much greater INVOLVEMENT, since political decisions there affect them in a more immediate and direct way.
6. After the operation the patient's condition continued to IMPROVE dramatically. Doctors attributed his IMPROVED condition to a better understanding of the patient's disease and recent IMPROVEMENTS in operating procedures.
7. Although the government does not permit DESCRIMINATORY hiring practices, it is often difficult to prove that a case of DESCRIMATION has actually occurred.
8. The students thought the movie was so STIMULATING that they wanted to read more about the subject. It's not often that a film provokes and STIMULATES people so much that they want to study the topic on their own.
9. She often refers to her college days as one of the most MEANINGFUL experiences of her life. She claims that in college she learned the real MEANING of hard work and self-discipline.
10. More people are receiving professional TRAINING in the sciences than at any time in history. There are more TRAINED scientists doing research today than in all other centuries combined.

MAKING GENERALIZATIONS ABOUT WORD FORMS

Directions: *Refer back to the part of the word form list as indicated, then try to complete the statements that follow.*

1. Refer to the verbs in items 1–3. These three verbs all end in the suffix ____________ . This suffix indicates that a word is a ____________ .
2. Refer to the nouns in items 4–6. These three nouns end in the suffix ____________ . This suffix indicates that a word is a ____________ .

3. Refer to the verbs and nouns in items 7 and 8. The verbs end with the letters ______________ . The nouns end with the letters ______________ . To form a noun when the verb ends in ______________ , you drop the letter ______________ and add the suffix ______________ .

4. Refer to the nouns in items 9 and 10. Both nouns end in the suffix ______________ . To form a noun, the suffix ______________ is added to the ______________ .

Dictionary Skills: Multiple Definitions and Parts of Speech

Directions: *This exercise combines two skills: identifying a word's part of speech (whether a word is a noun, verb, adjective, or adverb) and identifying its meaning. First, read the dictionary definition of the word. Then, in the space provided in the sentences that follow, write the part of speech and the meaning of the boldface word in each sentence. The first one has been done as an example.*

deal (dēl) *v.* **dealt** (dĕlt), **dealing.** 1. To distribute. 2. To be occupied or concerned with; treat. 3. To do business with; trade. *n.* 1. A bargain or agreement. 2. A large quantity or amount. 3. A business transaction.

1. An international corporation **deals** with many nations, establishing new markets and developing advertising campaigns suited to the individual tastes of each country.

   verb - 3. to do business with

2. During the 1960s there was a great **deal** of social protest on the campuses of many North American universities.

   ____

3. His biggest problem as an administrator is that he doesn't **deal** with the feelings and needs of his employees.

   ____

just (jŭst) *adj.* 1. Honorable and fair in one's dealings and actions. 2. Accurate; well-founded. *adv.* 1. Precisely; exactly. 2. Only a moment ago. 3. Barely; scarcely; by a narrow margin. 4. Merely; only. 5. Really or positively, as in *It's just perfect!*

4. In some companies men receive promotions ahead of women even though the women may be **just** as qualified.

   ____

5. Although we invited a lot of people to the meeting, **just** five people showed up.

   ____

6. When the salesman asked if I needed any help I replied, "No, thanks. I'm **just** looking."

____

7. My friend is so lucky. She had **just** graduated from law school when she found a job with a prestigious law firm.

____

8. He was loved and respected by all his employees because he tried to be **just** in his treatment of everyone, regardless of the person's status.

____

practice (prăk′ tĭs) *v.* **-ticed, -ticing.** 1. To do or perform something habitually or customarily. 2. To exercise or perform repeatedly in order to acquire a skill. 3. To work at (a profession). *n.* 1. A habitual or customary way of doing things. 2. Repeated performance of an activity in order to learn or perfect a skill. 3. The business of a professional person.

9. The hiring **practices** of different government agencies may vary, but all are expected to comply with federal laws regarding equal opportunity.

____

10. Regardless of how much natural talent a person possesses, it's still necessary to **practice** many hours a day to become a world-class musician.

____

11. My wife is an experienced lawyer. She's been **practicing** law for more than fifteen years.

____

prompt (prŏmpt) *adj.* 1. On time; punctual. 2. Quick to act or respond. *v.* 1. To incite; to cause to act. 2. To give rise to; to inspire. 3. To assist with a reminder; to remind.

12. The department store offers **prompt** delivery of any item purchased at any of its locations.

____

13. The desire to pursue a professional career has **prompted** many people to delay marriage.

____

14. Class begins at the scheduled time because both the teacher and the students are always **prompt.**

____

rise (rīz) *v.* **rose, risen** (rĭz′ən), **rising.** 1. To assume a standing position. 2. To get out of bed. 3. To move from a lower to a higher position. 4. To increase in amount, value, etc. 5. To appear above the horizon. 6. To meet a demand or challenge. 7. To rebel; to revolt. *n.* 1. The act of rising; an ascent. 2. Occasion or opportunity, as in *give rise to change.* 3. An increase in price, worth, quantity, or degree. 4. Elevation in social status, prosperity, or importance.

15. Every year the cost of food and shelter **rises.**

____

16. Although she's faced with many difficult challenges, I'm sure she will **rise** to the occasion and do an excellent job.

____

17. His dramatic **rise** to power was possible only because he had the support of several important political groups.

____

18. The boxer **rose** slowly from the canvas after he'd been knocked down by a powerful punch.

____

19. The farmer was already at work in the fields when the sun **rose** over the mountains.

____

20. In discussing the life of Abraham Lincoln, people like to tell about how he **rose** from humble origins to become the sixteenth President of the United States.

____

Classifying and Categorizing Information

Exercise A: *In the following series of words, circle the one word that does not belong with the other words in the same group. In the space provided, write a title that explains why the other three words belong together. The first one has been done for you as an example.*

1. ***Communication media***	2. ______	3. ______
telephone	law	decade
newspaper	economics	century
airplane (circled)	protest	early
radio	politics	hour
4. ______	**5.** ______	**6.** ______
fulfillment	computer	injustice
happiness	steamship	exploitation
sadness	television	discrimination
conversation	car	unity
7. ______	**8.** ______	**9.** ______
traditional attitudes	money	ocean
birth control methods	house	tunnel
desire for self-fulfillment	health	river
day-care facilities	jewelry	sea

10. ______________
opera
popular song
violin
symphony

11. ______________
dirty air
loud noises
cancer
impure water

12. ______________
withdrawal
salary
deposit
loan

13. ______________
car
boat
truck
bicycle

14. ______________
leukemia
heart disease
pneumonia
blindness

15. ______________
continent
city
population
island

Exercise B: *Divide these phrases into three different groups in the columns provided. Then give each group a general title or name. Be sure that all the phrases in your group relate to each title.*

second income
right to vote
unemployment rate
final exam
law student
election year
standard of living
cost of living
presidential debate
social movement
foreign language
peace demonstration
intellectual development
material possessions
career training
government leaders
rate of inflation
student-teacher relationships

Group I	Group II	Group III
1.	1.	1.
2.	2.	2.
3.	3.	3.
4.	4.	4.
5.	5.	5.
6.	6.	6.
______________	______________	______________
(Title for Group I)	(Title for Group II)	(Title for Group III)

The Chaser

JOHN COLLIER (1901–1980)

John Collier was born in London, England, in 1901. His work as a writer took many forms: poet, journalist, reviewer, novelist, and Hollywood filmscript writer. He is also the author of some fifty short stories, many of which have appeared in leading literary magazines of the time.

The themes of magic, power, sex, and greed are often found in Collier's writings. In "The Chaser" these themes are combined to create an unusual short story with a particularly amusing and thought-provoking conclusion.

Alan Austen, as nervous as a kitten, went up certain dark and creaky stairs in the neighborhood of Pell Street, and peered[1] about for a long time on the dim[2] landing before he found the name he wanted written obscurely on one of the doors.

He pushed open the door, as he had been told to do, and found himself in a tiny room, which contained no furniture but a plain kitchen table, a rocking-chair, and an ordinary chair. On one of the dirty buff[3]-colored walls were a couple of shelves, containing in all perhaps a dozen bottles and jars.

An old man sat in the rocking-chair, reading a newspaper. Alan, without a word, handed him the card he had been given. "Sit down, Mr. Austen," said the old man very politely. "I am glad to make your acquaintance."

"Is it true," asked Alan, "that you have a certain mixture that has -er-quite extraordinary effects?"

"My dear sir," replied the old man, "my stock in trade[4] is not very large—I don't deal in laxatives and teething mixtures—but such as it is, it is varied. I think nothing I sell has effects which could be precisely described as ordinary."

"Well, the fact is—" began Alan.

"Here, for example," interruped the old man, reaching for a bottle from the shelf. "Here is a liquid as colorless as water, almost tasteless, quite imperceptible in coffee, milk, wine, or any other beverage. It is also quite imperceptible to any known method of autopsy."

"Do you mean it is a poison?" cried Alan, very much horrified.

"Call it a glove-cleaner if you like," said the old man indifferently.[5] "Maybe it will clean gloves. I have never tried. One might call it a life-cleaner. Lives need cleaning sometimes."

"I want nothing of that sort," said Alan.

"Probably it is just as well," said the old man. "Do you know the price of this? For one teaspoonful, which is sufficient, I ask five thousand dollars. Never less. Not a penny less."

"I hope all your mixtures are not as expensive," said Alan apprehensively.[6]

"Oh dear, no," said the old man. "It would be no good charging that sort of price for a love potion, for example. Young people who need a love potion very seldom have five thousand dollars. Otherwise they would not need a love potion."

"I am glad to hear that," said Alan.

"I look at it like this," said the old man. "Please[7] a customer with one article, and he will come back when he needs another. Even if it is more costly. He will save up for it, if necessary."

"So," said Alan, "you really do sell love potions?"

"If I did sell love potions," said the old man, reaching for another bottle, "I should not have mentioned the other matter to you. It is only when one is in a position to oblige that one can afford to be so confidential."[8]

"And these potions," said Alan. "They are not just—just—er—"

"Oh, no," said the old man. "Their effects are permanent, and extend far beyond casual impulse. But they include it. Bountifully, insistently. Everlastingly."[9]

[1]**peered:** looked

[2]**dim:** not bright

[3]**buff:** brownish yellow

[4]**stock in trade:** merchandise; goods

[5]**indifferently:** without interest

[6]**apprehensively:** nervously; fearfully

[7]**please:** satisfy

[8]**confidential:** trusting

[9]**everlastingly:** forever

"Dear me!" said Alan, attempting a look of scientific detachment. "How very interesting!"

"But consider the spiritual side," said the old man.

"I do, indeed," said Alan.

"For indifference," said the old man, "they substitute devotion. For scorn, adoration. Give one tiny measure of this to the young lady—its flavor is imperceptible in orange juice, soup, or cocktails—and however gay and giddy[10] she is, she will change altogether. She will want nothing but solitude, and you."

"I can hardly believe it," said Alan. "She is so fond of parties."

"She will not like them any more," said the old man. "She will be afraid of the pretty girls you may meet."

"She will actually be jealous?" cried Alan in rapture.[11] "Of me?"

"Yes, she will want to be everything to you."

"She is, already. Only she doesn't care about it."

"She will, when she has taken this. She will care intensely. You will be her sole interest in life."

"Wonderful!" cried Alan.

"She will want to know all you do," said the old man. "All that has happened to you during the day. Every word of it. She will want to know what you are thinking about, why you smile suddenly, why you are looking sad."

"That is love!" cried Alan.

"Yes," said the old man. "How carefully she will look after you! She will never allow you to be tired, to sit in a draught,[12] to neglect your food. If you are an hour late, she will be terrified. She will think you are killed, or that some siren[13] has caught you."

"I can hardly imagine Diana like that!" cried Alan, overwhelmed with joy.

"You will not have to use imagination," said the old man. "And, by the way, since there are always sirens, if by any chance you should, later on, slip[14] a little, you need not worry. She will forgive you, in the end. She will be terribly hurt, of course, but she will forgive you—in the end."

"That will not happen," said Alan fervently.

"Of course not," said the old man. "But, if it did, you need not worry. She would never divorce you. Oh, no! And, of course, she herself will never give you the least, the very least, grounds[15] for—uneasiness."

"And how much," said Alan, "is this wonderful mixture?"

"It is not as dear,[16]" said the old man, "as the glove-cleaner, or life-cleaner, as I sometimes call it. No. That is five thousand dollars, never a penny less. One has to be older than you are, to indulge in that sort of thing. One has to save up for it."

"But the love potion?" said Alan.

"Oh, that," said the old man, opening the drawer in the kitchen table, and taking out a tiny, rather dirty-looking phial.[17] "That is just a dollar."

"I can't tell you how grateful I am," said Alan, watching him fill it.

"I like to oblige," said the old man. "Then customers come back, later in life, when they are rather better off, and want more expensive things. Here you are. You will find it very effective."

"Thank you again," said Alan. "Good-by."

"Au revoir,"[18] said the old man.

[10]**gay and giddy:** happy and silly

[11]**rapture:** ecstasy; delight

[12]**draught:** current of air

[13]**siren:** seductive woman

[14]**slip:** make a mistake

[15]**grounds:** reasons

[16]**dear:** expensive (British)

[17]**phial:** small glass bottle

[18]**Au revoir:** See you again (French)

QUESTIONS

1. Where does the story take place? Describe what the place looks like.
2. Why did Alan Austen go there?
3. The old man showed Alan two bottles. What was in the first bottle? What qualities or powers did the second bottle possess?
4. What qualities does Alan want a woman to have? What is his concept of the ideal woman?
5. What is the cost of the two bottles? Why do you think one bottle costs so much more than the other?
6. At the end of the story the old man says good-bye to Alan by using the French expression "au revoir." The French word means literally "to see again." Why do you think the old man says "au revoir" at the story's end?
7. The title of the story is "The Chaser." A chaser is a second liquid that is drunk immediately after another liquid in order to eliminate or lessen the strong taste of the first. For example, beer is sometimes used as a "chaser" after a strong whiskey has been drunk. How does the title "The Chaser" apply to the story?
8. What do you think is the message of this story?
9. Compare the story "The Chaser" with the folktale "How the Ethiopian Woman Tamed Her Husband" in terms of the following. What similarities and differences do you see?
   a. The setting (where the stories take place)
   b. The characters (who are they, what qualities they have)
   c. The plot (what the important events are, at the beginning, at the end)
   d. The message or main theme

Directions: *In the space provided, write the one word or phrase from the right-hand column that has the same meaning as the boldface word on the left. Do not use a dictionary; refer to the story.*

1. a **dim** room	***not bright***	great happiness
2. a **tiny** room	________	satisfy
3. a **plain** table	________	reasons
4. to be **imperceptible** in coffee	________	anxiety, worry
5. to **seldom** have money	________	not bright
6. to **please** a customer	________	very small
7. a casual **impulse**	________	lack of interest
8. a feeling of **detachment**	________	ordinary
9. to show **scorn**	________	rarely, infrequently
10. **grounds** for divorce	________	sudden desire, urge
11. overwhelmed with **joy**	________	not noticeable
12. a feeling of **uneasiness**	________	rejection, contempt

3

READING INTO IT: THE MEDIUM AND THE MESSAGE

N.Y. Public Library Picture Collection

A U.S. Army private during the Civil War (1861–1865)

U.S. Army photograph by Oscar E. Porter

The typical military look of the Vietnam War era

N.Y. Public Library Picture Collection

A Vietnam War protester during the 1971 March on Washington

Understanding Vocabulary in Context

Directions: *Read each group of sentences carefully. Then circle the one word on the left that has the same meaning as the boldface word. The boldface word in each sentence appears in the reading selection that follows this exercise.*

-problems
-characteristics
-foundations
-functions

1. There are many beautiful movie actresses in the world, but it's usually those women with unusual physical **features**—such as a tender yet sad smile; dark, penetrating eyes; or a mysterious look—who truly capture the public's attention and admiration.

-orchestra
-class
-survey
-disturbance

2. Politicians running for elected office will frequently conduct a study or **poll** in order to find out the public's opinion on various issues.

-preferred
-visited
-impressed
-viewed, saw

3. First impressions can be misleading. When I met my wife for the first time I **perceived** her as a rather silly, unintelligent person. Today I know her to be a bright and mature woman.

-duplicate
-avoid
-enjoy
-laugh at

4. Children often try to **emulate** or copy the behavior that they see on television.

-too much
-not enough
-correct
-serious

5. In sports, insufficient preparation and practice are often the reason for an athlete's poor performance. In boxing, for instance, a **lack of** training increases the chance of losing a fight or of suffering a serious injury.

-eliminate
-confuse
-communicate
-admire

6. To **convey** or express a particular thought, a writer will sometimes compare one idea with another.

-result in
-eliminate
-cure
-investigate

7. Lack of physical activity can **lead to** a variety of health problems. For example, problems with sleeping and concentrating are sometimes the result of not enough exercise.

-ceremony
-ancestry
-country
-rebellion

8. Their family has a proud and distinguished **heritage**. In each of the last four generations, at least one family member has had an important role in government or industry.

-elected members
-privileged members
-happy members
-sad members

9. The president's funeral was a sad yet impressive occasion. Senators, business leaders, important artists, and other members of society's **elite** were all in attendance.

-obligations
-interest
-free time
-hope

10. On weekends most people like to use their free time to go out and enjoy themselves or do the things they had no time for during the week. Others, however, remain home and do nothing. It's as if they don't know what to do with their moments of **leisure**.

Reading into It: The Medium and the Message

(1) As we live in a culture we consciously and unconsciously incorporate certain standard ways of behaving and conducting ourselves. From an early age we are all taught how to act upon meeting a stranger or how to behave at the dinner table. We learn that different social occasions require different ways of dressing; we don't wear the same clothes to a job interview that we'd wear to play in the park. By following or not following these forms, we project an image of ourselves to others around us, whether we like it or not. Sometimes we are consistent, and sometimes we change our styles. In either case we are communicating something about our own personalities.

"YOU SAY YES, I SAY NO"

(2) Without ever being formally taught, most of us comprehend the unspoken messages of our own culture. For instance, people in the United States learn that when we move the head up and down, it means "yes"; when we shake the head from side to side that means "no." No one has to be taught what these movements mean. Problems result, however, when people come into contact with other people who have a different way of expressing the same message.

(3) Here's one amusing case in point. An American visiting the country of Turkey can get into a lot of trouble if he or she doesn't know the local customs. In Turkey, the head movements to indicate "yes" and "no" are almost the exact opposite of those used in the United States. To indicate "yes," the Turkish people move their heads from side to side, similar to an American's signal for "no." To indicate "no" Turks will move their heads in an upward direction, with eyes rolling up toward the sky. To an American, this gesture for "no" resembles the American signal for "yes." Imagine what happens when the unaware American tourist asks the Turk if a particular street is the correct way to get back to the hotel. The nod of the Turk's head will certainly prove "misleading."

(4) The use of clothes can also be misleading, even for people from the same country. The clothing itself may be ambiguous and convey a "double message." Take, for example, the young lady who goes shopping at the supermarket wearing a jogging suit, high heeled shoes, and long, dangling jewelry. Dressing in these clothes not only communicates her awareness of the "leisure" fashion style, but also signals that her clothes are primarily decorative. She may be subconsciously dressing to attract members of the opposite sex and *not* to exercise on the gymnasium floor. Likewise, a young woman working in an office who accentuates her feminine physique by wearing tight-fitting sweaters or low-cut blouses communicates her interest in "manhunting" as much as in "career hunting." Employers are quick to notice this "double message" and rarely promote people who are not "all business." A certain style of dress clearly exists among the elite of the business world; people who do not respect this unwritten dress code rarely advance very far up the corporate ladder. The message here is clear: People who want to advance at a job need to pay careful attention to the nonverbal messages of those people they wish to emulate or impress.

(5) Men find themselves communicating "double messages" when they are expected to behave according to traditional "masculine" roles. For instance,

if a man does not stand "straight and tall" while he speaks forceful words, or if his voice fluctuates too much in tone, his words will probably lose their effect on the listener. By contrast, women's voices have been permitted a much wider range of tone, up and down the vocal scale, in order to express emotion. In general, their voices will rise and fall much more whenever they express feelings of enthusiasm, anger, or surprise. American men, on the other hand, are expected to control or limit their tone of voice as well as the movement of their hands. Hesitation, weakness, or insincerity are easily "read into" the words of men whose "body language" or tone of voice does not reinforce their spoken message.

THE ANSWERS ARE NOT ALWAYS THE ISSUE: THE KENNEDY-NIXON DEBATES

(6) A classic example of the importance of voice and "body language" has come out of the famous 1960 debates between John F. Kennedy and Richard M. Nixon, both candidates for U.S. president at that time. After the first debate, a poll was taken of two groups of people, one group who had watched the debate on TV and the other who had listened to the debate on radio. The majority of radio listeners thought Nixon was the winner. However, the majority of TV viewers thought Kennedy had definitely won. Experts believe that it was Kennedy's "good looks," "body language," (his use of gestures and facial expressions), and tone of voice that influenced the opinion of the TV viewers. Thus it's not always what you say that matters, but how you say it and how you look while you're saying it that really count.

REAL MEN DON'T WEAR PINK

(7) Colors, hair, and jewelry are also frequently determined by a person's sex. This is not always true for all cultures, and it's not even true now throughout the United States. In this country, it took the full force of the "flower power" movement of the anti–Vietnam War protests to bring about a change from these culturally strict norms. The "anti-military" attitudes of the 1960s and 1970s sought to break with the military's traditional masculine or "macho" position, thus making it more acceptable for men to wear floral designs on their shirts in pinks, purples, violets, and other "feminine colors." For some people, long hair and jewelry on men also became acceptable as a means of expressing this changed way of thinking. More facial hair also became common, precisely because it differed from the military norm. The business world, however, has been slow to change. In most offices today, wearing bright colors, jewelry, and long hair is still not acceptable for men.

WHEN IN ROME, DO AS THE ROMANS DO

(8) Certainly for people who are living in a new culture, it would be helpful to pay attention to the various ways of transmitting messages and to try not to judge other people's behavior too quickly. It may even be wise to request clarification from the natives of the land. One common source of misunderstanding between people of different cultures has to do with the use of space. North Americans, for example, are often perceived as "unfriendly," "distant," or "aloof" compared with other national groups, in part because they prefer more physical distance between people than some other groups such as Arabs, Greeks, and Latin Americans. People in the U.S. have a long-standing heritage of not touching each other physically even when they are emotionally close. This distancing can be confusing and upsetting to foreigners, who often mis-

interpret Americans' need for space and distance as a kind of personal rejection or insult.

(9) Even in different areas of the same country, different customs exist that lead to confusion and misinterpretation. People from big cities are often perceived as a different breed from their "country cousins." New Yorkers, for example, are constantly referred to as "unfriendly" or "cold" by tourists. Recent studies have shown that this idea has developed as a result of the New Yorker's lack of eye contact on the street. Very specific "unwritten rules" for eye contact exist in New York and other large metropolitan areas. Unfortunately for outsiders, these "rules" are almost never talked about and it may take some time to learn them. At distances where people cannot detect one another's facial features, New Yorkers are free to look at each other. But, as the other person comes closer and the distance is reduced, it is definitely "impolite" to continue to "stare" (or even to look). Anyone who does so is violating this unwritten code. Making direct eye contact when a person's features are clearly visible is "taboo" and is "asking for trouble." Fortunately, however, visitors to New York often escape an unpleasant situation because the native will look away at the appropriate time and consequently will avoid a confrontation.

(10) However, the visitor from the country, who is used to exchanging friendly greetings on the street, may read this action as coldness and a kind of personal rejection. New Yorkers, on the other hand, can take a quick dislike to "tourists" who observe them too closely, since it is perceived as an insult indicating that they are "strange" or "different." Many New Yorkers are proud of their tolerance of differences and reject others who openly express surprise and curiosity. People from big cities such as New York pride themselves on not paying attention to every little thing their neighbors do. With so many people living together so closely, they feel it is important to allow people their personal privacy, even on the street.

MSING THE MESSAGE OR IS THE MESSAGE MSLEADING?

(11) For women today, simply filling out an application form or writing a name on a letter sends a kind of message, and it's a message that can easily lead to misunderstanding. Until recently, the marital status of a woman was known by the way she signed her name or introduced herself. If a woman was married she referred to herself as *Mrs.*; if she was single she used *Miss*. Men, on the other hand, have always used the title *Mister* (or *Mr.* for short) regardless of whether they were married or single. There are important reasons for this difference. In most cultures of the world the role of men, whether as fathers or husbands, has been to protect women. In the United States, before women were allowed to vote (1920), they were not considered "legal people." They could not own property or inherit family wealth. They could not even be their children's legal guardian or have any legal "say" in running a business. The man was "head of household." It was thought that a woman was not "qualified" to assume adult responsibilities. Therefore, it was important to clearly identify a woman's status, for in that way one knew who was "legally" responsible for her, her father or her husband.

(12) Nowadays, however, many more women want to be seen as independent, capable individuals in their own right. Many of these women prefer to use the title *Ms.* before their names, a title that does not indicate a woman's marital status in the same way that *Mr.* does not distinguish a man's. Of course, many women continue to use the titles *Mrs.* and *Miss*; some out of habit, and others, perhaps, because they are proud of marrying a particular man. What-

ever the reason, women today communicate something about themselves by the title they choose to use. And as with other forms of nonverbal communication, their choices are open to interpretation and misinterpretation by others.

(13) If a woman uses *Mrs.*, is she communicating that she is proud to be married or is she simply showing that she's a member of an older generation? Or is she trying to show that she is against women's having too much independence? And the woman who uses *Miss,* is she trying to show others that she is unmarried but looking for a partner? Or is she just "anti–Women's Lib"? And the woman who prefers *Ms.*, is she trying to communicate her beliefs or merely hide her status? Is it her way of expressing support for equality for women? Is she trying to send a strong personal or political message? Or is she merely trying to hide the fact that she's not married? Is the use of *Ms.* *mis*leading? Some men think so.

(14) Many of today's application forms include all three titles for women. Compared to the simplicity of the one male form, three separate titles may seem a little strange and perhaps a little silly. It remains to be seen which titles will prevail in future generations. Will it be *Miss* and *Mrs.*, or simply *Ms*? Will all women be "msing" their titles or will the *Ms.* be missing?

Comprehension Questions

1. What is "body language"?
2. Why do American tourists have difficulty when they visit the country of Turkey?
3. Why do many foreigners, particulary Latin Americans and Arabs, think that North Americans are "cold" and unfriendly"?
4. According to the article, how are New Yorkers different from people from small towns? What reason does the article give to explain this difference?
5. What important lesson about nonverbal communication was demonstrated by the Kennedy-Nixon debates? Why did most TV viewers think Kennedy had won the debate?
6. Explain why a woman who wears a jogging suit, jewelry, and high-heeled shoes is giving an ambiguous or "double" message.
7. If a man doesn't stand "straight and tall" when he's speaking in an angry way, what kind of message is he sending? How do other people tend to interpret his behavior?
8. In American society, what associations do most people make with the colors pink and purple?
9. During the 1960s, why did it become more acceptable for men to wear long hair and jewelry?
10. Why have most cultures of the world created two titles to differentiate between married and single women?
11. Why do you think men find women's use of *Ms.* misleading? What is responsible for men's confusion about this recently created title?

Topics for Discussion and Composition

1. How do you feel if another person "stares" at you? What do you usually do?
2. Have you ever had an unusual experience because of the way *you* looked at another person? Describe what happened.
3. Have you ever been to another country or place where the local customs were very different concerning the use of *nonverbal* communication? How did you find out that the customs were different? How did you react? Did you ever have any misunderstandings because of these differences in customs?
4. The article mentioned differences in eye contact between people from big cities and people from small towns. What *other* differences exist between people from these two places?
5. What are your favorite colors? Do these colors represent anything special to you? Do the colors of the clothes you wear reflect your personality in any way?
6. Describe the room where you live. Give as many details as possible. Do you think your room communicates anything special about you or your personality?
7. Do you think there are such things as "feminine" and "masculine" colors? Explain.
8. "Vain trifles as they seem, clothes have, they say, more important offices than merely to keep us warm. They change our view of the world and the world's view of us . . . . There is much to support the view that it is clothes that wear us and not we them."—VIRGINIA WOOLF, *Orlando*. What ideas are being communicated about the use of clothes in this quote? Do you agree?
9. Describe the clothes your different teachers wear. Do you think their clothes reflect anything about their personalities? Explain.
10. In your culture, what general attitudes do you think exist about the following: men who have long hair; men who wear jewelry; women who wear short dresses or tight-fitting blouses; high tones of voice; low tones of voice; moving your hands a lot as you talk.
11. Are there any other forms of nonverbal communication that are considered "nonstandard" or unacceptable in your culture that most Americans would probably not know about? Do tourists to your country have problems with these different signals?
12. In your culture, how are people expected to behave in the following circumstances? What verbal and nonverbal behavior is expected? (What words are used? How do people use their eyes, their hands, their posture, etc.?)
    a. When you are introduced to another person for the first time
    b. When you say good-bye to someone
    c. When you see someone who is close to you that you haven't seen for a long time
    d. When two people are busy talking together and you need to speak to one of them about something private
13. When listening to another person speak, how do you know if the person is being sincere and honest? What nonverbal signs do you pay special attention to in addition to the actual words the person says?

Identifying the Main Points of an Article

Directions: *Listed next are ten general statements. Put a check next to the six statements that you think were the main ideas or concepts presented in the article "Reading into It: The Medium and the Message."*

_____ 1. People enjoy traveling to other cities and countries.

_____ 2. From an early age, people learn specific ways of behaving and conducting themselves.

_____ 3. When people from different countries come together, their gestures and behavior can be misunderstood unless they know each other's customs.

_____ 4. People's intentions can be misinterpreted because of the clothes they wear.

_____ 5. Most people prefer to watch television than listen to the radio, especially when a political debate is on the air.

_____ 6. The use of a person's voice or physical gestures is very important in the communication of a spoken message.

_____ 7. Different customs within the United States exist that can result in misunderstanding.

_____ 8. The anti-Vietnam War protests helped to bring American involvement in the war to an end.

_____ 9. New Yorkers are proud of the fact that their city is a major cultural center.

_____ 10. A woman's use of the titles *Miss, Mrs.*, and *Ms.* can easily be misinterpreted by other people.

SEEING RELATIONSHIPS: EXAMPLES AND ILLUSTRATIONS

Authors frequently use specific examples to support or illustrate a general idea or point of view. The following paragraph, paraphrased from chapter 2, shows how an author tries to clarify the main point. What main point is the author trying to make? What specific examples are given? Underline them. Circle the specific words that are used to introduce or indicate each *different* example.

There are many reasons why women's roles have changed so much in recent years. One reason has to do with advances in medical technology. Birth control methods make it possible for women to establish themselves in careers before having children. In addition, the greater availability of day-care centers has made it easier for women to work outside the home. Another reason has to do with the high cost of living and inflation. Many families rely on a second income, a wife's earnings, to maintain a standard of living. Moreover, many more men accept the fact that women are able to work at most jobs as well as men. As the number of working women increases, social acceptance increases as well.

Words used to indicate examples: for example, for instance, a case in point, an illustration, to illustrate

Words used to indicate that more examples are being given: in addition, furthermore, moreover, also, another, as well, too, as well as, first, second, third, fourth, etc.

Directions: *In the blanks provided, copy the six sentences that you identified as the main points of chapter 3. Be sure to rewrite one sentence next to each of the six numbers given. (You may want to check your answers with your teacher before doing this.) Then, using the information in the article, write as many different examples as you can that you think illustrate or support each main point. The first one has been done for you as a model.*

1. ***From an early age, people learn specific ways of behaving and conducting themselves.***
   a. ***How to act when we meet a stranger***
   b. ***How to behave at a dinner table***
   c. ***How to dress for different social occasions***
2. ____________________
   a. ____________________
   b. ____________________
   c. ____________________
3. ____________________
   a. ____________________
   b. ____________________
   c. ____________________
4. ____________________
   a. ____________________
   b. ____________________
   c. ____________________
5. ____________________
   a. ____________________
   b. ____________________
   c. ____________________
6. ____________________
   a. ____________________
   b. ____________________
   c. ____________________

Vocabulary Development Puzzle

Directions: *Complete each word in the following sentences. Use the letters already in the spaces to help you. Only one letter may be used for each blank space. Notice that some of the spaces have numbers directly under them. As you complete each sentence, recopy the numbered letters into their corresponding spaces in the "message" that follows these directions. If all of your sentences have been correctly answered, then the words created in that final sentence should deliver a message. Good luck.*

Message:

_ _ _ _ _ _ _ _ _ _ i _ _   _ _   _   _ _ _
1 2 3 4 5 6 7 8 9 10 11 12 13   14 15   16   17 18 19

_ _ _ e   _ _ _   _ _ _ _   _ _ _   _ _ _
20 21 22 23   24 25 26   27 28 29 30   31 32 33   34 35 36

_ _ _ _   _ _ _ _
37 38 39 40   41 42 43 44

1. Visitors to New York City often p e(23) r c e(23) i(11) v e(23) of New Yorkers as unfriendly because of their lack of eye-contact on the street.
2. If a man's t o n(26) e(23) of voice is too high, people often don't take him seriously, even if he's expressing anger.
3. After a political debate, newspapers will often conduct a p o(18) l(17) l(17) or survey in order to find out the public's opinion.
4. Physical gestures, such as a nod of the head or a movement of the hand, are used by people to express or c o(21) n(6) v e y(31) their feelings.
5. In New York and other large cities, it's considered impolite to s t(10) a r(40) e at another person on the street.
6. People with attractive bodies sometimes wear tight-fitting clothes to accentuate or show off their p h(28) y(44) s(15) i q u(25) e s(15).
7. Differences between cultures can frequently l _(29) _(16) _(43) to misunderstanding.
8. When visiting another country, it's sometimes better not to j u(39) d g e(29) the other people until you know more about their customs.
9. Many foreigners are not a w(27) a r e(36) that many Americans prefer to keep a certain distance when they're talking to other people.

10. The use of *Ms.* can be a _3_ _41_ _14_ g _34_ _2_ _34_ s, and as a result, people sometimes don't know if a woman is trying to hide her marital status or if she's showing her support for "Women's Lib."

11. Although a political debate is supposed to give the public an opportunity to hear the participants' opinions on specific i _35_ _35_ _33_ e _35_, people often pay more attention to the speakers' good looks and body language than to their ideas and answers.

12. As children, we learn that there are s _19_ a _13_ _43_ a r _43_ ways of behaving and conducting ourselves.

13. Turkish people usually move their hands in an _5_ p _27_ a r _43_ direction to signal "no."

14. It's become more acceptable for North American men to wear long hair, bright colors, and j _29_ _27_ _29_ l r _37_ than it used to be.

15. In the business world, employers rarely p _22_ _32_ _4_ _32_ t e people to higher positions if they don't conform to the accepted dress code.

16. Many of today's _9_ p p l _7_ _8_ _9_ t _7_ _12_ _30_ forms include three separate titles for women.

17. In the United States prior to 1920, women did not have the right to v _42_ _19_ e.

18. In the United States, many people consider the colors pink and purple to be "f _24_ _20_ i _13_ i _13_ ___" colors.

19. In the United States, the Spanish word "m ___ _1_ h _38_" is also used to refer to someone who tries to be "tough" and "masculine" in the traditional sense.

Word Forms

PREFIXES

Directions: *Study the list of prefixes and their meanings. Then use one of the prefixes to form a word that correctly completes each of the sentences. The first item has been done for you as an example.*

Prefix	Meaning	Examples
en, in	in, inside	to insert money, to encage a bird
anti, contra	against	an anti-labor group, to use contraception
inter	between	an interstate highway
multi	many	a multitude of people
ex, extra	out, outside	to exclude a person, an extraordinary event
co, col com, con	together with	a coauthor, to collaborate on a task, a community, to concur on an idea

1. It's still generally not acceptable for businessmen to wear bright, ***multi-*** colored clothes to work, especially if the colors are pink and purple.
2. During the 1960s many young people wore long hair to express their __ANTI__ -war sentiments and attitudes.
3. Although she is serious about wanting a higher position at work, she's definitely sending a __CONTRA__ dictory message to her employers by wearing sexy, tight-fitting clothes.
4. With crime continuing to rise in some cities, communities are organizing volunteer citizen patrols as an __ANTI-__ crime measure.
5. When we are very young we learn to __IN__ corporate specific ways of behaving and conducting ourselves in order to __COM__ form with the rules and expectations of society.
6. In public-speaking classes, students are taught the important role that tone of voice plays in __INTER__ personal relations.
7. In trying to learn a foreign language, particularly as an adult, it's necessary to __IN__ vest a great deal of time and effort.
8. A dentist needs to use special surgical instruments to __EX__ tract a patient's tooth.
9. A spirit of __CO__ operation is necessary if the nations of the world are going to __CO__ -exist in peace.
10. There is usually a brief rest between the first and second parts of a concert. During this short __INTER__ mission many people exit the concert hall to smoke or just to get some fresh air.

Directions: *Complete the following groups of sentences by using the correct form of each word given in the word form list. Be sure that the number of each word form corresponds to the sentence-group number. Change the form of the verb or noun when necessary. The first sentence has been done for you as an example.*

	Noun	Infinitive of Verb	Adjective	Adverb
1.	clarity, clarification	to clarify	clear	clearly
2.	simplicity, simplification	to simplify	simple	simply
3.	identity, identification	to identify	identical	identically
4.	reliance	to rely	reliant, reliable	reliably
5.	tolerance	to tolerate	(in)tolerant, (in)tolerable	tolerably
6.	inheritance	to inherit	(in)heritable	
7.	pride	to pride oneself	proud	proudly
8.	perception	to perceive	perceptive	perceptively
9.	comparison	to compare	comparative	comparatively

1. When other people's ideas are not ____***clear***____ to you, it's often wise to ask them to try to ____***clarify***____ what they've said. If you don't ask for a ____CLARIFICATION____ , you can easily walk away with a misleading impression of the other person.

2. With the titles *Miss, Mrs.,* and *Ms.,* completing a job application is no longer such a ____SIMPLE____ task for women. Men, on the other hand, ____SIMPLY____ have to put a check next to *Mr.* Maybe someday they'll find a way to ____SIMPLIFY____ the situation for women as well.

3. Those two brothers are ____IDENTICAL____ twins. Even their family has problems trying to ____IDENTIFY____ who's who. They walk and talk almost ____IDENTICALLY____ , and their physical features are also ____IDENTICAL____ . From a distance, even their own parents have problems making an accurate ____IDENTIFICATION____ .

4. In previous centuries people ____RELIED____ on animals and their own muscle power to do their work. Today, however, people seem to have an almost total ____RELIANCE____ on machines and other forms of technology. In fact, most people are totally ____RELIANT____ on a car, bus, or train to take them to and from work every day. That's why ____RELIABLE____ sources of transportation are so important to them.

5. Growing up in a family of seven children, I learned how to __TOLERATE__ a lot of noise and commotion at home. My husband has absolutely no __TOLERENCE__ for noise. He finds it __INTOL__ whenever I play loud music in the house.
6. Although it's commonly accepted that all people __INHERIT__ their physical characteristics from their parents, no one can say to what extent our personalities and intelligence are __INHERITABLE__ .
7. New Yorkers are __PROUD__ of their diversity and fast-paced life-style. They take great __PRIDE__ in knowing that their city is one of the cultural and financial centers of the world. They also __PRIDE THEMSELVES__ on their ability to deal with hardship and crisis, and will even speak __PROUDLY__ about what a crazy place their city is.
8. After listening to the debate, the TV commentators all had different __PERCEPTIONS__ as to which candidate had won the debate. One of the program commentators made a very __PERCEPTIVE__ comment. He said that most people watching a debate __PERCEIVE__ what they want to __PERCEIVE__ , regardless of what the candidates actually say.
9. It's often quite interesting to __COMPARE__ your own culture with other cultures of the world. Although this is a __COMPARATIVELY__ simple method or technique, it can lead to some very stimulating insights and conclusions. By making __COMPARISON__ with other groups, we are often able to learn a great deal about ourselves.

MAKING GENERALIZATIONS ABOUT WORD FORMS

Directions: *Refer back to the part of the word form list as indicated, then try to complete the statements that follow.*

1. Refer to the verbs in items 1–3. All three verbs end in the suffix ____________ . The suffix ____________ indicates that the word is a ____________ .
2. Refer to the nouns in the items 1–3. Three of the nouns end in the suffix ____________ . The other three nouns end in the

suffix ______________________ . The suffixes *ity* and *ation* both indicate that a word is a ______________________ .

3. Refer to the nouns in items 4–6. The three nouns end in the suffix ______________________ . The suffix ______________________ indicates that a word is a ______________________ .

4. Refer to the adjectives in items 4–6. These three adjectives end in the suffix ______________________ . The suffix ______________________ indicates that a word is a ______________________ .

Dictionary Skills: Multiple Definitions and Parts of Speech

Directions: *This exercise combines two skills: identifying a word's part of speech (whether a word is a noun, verb, adjective, or adverb) and identifying its meaning. First, read the dictionary definition of the word. Then in the space provided after each sentence, write the part of speech and the meaning of the boldface word in each sentence. The first one has been done as an example.*

breed (brēd) *v.* **bred** (brĕd), **breeding.** 1. To produce (offspring); reproduce. 2. To bring about cause. 3. To raise (animals). *n* 1. A homogeneous group of animals within a species, developed by humans. 2. A type or kind. breeder, *n.*

1. The German shepherd is one **breed** of dog that has been successfully trained to provide help for the blind.

   n.-1. A homogeneous group of animals within a species.

2. The management believes that if only a few people earn a very high salary, it will **breed** feelings of resentment and dissatisfaction among the other employees.

   ____

3. On their farm they **breed** chickens, rabbits, and other animals.

   ____

head (hĕd) *n.* 1. The upper extremity of the body, containing the brain and in vertebrates, the eyes, ears, nose, and mouth. 2. Intellect; mind. 3. Self-control. 4. The obverse side of a coin. 5. A leader; chief; commander. 6. The foremost position: the head of the line. 7. A turning point, crisis. *adj.* 1. Most important; principal; commanding. 2. To be found at the top or front. *v.* 1. To be chief of; command. 2. To aim; to send in the direction of. 3. To proceed; to go in the direction of, as in *head for town.*

4. It doesn't surprise me that she's an excellent student. She's always had a good **head** on her shoulders.

   ____

5. He ran into the wall and severely injured his **head.**

6. The **head** car caused the accident when it suddenly stopped without any warning.

7. I'm a little tired. I think I'm going to **head** home as soon as I finish this last bit of work.

8. As **head** of the company, she was responsible for making all the important financial decisions.

9. When the man saw the accident he refused to panic. He was able to keep his **head** and calmly call the police.

movement (mo͞ov′ment) *n.* **1. a.** An act of moving; a change in position. **b.** A maneuver in which military or naval units are moved toward some tactical or strategic objective. **2.** A manner of moving. **3.** The activities of an organized group toward the achievement of a specific or common goal. **4.** The course or trend of affairs in a particular field. **5.** A principal division or section of a musical composition.

10. The first **movement** of Beethoven's Fifth Symphony has one of the most recognizable beginnings in all of classical music.

11. The heads of state never imagined that a **movement** which had begun as a small protest would soon escalate into a full-scale revolution.

12. In the business world there seems to be a **movement** among big corporations to acquire financial interests in smaller companies whose products or services are totally unrelated to each other.

13. During the ballet, we were all astonished by the beautiful **movement** of the dancers as they leaped across the stage.

sign (sīn) *n.* **1.** An indication of something. **2.** An action or physical gesture used to convey an idea, desire, or command. **3.** A board or poster used to advertise or convey information. **4.** A figure or device that represents a word or phrase. **5.** A trace or vestige. *v.* **1.** To affix one's signature to. **2.** To approve (a document) by affixing one's signature. **3.** To hire or engage by written contract.

14. As the actress hurriedly left the theater she refused to **sign** autographs for any of her admirers.

15. The team announced that they'd **signed** their star player to a new four-year contract.

____

16. Using both his hands, the policeman give a **sign** that the street was closed to traffic.

____

17. It's easy to get lost in that city. There aren't enough **signs**, and those that do exist can be very misleading.

____

range (rānj) *n.* 1. The limits within which something varies, as in *the range of prices.* 2. The extent of the operation or action of something. 3. A place for shooting at targets: rifle *range.* 4. A large, open region for grazing livestock or cattle. 5. A chain of mountains. 6. A large stove used for cooking. *v.* **ranged, ranging.** 1. To extend in a particular direction. 2. To vary within limits.

18. The Andes Mountains is a vast **range** that extends across virtually the entire length of South America.

____

19. It's a very interesting organization; its members **range** from young college students to retired people from all walks of life.

____

20. The General cautioned his forces not to fire until the enemy came into **range.**

____

21. North American men generally keep the tone of their voices and their hand movements within a more restricted **range** than most women.

____

Generating Topic Sentences

Directions: *Read each group of sentences carefully. Then in the space provided, complete the general statement that expresses the central idea of all the sentences. In other words, your completed sentence should serve as a main idea or topic sentence for the sentences that precede it.*

a. People from rural America often look at each other as they pass in the street.
b. Israelis are also well known for staring at people walking on the street.
c. New Yorkers, on the other hand, usually look away when strangers come close.

1. People have different customs concerning _______________

____

a. American businessmen are expected to wear suits and ties during work hours.

b. The color of businessmen's clothes is usually dark, with shades of blue, brown, and gray the most common colors.

c. American businesswomen also tend to wear darker colors when at work.

d. Moreover, businesswomen's dresses are not supposed to be too short, and their blouses should not be too low or too tight.

2. In the business world, men and ______________________________

____

a. In Spanish-speaking countries, a married woman is referred to as *senora* and a single woman is *señorita*.

b. In French-speaking nations, *madame* is the title used for a married woman, while *mademoiselle* is used for an unmarried female.

c. In Germany, a married woman's title is *frau,* while a single woman uses the title *fräulein.*

3. In many countries, there are ______________________________

____

a. During his presidency, the public's image of John Kennedy was that of a warm, friendly, and personable man.

b. By contrast, Richard Nixon often seemed stiff and formal in public.

c. Although TV cameras found him smiling much of the time, Jimmy Carter always seemed a little uncomfortable and tense in public situations.

d. Ronald Reagan has presented still another public image—relaxed, casual, a "nice guy."

4. ____

____

a. In Alaska, for instance, people wear heavy fur coats to protect them from subzero temperatures.

b. In some Middle Eastern countries, where hot weather is the norm, people have traditionally worn loose-fitting garments.

c. In some European nations, as the weather becomes hot, people prefer to wear as few clothes as possible, especially when at the beach.

5. ____

____

Three Tales of Disbelief and Misadventure

Getting the Point

Jim walked into the lobby of the large office building. It was the first time he had ever visited his girl friend at work, and he was looking forward to seeing her office and meeting her co-workers. He decided he would use the bathroom before trying to locate her office. As he was looking around the lobby for the men's room he spotted the security guard, a middle-aged man who was clearly of Hispanic descent. The guard was busy fixing something on his desk when Jim interrupted.

"Excuse me, do you know where the men's room is?"

Without nodding or stopping his work, the guard pursed his lips. Seeing the guard's response, Jim wondered to himself, "What's the matter with this guy? How can he work here and not know where the bathroom is?"

The security guard looked at Jim, who continued to stand there, a puzzled expression on his face. The guard thought to himself, "What's the matter with this guy? He asks me for directions, and when I show him he just stands there. Maybe he's up to no good."

Jim frowned and asked impatiently, "Do you speak English?"

The guard answered, angry at having been asked such a question, "Of course I speak English. I wouldn't have this job if I didn't speak English."

"Then can you tell me where the bathroom is?" Jim asked.

"Down the hall," the guard replied.

As Jim walked down the hall he shook his head and thought to himself, "Why didn't he help me in the first place?"

QUESTIONS

Can you explain the misunderstanding between Jim and the security guard? Use these questions to help you:

1. How did the security guard indicate the direction of the bathroom?
2. How did Jim react when the guard "pointed" toward the bathroom?
3. Why did Jim think that the guard was not responding to his question the first time?
4. Why did the guard think that Jim was "up to no good"?

Refer to the *first* paragraph on page 224 for an explanation.

An American in Paris

Nancy had just left her luggage at the hotel. It was her first time in a big city. As she stepped outside onto the street she felt both excited and scared at being alone in Paris for two weeks. This was the city she had always dreamed of visiting. For her, Paris was the city of elegance and romance. As she headed up the Boulevard Saint Germain she couldn't believe what she saw. Two women, one quite a few years older than the other, were walking toward her, their arms linked together. They were laughing and talking animatedly as they walked, oblivious to the people around them. Nancy stared at them and then discreetly looked away. She had never seen two women act this way in public before. She walked a few more blocks, and again she encountered a similar sight. This time two women, about the same age, were holding hands as they strolled past. Nancy's body stiffened. She tried to appear as though she hadn't noticed them, but she couldn't believe what was happening. She'd wanted so much to enjoy this first tour of Paris, but she had to be honest with herself. She never thought Paris would be like this. As she headed back to the hotel she thought, "If all of Paris is like this, it's going to be a strange two weeks."

QUESTIONS

How do you explain Nancy's change in attitude about being in Paris? Use these questions to help you:

1. How did Nancy react each time she saw the women walking together?
2. What were the women doing?
3. How do you think Nancy interpreted their behavior?

The Shadow of Your Smile

The class had begun fifteen minutes earlier when Wei Hsiao entered the room. As he quietly made his way to an empty seat, Mr. Simon, the teacher, spotted him and thought, "That student doesn't care much about the class. He's either late to class or he doesn't hand in his homework. I better do something." With that thought, Mr. Simon said, "Wei Hsiao, please see me after class."

At the end of the period the students copied down the homework assignment and filed out of the classroom. Wei Hsiao stood up and walked slowly toward his teacher's desk. Mr. Simon was alone, busy gathering up his papers and books. Wei Hsiao felt a little nervous at the thought of speaking to his teacher. He had never spoken directly to him before except in class.

Mr. Simon looked up and, frowning, said, "I'm afraid we need to talk."

Wei Hsiao smiled back, saying nothing.

Mr. Simon continued, "I'm not at all happy with your work. You're always late to class. You don't do the homework, or when you do, it's late."

Wei Hsiao continued to smile, offering no explanation.

Refer to the *second* paragraph on page 224 for an explanation.

Mr. Simon waited a moment and then his voice rose as he said, "If you keep this up you're going to fail the course. Doesn't that bother you?"

Wei Hsiao looked away, his expression unchanged, a smile still on his face.

Mr. Simon picked up his briefcase and, moving toward the door, he snapped, "I can see you obviously don't care about any of this. I don't have any more time to waste on you."

Wei Hsiao looked at the doorway, now empty, a slight smile still on his face.

QUESTIONS

Can you explain why Mr. Simon walked away from Wei Hsiao in the classroom? Use these questions to help you:

1. What were Mr. Simon's feelings toward Wei Hsiao when he first began to speak to him after class?
2. What was Wei Hsiao's reaction at that point?
3. How did Mr. Simon's feelings change during the conversation? How do you know?
4. Did Wei Hsiao's reaction change during the conversation? How do you think Mr. Simon interpreted Wei Hsiao's reaction?

Refer to the *third* paragraph on page 224 for an explanation.

4

CONFLICT IN BLACK AND WHITE

Library of Congress

Understanding Vocabulary in Context

Directions: *Read each group of sentences carefully. Then in the space provided, write a synonym or short definition for the boldface word. The first one has been done for you as an example. The boldface word in each sentence appears in the reading selection that follows this exercise.*

1. In trying to capture a dangerous criminal, the police will often offer a **reward**, sometimes worth thousands of dollars, for any information leading to the arrest and conviction of such a person.

   Definition or synonym: ***money given for doing something good***

2. I always felt that I could not trust my neighbor. When I overheard him intentionally lying to someone, it just **reinforced** my negative opinion of him.

   MAKE MORE SURE, CERTAIN. MAKE STRONGER

3. What a lazy, **shiftless** person she is! She's unemployed, yet she makes no effort to find a job.

   ____

4. It's easy to be wrong when you try to make a generalization about an entire group of people. For example, before coming to New York, I thought that all New Yorkers were cold and unfriendly. Now that I've lived here for a while, I realize that this **stereotype**, like all **stereotypes**, is not absolutely true. Many New Yorkers are really very warm and friendly.

   GENERAL PUBLIC OPINION

5. In every language there are often several words that have the same meaning, and it's actually possible to substitute one for the other. For some words, however, no other word exists that is exactly **equivalent**.

   EQUAL, SAME, SIMILAR.

6. The United States has some strange laws. For instance, the government permits cigarette companies to advertise their products in magazines and newspapers, yet it **bans** cigarette commercials on TV.

   TO BAN, FORBIDE

7. Although Americans like to criticize their country's postal service, you can usually depend on a letter reaching its proper destination. In some countries, however, the mail service is so **unreliable** that you never know if your letter will arrive at all.

   CAN'T TRUST, NOT DEPENDABLE, UNTRUSTWORTHY.

8. The young man was unfriendly, bitter, and angry, even though everyone else seemed happy and pleasant. I couldn't imagine why he had so much **hostility** toward everyone.

   ANGER, UNFRIENDLY PERSON

9. "You don't **intimidate** me," shouted the worker at her boss. "If you think I'm afraid of you and your threats, then you're crazy."

TO MAKE AFRAID to SCARE.

10. It's interesting to observe how two brothers can be so different. One can be completely independent and insist on doing things his own way, while the other can be so **submissive** that he just accepts whatever you tell him to do.

HUMBLE, ANASSERTIVE

Conflict in Black and White

THE ROOTS OF CONFLICT: SLAVERY AND THE CREATION OF STEREOTYPES

(1) Black and white. In the United States these two colors have been the source of racial conflict since the early 1600s. It was at that time that the first black people were kidnapped in Africa and sold into slavery to sea captains eager to make a profit in the human trade market. Those slaves who survived the long and difficult voyage across the ocean were then resold in America to wealthy landowners. These white landowners possessed large amounts of farmland and were in need of cheap labor to help them raise their crops. Of course farm machinery like today's did not exist, making farm work extremely laborious and difficult. Slaves were forced to labor all day under a hot sun, much like work horses and mules.

(2) To eliminate feelings of guilt and to justify their actions, slave owners found it easier to think of their slaves as "nonhuman" beings. To the white slave owner, those first Africans resembled monkeys as much as "men," with their dark skin color, bushy hair, and broad-shaped noses. The slave owner viewed these different physical features as "inferior." Furthermore, the slave owner perceived of these newly arrived slaves as "ignorant" since they neither spoke nor understood English. Slaves were considered by their owner as his property, like cattle or furniture, and if his slaves did not obey him, he would "fix" them so that they would. He was their "master," "superior" to them, and it was his job to teach them to "know their place."

(3) If a man wants to keep his property, he does not allow it to go free. He does not want it to be independent and strong, but rather, submissive and powerless. Knowledge is one kind of power. In many states, it was illegal to teach a slave how to read or write, for if slaves could read and write, they could also make their own "freedom papers."* They might even read about other slave revolts and unite together to fight for their freedom. Slave owners obviously did not want their property to run away or fight back. Consequently, they tried to intimidate their slaves and keep them illiterate. From childhood, slaves were taught that they were nothing, that they would always be nothing. Blacks, it was also believed, were naturally not as intelligent as white people. Therefore, it was not worth the trouble to try to educate them. Whites gave their slaves poorly constructed cabins with dirt floors and then said that black people were dirty by nature. Blacks, they said, did not deserve nice houses because they could not keep their own cabins clean. Owners did not give their

*Freedom papers were documents given to freed black people to show that they had been legally given their freedom and were not runaway slaves.

slaves any rewards or money for their labor and often beat them when they failed to do their work. They then accused blacks of being lazy, shiftless, and incompetent. These attitudes about blacks helped slave owners to justify the system of slavery and soon developed into stereotypes about an entire race of people.

(4) It is not surprising then that these conditions created strong feelings of hatred and hostility in blacks toward whites. They also caused fear and hostility in whites towards blacks, since whites were afraid that blacks would someday rebel. Most blacks were simply afraid of white people's power and mistreatment, and only some slaves tried to escape or did things to harm their owners. These actions, in turn, reinforced the owners' belief that black people were unreliable and untrustworthy. Often, whites found excuses for "lynching" and torturing blacks. Justice, it was clear, could not exist without equality, and equality could not exist with stereotypes of racial inferiority. Conflict between the two races increased as the stereotypes became more widespread and the mistreatment continued.

THE ROUTES OF CONFLICT: CIVIL WAR AND THE RECONSTRUCTION

(5) These racial stereotypes were in direct contradiction to the fundamental principles of the Constitution of the United States. The United States had been founded on the ideas that "all men are created equal" and that there should be "liberty and justice for all." People had come to the U.S. from all around the world in search of freedom. How could they call their country "the land of the free' when people actually had the right to own other human beings? Clearly, the concepts of freedom and slavery were in direct conflict with each other.

(6) By the mid-1820s, the states in the North had banned slavery. In the South, however, many states still insisted that people had the right to own slaves. Upon the election of Abraham Lincoln to the presidency in November of 1860, almost 100 years after the United States had become an independent nation, some of the states in the South seceded from the Union, declaring themselves independent from the rest of the U.S.A. These southern states called themselves The Confederacy, a confederation of independent states, each with its own separate government. The Confederacy would no longer accept policies made by some distant politician from "up North." The separation of the South was equivalent to a declaration of war. In 1865 the Civil War, (also known as the "War between the States") finally came to an end, but not before hundreds of thousands of men had died. The North had defeated the South, and slavery was banned in all parts of the United States.

(7) Although the Civil War was officially over, the hostility and tension between blacks and whites and North and South persisted. During the period of "reconstruction" that followed (1865–1877), the federal government gave black men some of the freedoms and privileges that white men had always enjoyed. Eventually, however, various states, particularly those in the South, enacted new laws to keep "the nigras in their place." These laws specified that blacks could not go to school with whites, that they could not eat at the same restaurants, that they could not vote unless their grandfathers had voted, that they could not use the same public rest rooms or waiting rooms at bus and train stations or drink from the same water fountains. Blacks continued to receive inferior accomodations and unequal treatment, since whites were still the ones who made the laws and held the power.

(8) Although blacks had "freedom" in a legal sense, most of them still did not have any education or economic independence. Consequently, they were

helpless to participate significantly in the political process to try to improve their status. Except for farm work, most former slaves had no skills. As a result, many blacks went back to work for the same white people who used to be their masters. Not many blacks could buy their own land or accumulate enough money to become economically independent. Instead they worked on the whites' land and gave to or shared with the owner the crops or money earned from the crops. In the South, "sharecropping" had become a way of life for many blacks. By 1900, thirty-five years after the end of the Civil War, conditions in the South had changed little for black people.

Comprehension Questions

Directions: *Answer the following questions based on the information in the article.*

1. When did slavery first begin in the United States?

2. What characteristics helped to make owners consider slaves nonhuman?

3. As a verb, the word **fix** has many different definitions. Here are some of them:

   (1) To tie securely; (2) To establish definitely, to **fix** a time; (3) To repair; (4) To take revenge upon; get even with; (5) To prearrange the outcome (of a game) by unlawful means; (6) To alter the sexual reproductive organs of an animal so that it cannot reproduce.

   Refer to paragraph 2 of the article. Which of the definitions could be applied to the way the word **fix** is used in the paragraph?

4. Explain the expression "knowledge is power." Give two examples of how the slaves could have been powerful if they had known how to read and write.

5. Refer to paragraphs 2 and 3. What are some of the different stereotypes that whites developed about blacks?

   a.

   b.

   c.

   d.

6. In your own words, explain the expression, "Equality cannot exist with stereotypes of inferiority."

7. During what years did the United States Civil War take place? What do you think the term *Reconstruction* means?

8. Refer to paragraph 7. List six of the ways that blacks were segregated from whites in some of the southern states after Reconstruction.

   a.

   b.

   c.

   d.

   e.

   f.

9. What is a "sharecropper"?

10. What do you think is the general purpose of the article?

Seeing Relationships: Explanation

The purpose of the article "Conflict in Black and White" was to try to explain why so much conflict has existed between blacks and whites in the United States. Can you identify the reasons given in the article that serve to explain the following events and circumstances?

1. Reasons slaves were brought from Africa to North America:

   a.

   b.

   c.

2. Reasons slave owners thought of slaves as "inferior" and "nonhuman":

   a.

   b.

   c.

3. Listed below are some specific stereotypes that whites developed about blacks. What explanation does the article give for why each stereotype developed? Reasons blacks were considered

   a. lazy:

   b. untrustworthy:

   c. less intelligent:

   d. dirty:

4. Reasons whites needed to create negative stereotypes about blacks:

   a.

   b.

5. Reasons whites were afraid of blacks:

   a.

   b.

6. Reason slavery was in conflict with the United States Constitution:

7. Reasons for the outbreak of the Civil War between the North and the South:

   a.

   b.

8. Reasons conditions did not change much for blacks after slavery ended:

   a.

   b.

   c.

   d.

Topics for Discussion and Composition

1. What characteristics come to mind when you think about each of the following groups?

North Americans	Latin Americans	New Yorkers
1.	1.	1.
2.	2.	2.
3.	3.	3.
4.	4.	4.

Asians	Arabs	Jews
1.	1.	1.
2.	2.	2.
3.	3.	3.
4.	4.	4.
Adolescents	**Mothers**	**Catholics**
1.	1.	1.
2.	2.	2.
3.	3.	3.
4.	4.	4.
Revolutionaries	**Politicians**	**Farmers**
1.	1.	1.
2.	2.	2.
3.	3.	3.
4.	4.	4.

2. Choose one of the groups above with which you have had a lot of contact. Have your experiences with people from this group reinforced or contradicted these stereotypes? Explain.
3. Do you agree that "knowledge is power"? What power have you gained as a result of increasing your knowledge? Give examples.
4. What other societies can you name that practiced slavery at other times in history? What differences do you see between slavery in those societies and slavery in the United States?
5. What are your roots? Describe your family's history.
6. Many people have more than one culture in their family background or life experience. What advantages are there in having a "mixed" background? What are some possible disadvantages?

Distinguishing Fact from Opinion

As you read, it is important that you be able to recognize the difference between facts and opinions. When an author presents you with new information, you must be able to determine how much of the information is really true and how much is the author's own point of view. The ability to distinguish between the two is an essential skill, especially when the subject is sensitive and complex, such as the theme of race relations.

What Is Fact? A fact is an objective statement that can be verified or shown to be true. A fact is something that can be observed; it is not influenced by emotion or personal prejudice.

What Is Opinion? An opinion is a subjective statement that indicates a personal point of view. A personal point of view cannot exist without the subject who holds that opinion. An opinion is a personal conclusion or judgement that cannot be proven. It may appear to be true, but it is open to debate since it cannot be verified in an objective way.

If you know how to distinguish facts from opinions, you will avoid learning wrong or misleading information. Because something appears in a book, that does not necessarily mean that it is correct.

Directions: *Study the definitions just given. Keep them in mind as you read each of the following statements. In the space provided, write "F" if you think the statement is a fact; write "O" if you think it is opinion.*

__*O*__ 1. Bushy hair is more beautiful than straight hair.

__*F*__ 2. The United States Civil War began in 1861.

_____ 3. Slaves did not deserve nice houses because they could not keep them clean.

_____ 4. Justice is the most important thing in a society.

_____ 5. Blacks have different physical characteristics than whites.

_____ 6. It was illegal in many states to teach a slave how to read or write.

_____ 7. The United States Civil War was the most terrible war in history because hundreds of thousands of men died.

_____ 8. It is better to be clean than dirty.

_____ 9. In fact, I think that all blacks were lazy and incompetent.

_____ 10. Most slaves worked on farms.

_____ 11. Whites are naturally inferior to blacks.

_____ 12. Today in the United States, most blacks are economically inferior to whites.

_____ 13. Slaves sometimes ran away to freedom.

_____ 14. Northern states banned slavery before the Civil War.

_____ 15. Knowledge is more powerful than money.

_____ 16. The first slaves spoke African languages that most whites did not understand.

_____ 17. Blacks should have the same opportunities as whites.

_____ 18. In the South, blacks could not use the same public rest rooms and water fountains as whites.

_____ 19. Whites enacted some good laws to keep blacks at the bottom of the economic scale.

_____ 20. Some southern states declared themselves independent from the rest of the United States.

Vocabulary Development

Directions: *Use the vocabulary to complete the sentences. Change the form of the word when necessary.*

scale	to justify	to reinforce
master	to found	to last
reward	to ban	to enact
stereotype	to share	to harm

1. The police are offering a $1,000 REWARD for any information leading to the capture of the escaped convict.
2. When I saw the way he mistreated his child, it REINFORCED my opinion that he is a bad parent.
3. United States involvement in World War II LASTED (CONTINUED) from 1941 until 1945.
4. Most people who live in the suburbs have a relatively high place on the country's economic SCALE .
5. There are special "obedience" schools where dogs are trained to obey their MASTERS .
6. Although the thieves took all the store owner's money, they did not HARM her physically.
7. The British were the first Europeans to FOUND a permanent settlement in North America.
8. Many restaurants and theaters are now ~~ARE~~ BANNING cigarette smoking because of the harm it can cause nonsmokers.
9. After his experience working with Mexicans, he no longer has the STEREOTYPE that they are all lazy and unpunctual.
10. In 1875 the Congress of the United States ENACTED a law to guarantee equal rights to blacks in public accommodations, an act invalidated by the Supreme Court in 1885.
11. Although Thomas Jefferson, the third U.S. president, wrote the words "All men are created equal," he did own slaves during his lifetime. He found it difficult to JUSTIFY his ownership of slaves, and upon his death his slaves were given their freedom.

guilty	crops	profit
eager	former	principle
voyage	untrustworthy	illiterate
	therefore	

1. She recently changed her profession. She claimed that her ______________ career did not offer her enough challenges.

2. People who have served time in prison often find it difficult to get jobs because many employers think that former criminals are ______________ .

3. Today, most American families living in cities are having fewer children. ______________ , the need for large elementary schools has decreased.

4. Although some students graduate from high school, they are virtually ______________ , never having learned to read or write well.

5. During the 1600s the ______________ by boat across the Atlantic Ocean took several months.

6. Sea captains from many different countries, ______________ to make money in the slave market, went to Africa to buy slaves.

7. When sea captains brought slaves to North America, they were able to resell these men and women and make a ______________ .

8. The United States government was founded on the ______________ that "all men are created equal."

9. Jefferson probably felt ______________ about owning slaves since he asked that all his slaves be freed when he died.

10. A farmer needs fertile land and a good climate to grow ______________ .

Word Forms/Sequencing Ideas

Directions: *1. Complete each group of sentences by writing in the appropriate blank space the correct word from those in parentheses. Change the form of the verb or noun where necessary.*

2. After completing all the sentences, number them in order, so that each group of sentences forms a well-organized paragraph. Write the number in the blank space at the left of each sentence. The first one has been done for you as an example.

1. **(to discuss, discussion)**

__2__ During class we all talked about our own experiences and **discussed** some of the ways people can misinterpret our actions.

3 At the end of the class the teacher said he wanted to continue the **discussion** next time.

1 When we entered the class, the teacher said, "Today I'd like us to **discuss** the importance of nonverbal communication."

2. **(to enslave, slave, slavery)**

_____ It was there that the great pyramids of the Egyptian Pharoahs were built by the labor of SLAVES.

_____ Although the institution of SLAVERY began in North America as early as the 1600s, it was certainly not the first time in history that people were used as SLAVES.

_____ It was common for nations to SLAVE people that they had conquered or defeated in war.

_____ Later in history two other powerful groups, the ancient Greeks and the ancient Romans, also SLAVED people.

_____ A much earlier example of SLAVERY on a large scale is to be found in ancient Egypt.

3. **(to develop, developing, development)**

_____ In India, on the other hand, a long rainy season makes it difficult for the Indian people to DEVELOP their agriculture.

_____ The economic DEVELOPMENT of a country often depends on its climate and natural resources.

_____ Likewise, problems with climate in some of the DEVELOPING nations of North Africa have also limited economic DEVELOPMENT in this part of the world.

_____ For example, the abundant resources and fertile land of the United States have played a major role in the DEVELOPMENT of the country.

4. **(to rebel, rebellion, rebellious)**

_____ One famous REBELLION was organized by John Brown, a white man who provided slaves with the weapons necessary TO REBEL.

_____ Both Turner and Brown were put to death for their REBELLIOUS actions.

_____ Nat Turner, a REBELLIOUS slave, was responsible for another well-known REBELLION.

_____ However, Turner's and Brown's attempts _____TO REBEL_____ were later chronicled in two famous works of literature, *John Brown's Body* and *The Confessions of Nat Turner.*

_____ During the course of slavery in the South, there were several _____REBELLIONS_____ by slaves that have become very famous.

5. **(power, powerful, powerless)**

_____ Today, the two great military _____POWERS_____ of the world are the Soviet Union and the United States.

_____ For instance, during the 1500s the country of Spain possessed one of the world's largest and most _____POWERFUL_____ naval forces.

_____ One of the interesting things about history is how the world's nations gain and lose _____POWER_____ over a long period of time.

_____ Nowadays, countries like Spain and England would probably be _____POWERLESS_____ to stop an invasion by these other two super _____POWERS_____.

_____ However, after Spain's navy was defeated by England in 1588, Spain lost much of its military _____POWER_____.

_____ Looking at these examples from history, one can only conclude that the Soviet Union and the United States will not always be the most _____POWERFUL_____ nations on earth.

6. **(to symbolize, symbol, symbolic, symbolically)**

_____ Given to the United States as a gift from the government of France, the statue _____SYMBOLIZE_____ freedom and justice.

_____ Most nations of the world have different _____SIMBOLS_____ that they use to express their national spirit and identity.

_____ The bald eagle is one _____SIMBOL_____ of the United States, and can be found _____SYMBOLICALLY_____ pictured on the back of all quarters and one-dollar bills.

_____ In the United States, for example, there are many _____SIMBOLIC_____ expressions of this country's heritage as a free and independent nation.

_____ This large and powerful bird _____SIMBOLIZES_____ freedom and strength.

_____ Another famous _____SIMBOL_____ of freedom is the Statue of Liberty, located in the harbor of New York City.

Dictionary Skills: Etymology

Roots Revisited: Just as people have ancestors, so too do the words of a language have different origins that go far back in time. Many words in the English language originated from much older languages such as Greek, Latin, and Middle and Old English.

Take the word *reconstruction* as an example. Each part of the word comes from the *Latin,* and each has a particular meaning.

re•con•struct•ion: re (L, again), con (L, together), struct (L, *struere,* to pile up, to build), ion, the result of being

The word *reconstruction* means, literally, *the result of being piled together again.*

Not all words in English come from other languages; some words have interesting or amusing stories behind them. Take the word *boycott,* for instance. To *boycott* is to refuse to have business or social relations with another individual or group, often as a means of protest. The word *boycott* comes from the name of a man, Charles Boycott, who was a land agent for the Earl of Ere, a wealthy landowner in Ireland. It was Boycott's responsibility to collect rent from his neighbors who lived on the Earl's land. His neighbors, however, felt that the rent was too high, and in 1881, they refused to pay Boycott their rent. From this isolated event of over a century ago, Boycott's name became a word used in everyday speech. In chapter 5, you will read about a different kind of boycott that helped change the course of history.

Directions: *Use an all-English dictionary to find the origin or etymology of each of the words listed. When possible, write the letters that indicate the language these words come from. (You may need to refer to the etymology guide at the front of the dictionary to identify what language each letter represents. For example, the letter L indicates that a word comes from Latin.) When appropriate, write the literal meaning of each word in the space provided.*

1. Mister ____________________
2. Slave ____________________
3. Guilt ____________________
4. Lynch ____________________
5. Torture ____________________
6. Secede ____________________
7. Negro ____________________
8. Labor ____________________
9. Abraham ____________________
10. Lincoln ____________________

NAMES AND ORIGINS

1. What is the origin of your name? Were you named after someone in particular?

2. Many names have specific meanings. Does your name have a particular meaning? Has your name influenced you in any way?

3. Do you have any nicknames? Does your family call you by a different name from the name that appears on your birth certificate? What is the origin of your nickname?

4. Have you ever changed your name? Did this change affect your self-image in any way?

Paraphrasing

One important skill in reading is the ability to state in your own words what you have read. This skill is called paraphrasing. Being able to express concisely in your own words the essential idea of a passage helps you to better understand and remember what you've read.

Here is an example of paraphrasing. Notice how the words of a long statement are reduced to a much shorter form while the important idea of the statement is still expressed.

Statement: Finally, in 1861, almost one hundred years after the United States had become an independent nation, some of the states in the South seceded from the United States, declaring themselves to be separate and independent from the rest of the country.

Paraphrase: In 1861, some Southern states separated from the rest of the United States.

Directions: *The following statements can be reduced to a simpler, more direct form. In the space provided, paraphrase each statement by using your own words as much as possible to express the central idea in a brief, direct way. The first item has been done as an example.*

1. In general, slaves rarely received any money, vacations, or special privileges in exchange for the long hours they were forced to work.

   Slaves rarely received rewards for their work.

2. During the years following the United States Civil War, blacks in the South were not allowed to use the same restaurants, public toilets, or waiting rooms as white people. In fact, blacks even had to drink from separate water fountains.

   ____

3. Slavery in North America developed for several reasons, many of them economic; sea captains were anxious to make money by bringing kidnapped slaves from Africa and selling them to white landowners for a profit. These landowners were in need of cheap labor, and slavery was a convenient economic solution to their problem.

   ____

4. To the white slave owner, African slaves were somehow inferior, in part because of their dark skin color, bushy hair, broad-shaped noses, and other physical differences.

---

5. Whites tended to think that all blacks were the same, that most blacks were naturally less intelligent, less trustworthy, and less hard-working than white people.

---

6. It was against the law in some states to teach a slave to read and write. In addition, slaves were forced to live in dirt-floor cabins and were given no rewards for their hard work. Slaves who were caught trying to escape were treated severely, often beaten and tortured by their owner.

---

7. The United States was founded on the principles of "all men are created equal" and "liberty and justice for all." How could people call their country the "land of the free" when they were allowed to own other human beings?

Mr. Know-All

WILLIAM SOMERSET MAUGHAM

(1874–1965)

Born in 1874 in Paris, France, of English parents, William Somerset Maugham had a long and varied life. An orphan at the age of ten, Maugham was educated at King's School in England and Heidelberg University in Germany. Of his childhood he says, "The accident of my birth in France . . . instilled in me two modes of life, two liberties, two points of view (and) prevented me from ever identifying completely with instincts and prejudices of one people or another."

Maugham was a prolific writer who enjoyed great commercial success early in life. During his life he traveled extensively through Europe, the Orient, and the South Seas. His travels and his work as a British spy during the two world wars provided him with stories that helped make him the most widely read English writer since Charles Dickens. In addition to being a novelist and playwright of distinction, Maugham was a master of the short story. "Mr. Know-All," the short story presented here, is set after the end of the first world war (1914–1918) at a time when Prohibition (a period when alcoholic drinks were illegal) was still in effect. The story, along with two others, was made into a film, Trio, *in 1950. Although the story of "Mr. Know-All" takes place more than sixty years ago, its message remains as timely and important as when it was first written.*

I was prepared to dislike Max Kelada even before I knew him. The war had just finished and the passenger traffic in the ocean going liners was heavy. Accommodation was very hard to get and you had to put up with whatever the agents chose to offer you. You could not hope for a cabin to yourself and

I was thankful to be given one in which there were only two berths.[1] But when I was told the name of my companion my heart sank. It suggested closed portholes and the night air rigidly excluded. It was bad enough to share a cabin for fourteen days with anyone (I was going from San Francisco to Yokohama), but I should have looked upon it with less dismay[2] if my fellow passenger's name had been Smith or Brown.

When I went on board I found Mr. Kelada's luggage already below. I did not like the look of it; there were too many labels on the suitcases, and the wardrobe trunk was too big. He had unpacked his toilet things, and I observed that he was a patron of the excellent Monsieur Coty; for I saw on the washing-stand his scent, his hairwash and his brilliantine. Mr. Kelada's brushes, ebony with his monogram in gold, would have been all the better for a scrub.[3] I did not at all like Mr. Kelada. I made my way into the smoking-room. I called for a pack of cards and began to play patience.[4] I had scarcely started before a man came up to me and asked me if he was right in thinking my name was so and so.

"I am Mr. Kelada," he added, with a smile that showed a row of flashing[5] teeth, and sat down.

"Oh, yes, we're sharing a cabin, I think."

"Bit of luck, I call it. You never know who you're going to be put in with. I was jolly[6] glad when I heard you were English. I'm all for us English sticking[7] together when we're abroad, if you understand what I mean."

I blinked.

"Are you English?" I asked, perhaps tactlessly.[8]

"Rather. You don't think I look like an American, do you? British to the backbone, that's what I am."

To prove it, Mr. Kelada took out of his pocket a passport and airily waved it under my nose.

King George has many strange subjects. Mr. Kelada was short and of a sturdy build, clean-shaven and dark skinned, with a fleshy, hooked nose and very large lustrous[9] and liquid eyes. His long black hair was sleek[10] and curly. He spoke with a fluency in which there was nothing English and his gestures were exuberant.[11] I felt pretty sure that a closer inspection of that British passport would have betrayed[12] the fact that Mr. Kelada was born under a bluer sky than is generally seen in England.

"What will you have?" he asked me.

I looked at him doubtfully. Prohibition was in force and to all appearances the ship was bone dry. When I am not thirsty I do not know which I dislike more, ginger ale or lemon squash. But Mr. Kelada flashed an oriental smile at me.

"Whisky and soda or a dry martini, you have only to say the word."

"From each of his hip pockets he furnished a flask[13] and laid it on the table before me. I chose the martini, and calling the steward he ordered a tumbler of ice and a couple of glasses.

"A very good cocktail," I said.

"Well, there are plenty more where that came from, and if you've got any

[1]**berths:** sleeping places
[2]**dismay:** discouragement, apprehension
[3]**scrub:** cleaning by rubbing hard
[4]**patience:** a card game played by one person
[5]**flashing:** bright; shiny
[6]**jolly:** very (British)
[7]**sticking:** staying
[8]**tactlessly:** without sensitivity
[9]**lustrous:** shiny; bright
[10]**sleek:** smooth; shiny
[11]**exuberant:** full of life; uninhibited
[12]**betrayed:** exposed
[13]**flask:** small bottle

friends on board, you tell them you've got a pal[14] who's got all the liquor in the world."

Mr. Kelada was chatty[15]. He talked of New York and of San Francisco. He discussed plays, pictures, and politics. He was patriotic. The Union Jack[16] is an impressive piece of drapery, but when it is flourished[17] by a gentleman from Alexandria or Beirut, I cannot but feel that it loses somewhat in dignity. Mr. Kelada was familiar. I do not wish to put on airs,[18] but I cannot help feeling that it is seemly[19] in a total stranger to put mister before my name when he addresses me. Mr. Kelada, doubtless to set me at my ease, used no such formality. I did not like Mr. Kelada. I had put aside the cards when he sat down, but now, thinking that for this first occasion our conversation had lasted long enough, I went on with my game.

"The three on the four," said Mr. Kelada.

There is nothing more exasperating[20] when you are playing patience than to be told where to put the card you have turned up before you have a chance to look for yourself.

"It's coming out, it's coming out," he cried. "The ten on the knave."

With rage and hatred in my heart I finished.

Then he seized[21] the pack.

"Do you like card tricks?"

"No, I hate card tricks," I answered.

"Well, I'll just show you this one."

He showed me three. Then I said I would go down to the dining-room and get my seat at the table.

"Oh, that's all right," he said, "I've already taken a seat for you. I thought that as we were in the same stateroom[22] we might just as well sit at the same table."

I did not like Mr. Kelada.

I not only shared a cabin with him and ate three meals a day at the same table, but I could not walk round the deck without his joining me. It was impossible to snub[23] him. It never occurred to him that he was not wanted. He was certain that you were as glad to see him as he was to see you. In your own house you might have kicked him downstairs and slammed[24] the door in his face without the suspicion dawning on him that he was not a welcome visitor. He was a good mixer, and in three days knew everyone on board. He ran everything. He managed the sweeps,[25] conducted the auctions, collected money for prizes at the sports, got up quoit and golf matches, organized the concert and arranged the fancy-dress ball.[26] He was everywhere and always. He was certainly the best hated man in the ship. We called him Mr. Know-All, even to his face. He took it as a compliment. But it was at mealtimes that he was most intolerable. For the better part of an hour then he had us at his mercy. He was hearty, jovial,[27] loquacious[28] and argumentative. He knew everything better than anybody else, and it was an affront to his overweening[29] vanity that you should disagree with him. He would not drop a subject, however unimportant,

[14]**pal:** friend (informal)
[15]**chatty:** talkative
[16]**Union Jack:** British flag
[17]**flourished:** shown; exhibited
[18]**put on airs:** show off
[19]**seemly:** proper
[20]**exasperating:** upsetting; annoying
[21]**seized:** took away suddenly
[22]**stateroom:** cabin
[23]**snub:** reject; ignore
[24]**slammed:** closed with force
[25]**sweeps:** gambling
[26]**ball:** dance
[27]**jovial:** full of good humor
[28]**loquacious:** talkative
[29]**overweening:** excessive

till he had brought you round[30] to his way of thinking. The possibility that he could be mistaken never occurred to him. He was the chap[31] who knew. We sat at the doctor's table. Mr. Kelada would certainly have had it all his own way, for the doctor was lazy and I was frigidly indifferent, except for a man called Ramsay who sat there also. He was as dogmatic[32] as Mr. Kelada and resented bitterly the Levantine's cocksureness[33]. The discussions they had were acrimonious[34] and interminable.

Ramsay was in the American Consular Service and was stationed at Kobe.[35] He was a great heavy fellow from the Middle West, with loose fat under a tight skin, and he bulged out of his ready-made clothes. He was on his way back to resume his post, having been on a flying visit to New York to fetch[36] his wife who had been spending a year at home. Mrs. Ramsay was a very pretty little thing, with pleasant manners and a sense of humor. The Consular Service is ill paid, and she was dressed always very simply; but she knew how to wear her clothes. She achieved an effect of quiet distinction. I should not have paid any particular attention to her but that she possessed a quality that may be common enough in women, but nowadays is not obvious in their demeanour.[37] It shone in her like a flower on a coat.

One evening at dinner the conversation by chance drifted[38] to the subject of pearls. There had been in the papers a good deal of talk about the cultured pearls which the cunning[39] Japanese were making, and the doctor remarked that they must inevitably diminish the value of real ones. They were very good already; they would soon be perfect. Mr. Kelada, as was his habit, rushed the new topic. He told us all that was to be known about pearls. I do not believe Ramsay knew anything about them at all, but he could not resist the opportunity to have a fling[40] at the Levantine, and in five minutes we were in the middle of a heated argument. I had seen Mr. Kelada vehement and voluble[41] before, but never so voluble and vehement as now. At last something that Ramsay said stung him, for he thumped[42] the table and shouted.

"Well, I ought to know what I am talking about, I'm going to Japan just to look into this Japanese pearl business. I'm in the trade and there's not a man in it who won't tell you that what I say about pearls goes. I know all the best pearls in the world, and what I don't know about pearls isn't worth knowing."

Here was news for us, for Mr. Kelada, with all his loquacity, had never told anyone what his business was. We only knew vaguely that he was going to Japan on some commercial errand[43]. He looked around the table triumphantly.

"They'll never be able to get a cultured pearl that an expert like me can't tell with half an eye." He pointed to a chain that Mrs. Ramsay wore. "You take my word for it, Mrs. Ramsay, that chain you're wearing will never be worth a cent less than it is now."

Mrs. Ramsay in her modest way flushed[44] a little and slipped the chain

[30]**brought you round:** persuaded you
[31]**chap:** guy; man (British)
[32]**dogmatic:** strongly opinionated
[33]**cocksureness:** overconfidence
[34]**acrimonious:** bitter
[35]**Kobe:** a city in Japan
[36]**fetch:** get
[37]**demeanour:** behavior; manner
[38]**drifted:** moved
[39]**cunning:** clever
[41]**voluble:** talkative; loud
[42]**thumped:** hit; pounded
[43]**errand:** trip
[44]**flushed:** turned red

inside her dress. Ramsay leaned forward. He gave us all a look and a smile flickered[45] in his eyes.

"That's a pretty chain of Mrs. Ramsay's, isn't it?"

"I noticed it at once," answered Mr. Kelada. "Gee, I said to myself, those are pearls all right."

"I didn't buy it myself, of course. I'd be interested to know how much you think it cost."

"Oh, in the trade somewhere round fifteen thousand dollars. But if it was bought on Fifth Avenue I shouldn't be surprised to hear anything up to thirty thousand was paid for it."

Ramsay smiled grimly.

"You'll be surprised to hear that Mrs. Ramsay bought that string at a department store the day before we left New York, for eighteen dollars."

Mr. Kelada flushed.

"Rot[46]. It's not only real, but it's as fine a string for its size as I've ever seen."

"Will you bet on it? I'll bet you a hundred dollars it's imitation."

"Done."

"Oh, Elmer, you can't bet on a certainty," said Mrs. Ramsay.

She had a little smile on her lips and her tone was gently deprecating[47].

"Can't I? If I get a chance of easy money like that I should be all sorts of a fool not to take it."

"But how can it be proved?" she continued. "It's only my word against Mr. Kelada's."

"Let me look at the chain, and if it's imitation I'll tell you quickly enough. I can afford to lose a hundred dollars," said Mr. Kelada.

"Take it off, dear. Let the gentlemen look at it as much as he wants."

Mrs. Ramsay hesitated a moment. She put her hands to the clasp.

"I can't undo it," she said. "Mr. Kelada will just have to take my word for it."

I had a sudden suspicion that something unfortunate was about to occur, but I could think of nothing to say.

Ramsay jumped up.

"I'll undo it."

He handed the chain to Mr. Kelada. The Levantine took a magnifying glass from his pocket and closely examined it. A smile of triumph spread over his smooth and swarthy[48] face. He handed back the chain. He was about to speak. Suddenly he caught sight of Mrs. Ramsay's face. It was so white that she looked as though she were about to faint[49]. She was staring at him with wide and terrified eyes. They held a desperate appeal; it was so clear that I wondered why her husband did not see it.

Mr. Kelada stopped with his mouth open. He flushed deeply. You could almost see the effort he was making over himself.

"I was mistaken," he said. "It's very good imitation, but of course as soon as I looked through my glass I saw that it wasn't real. I think eighteen dollars is just about as much as the damned thing's worth."

He took out his pocketbook and from it a hundred dollar note. He handed it to Ramsay without a word.

[45]**flickered:** shone unsteadily

[46]**rot:** nonsense; garbage

[47]**deprecating:** disapproving

[48]**swarthy:** dark

[49]**faint:** lose consciousness

"Perhaps that'll teach you not to be so cocksure[50] another time, my young friend," said Ramsay as he took the note.

I noticed that Mr. Kelada's hands were trembling.[51]

The story spread over the ship as stories do, and he had to put up with[52] a good deal of chaff[53] that evening. It was a fine joke that Mr. Know-All had been caught out[54]. But Mrs. Ramsay retired to her state-room with a headache.

Next morning I got up and began to shave. Mr. Kelada lay on his bed smoking a cigarette. Suddenly there was a small scraping sound and I saw a letter pushed under the door. I opened the door and looked out. There was nobody there. I picked up the letter and saw it was addressed to Max Kelada. The name was written in block letters. I handed it to him.

"Who's this from?" He opened it. "Oh!"

He took out of the envelope, not a letter, but a hundred-dollar note. He looked at me and again he reddened. He tore the envelope into little bits and gave them to me.

"Do you mind just throwing them out of the porthole?"

I did as he asked, and then I looked at him with a smile.

"No one likes being made to look a perfect damned fool," he said.

"Were the pearls real?"

"If I had a pretty little wife I shouldn't let her spend a year in New York while I stayed at Kobe," said he.

At that moment I did not entirely dislike Mr. Kelada. He reached out for his pocketbook and carefully put in it the hundred-dollar note.

QUESTIONS

1. Who is telling the story? What is the person's nationality?
2. Describe the story's setting. Where do the events of the story take place?
3. Who is Mr. Kelada? Describe his physical appearance. Where do you think he's from?
4. What emotional conflict exists in the story? How is the conflict first introduced to the reader?
5. What is the initial reason for the conflict? What words and examples are used to demonstrate the narrator's feelings toward Mr. Kelada?
6. How is the conflict developed during the story? What other examples or situations are presented to illustrate the conflict?
7. Who are Mr. and Mrs. Ramsay? What description is given about their appearance? What kind of person is Mrs. Ramsay?
8. What was Mrs. Ramsay's reaction while Mr. Kelada and her husband discussed the pearls? Why is her reaction important to the rest of the story?
9. What was Mr. Kelada's reaction to Mrs. Ramsay's pearls? How did his reaction change? What caused him to change his mind?
10. Where did Mrs. Ramsay get the pearls she was wearing? What happens in the story that permits the reader to know the true value of the pearls?

[50]**cocksure:** confident

[51]**trembling:** shaking

[52]**to put up with:** to tolerate

[53]**chaff:** ridicule; teasing

[54]**caught out:** embarrassed

11. How does the narrator feel toward Mr. Kelada at the end of the story? What is responsible for this change in attitude?

12. How does this story relate to some of the themes introduced in the article "Conflict in Black and White"? What message or lesson do you think the story "Mr. Know All" is attempting to communicate?

Directions: *Use the following words from the story to complete the sentences below:*

dismay	to stick	to faint	exuberant	errand
demeanor	to seize	to arrange	exasperating	worth

1. The narrator had a feeling of disappointment and ____________________ when he realized his fellow passenger was named Kelada.

2. Mr. Kelada thought that he and the narrator should ____________________ together on the ship since they were both English citizens.

3. Mr. Kelada had a very friendly ____________________ ; he was constantly talking and enjoyed expressing an opposing point of view.

4. The narrator found Mr. Kelada ____________________ because Mr. Kelada never left him in peace.

5. When the narrator had finished his card game, Mr. Kelada ____________________ the cards and proceeded to show him several card tricks.

6. The narrator considered Mr. Kelada's gestures to be ____________________ , probably because Mr. Kelada moved his hands a lot as he talked.

7. Mr. Kelada enjoyed mixing with the other people on the ship, and he ____________________ many activities for his fellow voyagers.

8. Mr. Kelada informed everyone that he was going to Japan on a commercial ____________________ in order to investigate the pearl business there.

9. When Mr. Ramsay started to show Mr. Kelada the pearls, Mrs. Ramsay turned completely pale. She looked as if she was going to ____________________ .

10. Mr. Kelada was right about the true ____________________ of the pearls; they really were an expensive piece of jewelry.

5

"I HAVE A DREAM"

UPI/Bettmann Archive

Understanding Vocabulary in Context

Directions: *Read each group of sentences carefully. Then in the space provided, write a synonym or short definition for each boldface word. The boldface word in each sentence appears in the reading selection that follows this exercise.*

1. One can't always judge people by what they say they will do. People's **deeds** or actions reveal more about their characters than mere words.

   Definition or synonym: ACTIONS

2. He was a combat soldier and was in the most dangerous situation he had ever faced; with the enemy approaching from all sides and no way to escape, his **plight** seemed hopeless.

   BAD SITUATION

3. Even before the case was concluded it was clear that the judge would give the mother custody of the children. The father knew he had no legal choice except to **comply with** the judge's decision.

   TO ACCEPT / AGREE TO DO SOMETHING

4. As news of the assassination spread, people ran through the streets, breaking windows, setting fire to cars, and destroying everything in their path. It took the police ten hours to end this, the worst **riot** in the city's history.

   MOTIVATIVE DEMONSTRATION,

5. At different periods in history, groups of people have been under the **rule** of more powerful nations. For example, the ancient Romans controlled much of Europe, just as the Greeks once governed parts of Asia.

   POWER, LAW, AUTORITHY

6. As young men preparing to become ministers of the church, we were taught how to deliver the Sunday **sermon**, a speech used during the church service to express a special religious or moral message.

   A SPEECH.

7. The Nobel Prize is actually several **awards**. These **awards** are given annually in recognition of contributions in the fields of literature, science, and peace.

   PRIZES / PRIZE

8. In preparing her critically acclaimed novel, the writer dedicated four years of her life to researching the book's subject, and then **devoted** another three years to the actual writing of the book.

   SPEND TIME DOING SOMETHING.

9. The judge stared at the convicted criminal and said, "You have been found guilty of possession of an illegal weapon. State law requires that I **sentence** you to one year in prison."

   TO TELL WHAT THE PUNISHMENT WILL BE.

10. The professor's enthusiam for his subject was **contagious**. Students who were normally disinterested in their schoolwork suddenly became excited and enthusiastic when they entered his class.

    ABLE TO SPREAD

    CAN BE SPREAD

"I Have a Dream"

and if ever i touched a life i hope that life
knows
that i know that touching was and still is and
always will be the true
revolution—NIKKI GIOVANNI
from the poem "When I Die" (1972)

A PROUD HERITAGE

(1) On December 19, 1899, a few days before the turn of the century, a son was born to a poor black sharecropper in Stockbridge, Georgia. He was one of eleven children of James Albert King and his wife. When the children were old enough, they all had to work in the fields to help support the family. Consequently none of them received much schooling. This son, Martin, called "Mike" by his family, was especially good at arithmetic, and when he was 15 years old he discovered that the white landowner was cheating his family. He was angry and upset about his family's plight. He decided to get an education and make conditions better for his people. Mike left home and worked at various kinds of manual labor while he went to school at night. He had become a man of 26 before he finally graduated from high school, and it took him another five years to get his college diploma. By that time he was a minister in his church, and he had married. On January 15, 1929, a second child was born to "Mike" and Alberta King. They named him Martin Luther King, Jr.

KING'S EARLY YEARS

(2) As a child, Martin Luther King, Jr., loved to hear his father speak in church. He was very proud of his father and wanted to learn to use big words the same way his father did. When Martin Jr. was only five years old he wanted to go to school so badly that he convinced his mother to let him go, even though the minimum age was six. The story is told that the teacher discovered his true age when he told his classmates that at his last birthday there were five candles on the cake. He was sent home to wait another year.

(3) M.L. (as he was called at home) learned quickly, both in school and out. He had two white friends who lived nearby. Suddenly the boys' parents did not allow them to play with M.L. anymore because he was "colored." All around the city there were signs that read, "For Whites Only" or "Colored," because local laws required segregation of whites and blacks. The "colored" or Negro people were treated as if they were inferior. It was common for a white person to call a black man "boy," even if the black was decades older than the white. There were many restaurants that would not serve food to Negroes. If blacks were far from home they simply had to go hungry until they could find a place to eat. Of course public rest rooms were not available to blacks either, and what was available was greatly inferior to the facilities available to whites. Blacks were nearly always given inferior accommodations if they were accommodated at all.

(4) For two years M.L. had the opportunity to attend a special private "laboratory" school that Atlanta University had developed as an experimental project. There were not many students in the classes, and each student received much individual attention. The teachers at the school wanted to show the world that the stereotypes about Negroes were not true; they wanted to prove that Negro children could learn just as quickly as white children if given

an equal opportunity. M.L. learned quickly. He also learned about the history of his people. He was inspired by the deeds of the great men and women who had devoted their lives to improving the conditions of Negroes in the United States, and he dreamed that one day maybe he too could do something to help his people.

KING EMERGES AS A LEADER

(5) When M.L. was in college and later in divinity school he studied the writings and works of two men (in addition to Jesus Christ) who profoundly influenced his own thinking. These men were Henry David Thoreau (1817–1862), a writer and philosopher from Concord, Massachusetts, and Mohandas K. Gandhi (1869–1948), "The Mahatma" ("Great Soul"), who had worked to free his own Indian people from the colonial rule and domination of Great Britain. Both of these men believed in nonviolent protest as a means of changing unjust laws. At different times in their lives both men were arrested and imprisoned for peaceful disobedience to unjust laws. Here was an idea that Martin Luther King, Jr., could associate with his own sense of purpose and religion. If he could use nonviolent resistance to change the unjust laws of racial segregation, maybe he could improve the conditions of his people in the South. Martin Luther King, Jr., was already married and a young minister at the Dexter Avenue Baptist Church in Montgomery, Alabama, when the opportunity came.

(6) Thursday evening, December 1, 1955, Mrs. Rosa Parks, a black woman, was returning home from work by bus when she was told to give her seat to a white man who had gotten on the bus after her. She was very tired and simply decided not to move. She was arrested. News of the event spread quickly within the black community. Dr. Martin Luther King, Jr., received a call to attend a meeting of Negro leaders the next evening. It was decided to boycott the Montgomery, Alabama, buses. The leaders felt that it was unjust for Negroes to have to give their seats to whites or move to the back of the bus if both groups of people paid the same amount of money for the ride. The boycott of the buses proved effective as black citizens refused to ride. The boycott lasted for many months. Meanwhile, white leaders in Montgomery tried to terrorize the blacks with violence and arrests in an effort to end the boycott. But the Negroes continued to ride together in "car pools" or to hitchhike. Eventually the Supreme Court of the United States ruled that Alabama's bus segregation laws were unconstitutional. This was the first personal political victory for Dr. Martin Luther King; there would be many more to come.

(7) Dr. King became a very famous leader in the Civil Rights Movement of the 1950s and 1960s precisely because of the success of his nonviolent resistance to unjust laws. The boycott in Montgomery awakened the nation to the power of nonviolent resistance; success slowly followed success as civil rights activists peacefully challenged the traditional concept of segregation in the South. The method was effective; the success was contagious. Many schools and colleges were forced to integrate. Blacks sat at lunch counters in restaurants for days until they were served. Blacks, together with sympathetic whites, took "freedom rides" to the South on interstate buses. These rides and the violence they provoked, dramatized the unjust situation. Later, police and local authorities were made to comply with federal regulations against segregation. At the same time there was a massive effort to register blacks to vote. This action greatly threatened whites, for if more blacks actually voted, they would finally have the political power to bring about real change. Everywhere they went, black people encountered hate and violence because of their noncompliance with segregation. Through it all, Dr. King's philosophy prevailed.

KING'S LEGACY

(8) On August 28, 1963, 250,000 people assembled in the nation's capital. The huge demonstration became known as the "March on Washington." At that demonstration Dr. King told the world, "I have a dream" that equality would come "to all of God's children . . . black and white, Jew and Gentile, Protestant and Catholic." He said he wanted everyone to be able to "join hands and sing in the words of the old Negro spiritual, 'Free at last! Free at last! Thank God Almighty, we are free at last!' " A year later Dr. Martin Luther King earned one of the world's highest awards, the Nobel Peace Prize. He was just thirty-five years old.

(9) But slowly new, younger black leaders came forward, some of them angry with the slowness of change. Some of these leaders spoke of more aggressive kinds of resistance. In the summers of 1964 and 1965 riots broke out in countless cities throughout the country in the states of California, Michigan, New Jersey, New York, and Pennsylvania, to name a few. Dr. Martin Luther King felt discouraged. Better than anyone, he knew the frustrations of nonviolent protest, but he believed in the method, despite its decline in popularity.

(10) In 1964, less than a year after President Kennedy's assassination, the Civil Rights Act was passed by the Congress of the United States. This law prohibited discrimination on the basis of race, color, or national origin. Despite the new law, discrimination against blacks did not disappear overnight. Still more protest was necessary to insure equal rights for all people. However, peaceful protest and nonviolent resistance continued to receive violence in return.

(11) By 1965, several civil rights leaders had been assassinated, including Medgar Evers and Malcolm X, and scores, if not hundreds, of followers had died from violent acts of fanatical segregationists. It is reported that at the time of President Kennedy's assassination on November 22, 1963, Dr. King had a premonition that he too would die from an assassin's bullet, and that it would be before his fortieth birthday. On April 4, 1968, King's premonition came true. The night before his death he spoke to a group of sanitation workers in Memphis, Tennessee. The workers had been on strike for nondiscriminatory working conditions, and there had been a march the week before that had ended in violence. The eruption into violence had discouraged Dr. King, and for nearly a week he had been in a state of severe depression. But that night Dr. King spoke gloriously to the workers and told them what was in his heart.

> We've got some difficult days ahead. But it really doesn't matter with me now. Because I've been to the mountain top. I won't mind. Like anybody I would like to live a long life. Longevity has its place. But I'm not concerned with that now, I just want to do God's will. And He's allowed me to go up to the mountain. And I've looked over, and I've seen the promised land. I may not get there with you, but I want you to know tonight that we as a people will get to the promised land. So I'm happy tonight. I'm not fearing any man. "Mine eyes have seen the glory of the coming of the Lord. . . ."

(12) The next night as he stood alone for a moment on a motel balcony to say good-bye to some co-workers, Dr. Martin Luther King, Jr., was fatally shot. James Earl Ray was later convicted of the crime and was sentenced to "life" in prison. In a sermon that he had delivered exactly three months earlier, Dr. King had specified what he hoped others would say about him at his funeral.

> If any of you are around when I have to meet my day, I don't want a long funeral. And if you get somebody to deliver the eulogy, tell him not to talk too long. . . . Tell them not to mention that I have a Nobel Peace Prize. That isn't important. Tell

them not to mention that I have three or four hundred other awards. That's not important. Tell them not to mention where I went to school. I'd like for somebody to say that day, that Martin Luther King, Jr. tried to love somebody. I want you to say that day I tried to be right on the war question. I want you to be able to say that day, that I did try to feed the hungry. And I want you to be able to say that day, that I did try in my life to clothe those who were naked. I want you to say on that day that I did try in my life to visit those who were in prison. I want you to say that I tried to love and serve humanity.

POSTSCRIPT

On November 2, 1983, a law honoring Dr. King was signed, effective January 1986, making the third Monday of January a national holiday. He is the only U.S. citizen other than George Washington to be recognized in this way.

Comprehension Questions

1. Describe Martin Luther King, Jr.'s family heritage.
2. What kind of relationship did King have with his father when he was a young boy?
3. What incident in the story demonstrates that King was eager to learn as a child?
4. As a child, King attended a special school founded by Atlanta University. Why was this school called a "laboratory school?"
5. What personal experiences did King have that probably motivated him to want to help his people?
6. What historical success did Mahatma Gandhi help to achieve? How did Gandhi's achievement influence King?
7. Who was Rosa Parks? What significance does she have in the story?
8. What was King's first major political victory?
9. What specific changes took place in the South during the 1960s as a result of the Civil Rights Movement?
10. What events took place in the 1960s that were in direct contrast to King's philosophy? What was King's reaction to them?
11. How did King feel about dying? Why did he feel this way?

Topics for Discussion and Composition

1. Do you have a *dream*? What is your dream?
2. Martin Luther King, Jr., had Jesus, Gandhi, and Thoreau as models. Who is your hero? Why do you admire him or her?
3. King's father was an important influence in his life. How have your parents influenced you?

4. In your lifetime, what important changes have you seen take place in society? What caused these changes to occur?
5. What personal experiences of discrimination have you had in your life? Describe your reaction.
6. Do you think there are some situations that justify the use of violence? Explain your answer.
7. During the 1960s H. Rapp Brown, a black leader, once said, "Violence is as American as cherry pie." What do you think he meant by this?
8. Eldridge Cleaver, author of *Soul on Ice,* is reported to have said, "If you're not part of the solution, you're part of the problem." What do you think he meant by this? Do you agree with him?
9. Martin Luther King, Jr., was not allowed to go to school until he was six years old because he was "too young." Do you think children should be allowed to enter school early if they want to, even if they are "underage"? Why or why not?
10. What things can parents do to help their children become good students in school? Give as many examples as you can.
11. What is the most difficult obstacle you have had to overcome during your life? How did you try to overcome it? Were you successful?
12. Why do you think King had a premonition that he was going to be assassinated?
13. Have you ever had a premonition that eventually came true? Describe what happened.
14. In the article "I Have a Dream," King speaks about how he wanted other people to remember him. If you had the chance to write your own eulogy, what would you want others to say about you after you died?

Paragraph Analysis: Identifying Unstated Main Ideas

An author usually presents the central idea of a paragraph in one complete sentence somewhere within each paragraph. This sentence includes the principal elements of the paragraph. The rest of the paragraph serves to support and elaborate on the main idea. Very often the first sentence of the paragraph will contain the idea of the entire paragraph. However, sometimes the main idea is not stated by the author in one simple sentence. In this case the reader must combine elements from several sentences to formulate one central idea. This is called an ***unstated main idea.***

Directions: *Choose the one sentence that best gives the important elements of the following paragraphs from the article in this chapter. You will need to refer directly to the story. The first one has been done for you as an example.*

Paragraph 1.

_____ Martin Luther King, Jr., was born on January 15, 1929, in Atlanta, Georgia.

_____ Martin Luther King, Sr., discovered that the white landowner was cheating his father.

__✓__ Martin Luther King, Jr.'s grandfather was a poor sharecropper, yet his father became a minister.

_____ Martin Luther King, Jr.'s father left home and later got married.

Paragraph 2.

_____ King loved to hear his father speak in church.

_____ King admired his father and was anxious to learn.

_____ King was sent home from school because he was too young.

_____ King wanted to use big words like his father.

Paragraph 3.

_____ King learned of discrimination in the South from his own experience.

_____ King had two white friends who lived nearby.

_____ Blacks could not eat in the same restaurants as whites.

_____ Blacks were always given accommodations inferior to those of whites.

Paragraph 4.

_____ Atlanta University developed an experimental school for black children.

_____ King learned about Negro history when he was young.

_____ King attended a special school where he began to dream about helping his people.

_____ King's teachers wanted to show the world that blacks could be successful if given an equal opportunity to learn.

Paragraph 5.

_____ King attended college and divinity school and later became a minister.

_____ Thoreau and Gandhi believed in nonviolent protest against unjust laws.

_____ The work of Gandhi and Thoreau helped King to develop his own philosophy of how to help improve conditions for his people.

_____ King had a strong sense of purpose, and was a devoted father and minister in Montgomery, Alabama.

Paragraph 6.

_____ The arrest of Rosa Parks resulted in a boycott of buses by blacks and the eventual desegregation of buses in Alabama.

_____ Before 1955, buses in Alabama were segregated.

_____ Martin Luther King, Jr., helped to organize a boycott against public buses.

_____ White leaders tried to terrorize blacks in an effort to end the boycott and establish their superiority.

Paragraph 7.

_____ More and more blacks in the South began to register to vote.

_____ The bus boycott in Montgomery was very successful.

_____ King became a famous leader in the Civil Rights Movement as non-violent resistance gradually succeeded.

_____ Many schools and colleges were forced to integrate, and restaurants began to serve more blacks.

Class Activity: *In the space provided, list what you think are the five most significant events of Dr. King's life that were mentioned in the article. List the events in chronological sequence, that is, the order in which the events occurred in his life. Compare your answers with those of your classmates.*

1.
2.
3.
4.
5.

Distinguishing Fact, Opinion, and Interpretation

In the preceding chapter we saw the importance of being able to distinguish the difference between a fact and an opinion. You will remember that a fact is an objective statement that can be verified. An opinion is a subjective statement that indicates a person's own feelings about something.

WHAT IS AN INTERPRETATION?

Unlike a fact, an interpretation is information that cannot be verified. In order to help the reader understand the relationship between various facts, an author will sometimes offer an interpretation based on the facts. The facts are true, but the author's interpretation may be open to debate.

An interpretation is different from an opinion in this way: an interpretation is an attempt to give more meaning and insight to the facts; an opinion represents the personal feelings of an author. In an interpretation, the writer tries to avoid giving a personal opinion.

In the social sciences, interpretations are continuously changing. Although the facts may remain the same, different people may see the relationships between them in a new and insightful way. Sometimes, as new facts become available, people are forced to change their interpretations as a result.

REVIEW OF TERMS

A **fact** is information that can be proven or verified in an objective way.
An **opinion** is a personal or subjective feeling about the facts.

An **interpretation** is an attempt to explain the relationship among facts in order to form an objective concept while avoiding personal feelings. This is done to clarify the author's view of the facts.

Directions: *Study the definitions just given. Keep them in mind as you read each of the following statements. In the space provided, write "F" for fact, "O" for opinion, and "I" for interpretation. The first three examples have been done for you. (In some cases, more than one answer may be possible depending on how you define key words in each statement.)*

__*F*__ 1. Martin Luther King, Jr., was born on January 15, 1929.

__*I*__ 2. After the Civil War, conditions did not change significantly for blacks.

__*O*__ 3. Conditions should have been much better for blacks after the Civil War.

_____ 4. In the South, black people were usually given inferior accommodations.

_____ 5. Black people should have used more violence in order to obtain better treatment.

_____ 6. King's study of Negro history helped him to formulate his dream of improving conditions for blacks in the United States.

_____ 7. The philosophies of nonviolent resistence of Gandhi and Thoreau had a strong influence on Martin Luther King.

_____ 8. Several civil rights activists were assassinated during the Civil Rights Movement of the 1960s.

_____ 9. Dr. Martin Luther King, Jr., is the most important black leader in the history of the United States.

_____ 10. Dr. King received the Nobel Peace Prize when he was thirty-five years old.

_____ 11. The success of the Montgomery bus boycott was a significant event because it helped produce unity among blacks.

_____ 12. Martin Luther King delivered his most beautiful speech during the demontration known as "the March on Washington."

_____ 13. The United States Congress passed the Civil Rights Act in 1964.

_____ 14. The assassination of Malcolm X and Medgar Evers made King recognize the probability that someone would assassinate him someday.

_____ 15. Martin Luther King was shot the day after he said. "I'm not fearing any man. 'Mine eyes have seen the glory of the coming of the Lord.' "

_____ 16. The use of nonviolent protest was a significant factor in King's ability to bring about change.

_____ 17. If Dr. Martin Luther King, Jr., had lived, he would have eventually been elected president of the United Sates.

_____ 18. King's ability to inspire people through his speeches made him an influential leader.

______ 19. Dr. Martin Luther King, Jr., was a famous civil rights leader.

______ 20. The 1964 Civil Rights Act was the most important piece of government legislation in American history.

Word Forms/Sequencing Ideas

Directions: *Complete each group of sentences by writing in the appropriate blank space the correct word from those in parentheses. Change the form of the verb or noun when necessary. Then number the sentences in order so that each group forms a well-organized paragraph. Write the number in the blank space at the left of each sentence.*

1. **(to assassinate, assassination, assassin)**

______ During the 1960s several American leaders were the victims of tragic __[ASSASSINATIONS]__ .

______ Just two months after King's __[ASSASSINATION]__ , the country was shocked to hear that Senator Robert Kennedy, President Kennedy's younger brother, had been __[ASSASSINATED]__ in Los Angeles, California.

______ The first __[ASSASSINATION]__ occurred in 1963 when President John F. Kennedy was fatally shot by an __[ASSASSIN]__ in Dallas, Texas.

______ In all three cases, the __[ASSASSINS]__ used a gun to commit the __[ASSASSINATION]__ .

______ In 1968, Dr. Martin Luther King, Jr., was the victim of a successful __[ASSASSINATION]__ attempt in Memphis, Tennessee.

2. **(to differ, difference, different, differently)**

______ Even though Northerners and Southerners speak __[DIFFERENTLY]__ , they are able to understand each other without many problems.

______ There are many __[DIFFERENCES]__ between the North and South of the United States.

______ Sometimes, however, the __[DIFFERENT]__ accents of the two groups do lead to an occasional misunderstanding.

______ For example, these two regions __[DIFFER]__ not only in terms of climate and natural resources, but also in their use of the English language.

3. **(to originate, originator, origin, original, originally)**

______ In fact, it's virtually impossible to know the exact __[ORIGIN/ORIGINATOR]__ of this unique philosophy.

_____ Years later King would use much the same method as Gandhi but in his own ___ORIGINAL___ way.

_____ Nonviolent resistance did not ___ORIGINATE___ in the United States.

_____ However, what we do know is that Mahatma Gandhi was one of the ___ORIGINATORS___ of nonviolent protest in the independence movement of India.

4. **(to succeed, success, successful, successfully)**

_____ It was in the year 1947 that Jackie Robinson ___SUCCEEDED___ in becoming the first black man to play professional baseball in the major leagues.

_____ A man of tremendous talent and courage, Robinson played ___SUCCESSFULLY___ for a period of ten years.

_____ One great ___SUCCESS___ in the effort to end racial discrimination in the United States occurred many years before the Civil Rights Movement of the 1960s.

_____ During those same years many other black players ___SUCCESSFULLY___ entered baseball, abolishing baseball's "color barrier" forever.

_____ The start of this inspirational ___SUCCESS - SUCCESSFUL___ story occurred in 1947.

5. **(to glorify, glory, glorious, gloriously)**

_____ The night before King was assassinated he spoke ___GLORIOUSLY___ to a group of sanitation workers.

_____ Dr. King never tried to ___GLORIFY___ his own contributions to the Civil Rights Movement.

_____ That last speech ended with these words from a famous hymn, "Mine eyes have seen the ___GLORY___ of the coming of the Lord."

_____ But certainly some of the movement's success was due to the fact that King was such a ___GLORIOUS___ orator.

Vocabulary Development Puzzle: King's Message

Directions: *Complete each missing word in the following sentences using only one letter for each blank space. Rewrite each numbered letter in the corresponding space of the sentence marked "King's Message." When you have completed all the letters of this sentence, you will have a message that was part of a speech given by Dr. Martin Luther King, Jr. The first item has been done for you as an example.*

King's Message:

_   _ _ _ _   _   _ _ _ _ _   t _ _ _   _ _ _
(1) (2 3 4 5) (6) (7 8 9 10 11) (12 13 14 15) (16 17 18)

b _ _ _ _ _ _ _ o _ _   _ _   _ _ _   _ _ _ _
(19 20 21 22 23 24 25 26 27 28 29) (30 31) (32 33 34) (35 36 37 38)

_ _ _ _ _ _   _   _ _ _ _ _ _ y   _ _   _ _ _ _
(39 40 41 42 43 44) (45) (46 47 48 49 50 51 52) (53 54) (55 56 57 58)

_ _ _.
(59 60 61)

1. After Rosa Parks was arrested, Negroes in Montgomery, Alabama, decided to b o y c o t t (19 27 52 _ 27 12 12) the buses in protest against discriminatory laws.
2. At the 1963 March on Washington, Dr. King _ _ _ _ v _ r _ _ (7 9 37 1 _ 9 _ 9 7) an inspirational speech. It was one of the most important and moving speeches he ever made.
3. The March on Washington was a _ u g _ (56 _ _ 40) demonstration, with more than a quarter of a million people in attendance.
4. When King's father was a teenager, he discovered that the white landowner was trying to c _ _ _ _ (_ 13 5 6 22) his family.
5. One of the world's most prestigious awards is the Nobel Peace _ _ _ z _ (8 1 _ _ 18).
6. Both Thoreau and Gandhi believed in civil _ i _ _ b _ _ i _ n c _ (7 _ 58 27 _ 40 7 _ 40 _ _ 40) as a method for changing unjust laws.
7. Gandhi's methods were very effective, and they helped India to become an _ _ d _ p _ _ d _ _ t (53 34 _ 47 _ 47 34 _ 47 34 _) nation.
8. During the 1960s, violent _ _ o t _ (25 57 _ _ 58) broke out in cities across the United States.
9. In the South prior to the 1960s, local laws did not _ _ _ o _ (60 49 49 _ 35) Negroes to use the same public facilities as white people.
10. As a child King _ _ _ _ n _ _ _ (3 16 16 24 _ 29 24 29) a special "laboratory school" in Atlanta, Georgia.
11. In the South, blacks and whites were not allowed to use the same restaurants, hotels, or public rest rooms. These are all examples of the _ _ g _ _ g _ _ i o _ (58 44 _ 46 44 _ 45 _ _ _ 34) that existed.
12. King _ e _ _ _ e _ (29 _ 4 21 15 _ 29) much of his life trying to improve conditions for his people.

13. During the 1960s, numerous black leaders emerged who wanted to use violence (4 57 21 38 41) instead of peaceful protest to change society.

14. King actually had a premonition (20 11 30 57 57 30) that he was going to be assassinated.

15. King was assassinated (33 58 58 33 58 58 33 29) while standing on a motel balcony. He was only thirty-nine years old.

16. King's convicted assassin, James Earl Ray, was given a sentence (5 55 5 41 5) of life in prison.

17. The night before he was fatally shot, King told a group of sanitation workers that he had been to the mountain top and that he had seen the promised (28 32 50 59) land.

18. The week before he died, King felt very depressed and discouraged (59 42 48 59) because a peaceful protest march had erupted into violence.

19. The Civil Rights Act of 1964 prohibited (8 42 17 36 39 36 51 7) discrimination on the basis of race (8 14), color, or national origin.

20. Both Dr. Martin Luther King, Jr., and his father (45 51 2 25) were church ministers (43 1 1 12 20).

21. King's grandfather worked as a sharecropper (58 26 46 41 46 46) on someone else's land.

22. Both King and Gandhi were arrested (10 25 25 29) many times for peaceful disobedience to the law.

23. The decision of the U.S. Supreme Court that segregation on buses was unconstitutional was the first major political victory (4 41 16 61) for Dr. King.

24. The philosophies of Jesus, Thoreau, and Gandhi all profoundly (27 31 27 54 61) influenced King's own thinking and ideas.

25. King wanted to be remembered as a person who tried to love and serve humanity (23 43 45 34 52).

Idiomatic Expressions

In English, many idiomatic expressions are formed by combining a verb and a preposition. Often, the meaning of the verb changes dramatically with each preposition used. In the following sentences, notice how each different preposition changes the meaning of the verb *look*, and thus the meaning of the entire sentence.

	Meaning
1. He **looks at** his father.	He **watches** his father.
2. He is **looking for** his father.	He's **searching** for his father.
3. He **looks up to** his father.	He **admires** his father.
4. He **looks after** his father.	He **takes care** of his father.

Directions: *Study the meaning of the verbs listed next. Notice how the prepositions change the meaning of the verbs. Then, complete the sentences by writing the appropriate expression in the space provided. Change the form of the verb when necessary. The first item has been done as an example.*

call for: require, need
call in: summon for consultation, ask to come
call off: postpone, cancel
call on: visit briefly
call up: telephone

1. As part of his job as a minister, King often went to hospitals and prisons to ___*call on*___ people in need of help and support.
2. King realized that in order to change social conditions in the United States, a nonviolent approach was ______________ .
3. The day Rosa Parks was arrested in Montgomery, Alabama, someone ______________ King and told him that there was going to be a meeting of black community leaders the following evening.
4. Once the Montgomery bus boycott had begun, black leaders refused to ______________ the boycott, even though local authorities tried to force them to end it.
5. During the course of the Civil Rights Movement, important lawyers were also ______________ when legal advice and assistance were needed.

go along with: agree, cooperate
go off: go away, leave, depart; explode
go back to: return
go over: examine completely; review
go by: pass
go down: decrease; be perpetuated, as in history

6. During the 1960s there were black leaders, such as Bobby Seales and H. Rapp Brown, who thought violence was necessary to change soci-

ety. These young leaders did not ______________________ with King's philosophy of peaceful protest.

7. As the years ______________________ , King's position in history seems to gain and grow in stature and importance.
8. What King and Gandhi were able to accomplish in their countries will ______________________ in history as two of the most successful social protest movements of the twentieth century.
9. As historians ______________________ King's life, it becomes clear how much his own philosophy was influenced by the thinking of others.
10. King was greatly discouraged when violence broke out. He knew that if violence became widespread, it would be difficult to ______________________ using peaceful methods of protest.

put down:	repress, stop
put off:	postpone
put on:	wear
put up:	construct, erect
put up with:	tolerate, bear

11. As violence broke out in big cities, the National Guard was called in to ______________________ the riots.
12. During his life King was forced to ______________________ many unpleasant situations. Once, as a high school student on a crowded bus, King was told to give his seat to a white person, just as Rosa Parks was told to do years later.
13. Governments sometimes ______________________ statues and monuments to commemorate the contributions and achievements of important men and women.
14. A minister usually ______________________ a special robe before leading the church service.

take after:	follow as an example; resemble in appearance or character
take out:	remove, extract
take over:	take control over
take up:	develop an interest in
take on:	oppose in competition (to be in opposition to)

15. As a high school student, King ____________________ public speaking and debating. Although he didn't know it at the time, his skill as a public speaker would someday help him to inspire and influence millions of people.
16. After King's death, many people mourned his loss. Some feared there would be no one with his status and influence who could ____________________ the leadership of the Civil Rights Movement.
17. The success of King and his followers is even more impressive when one considers how they were able to ____________________ an entire political and social system and still bring about change.
18. King ____________________ Gandhi, the great Indian leader, in the way in which he used nonviolent resistance to change unjust laws.

Outlining Activity

Directions: *Change each paragraph into an outline. Use the first phrase in each outline as a model to help you extract only the essential information from the paragraph.*

There have been many assassinations of famous men in the history of the United States. Perhaps the first assassination that will always remain in the minds of Americans is the assassination of the sixteenth president of the United States, Abraham Lincoln. Lincoln was shot by actor John Wilkes Booth while attending a play in Ford's Theater in Washington, D.C. The assassination took place in 1865, just five days after the United States Civil War had officially ended. Almost one hundred years later, in 1963, President John F. Kennedy was assassinated while riding in a motorcade in Dallas, Texas. Kennedy, the youngest man ever to be elected president, was only forty-six years old at the time. In 1968, two other famous Americans died from assassin's bullets. The great civil rights leader, Dr. Martin Luther King, Jr., was fatally shot while standing on a motel balcony in Memphis, Tennessee. Just two months later, Robert Kennedy, John Kennedy's younger brother, was killed in Los Angeles, California, after delivering a campaign speech there.

Historic Assassinations

1. Abraham Lincoln in 1865 in Washington, D.C.
2.
3.
4.

If any of you are around when I have to meet my day, I don't want a long funeral. And if you get somebody to deliver the eulogy, tell him not talk too long . . . Tell them not to mention that I have a Nobel Peace Prize. That isn't important. Tell them not to mention that I have three or four hundred other awards. That's not important. Tell them not to mention where I went to school. I'd like for somebody to say that day, that Martin Luther King, Jr. tried to love somebody. I want you to say that day that I tried to be right on the war question. I want you to be able to say that day, that I did try to feed the hungry. And I want you to be able to say that day, that I did try in my life to clothe those who were naked. I want you to say on that day, that I did try in my life to visit those who were in prison. I want you to say that I tried to love and serve humanity.—MARTIN LUTHER KING, JR.

What King Tried to Do during His Life

1. To love somebody.
2.
3.
4.
5.
6.

Dream Deferred

LANGSTON HUGHES (1902–1967)

Langston Hughes was born in Joplin, Missouri, in 1902. Often referred to as "the Negro Poet Laureate," he was a leading literary figure of the Harlem Renaissance of the 1920s. Although he graduated from high school in Cleveland, Ohio, and later attended Columbia University for one year, his real education came from life. He was employed as a seaman, waiter, laundry sorter, gardener, bus boy, and in other jobs.

Hughes received critical acclaim with the publication of his first collection of poems, Weary Blues, *in 1926. He is regarded as the leading black poet of his generation; his work poignantly expresses the hopes, fears, and concerns of blacks in the United States. He is the author of more than thirty-five books, including the novel* Not Without Laughter *(1930), a collection of short stories,* The Ways of White Folks *(1934), and two autobiographies,* The Big Sea *and* I Wonder as I Wander. *He died in New York City in 1967.*

What happens to a dream deferred?[1]

Does it dry up
like a raisin in the sun?
Or fester like a sore—[2]
and then run?

Does it stink like rotten meat?
Or crust[3] and sugar over—
like a syrupy sweet?

[1]postponed
[2]infection
[3]get hard

Maybe it just sags[4]
like a heavy load.

Or does it explode?

[4]sinks downward

FOR DISCUSSION

To what different things does the poet compare a dream deferred? Why do you think these comparisons are made? What do you think the poet's intention was when he wrote this poem?

From Nikki-Rosa

NIKKI GIOVANNI (1943–)

Born in Knoxville, Tennessee, in 1943, Nikki Giovanni is one of the best-known black poets of her generation. Her collections of poetry include My Home, Black Feeling, Black Talk/Black Judgment, *and* Cotton Candy on a Rainy Day. *Ms. Giovanni also holds many honorary degrees and is a board member of the Jackie Robinson Foundation. These lines are an excerpt from her poem* Nikki-Rosa.

I really hope no white person ever has
    cause
to write about me
because they never understand.
Black love is Black wealth and they'll
probably talk about my hard childhood
and never understand that
all the while[1] I was quite happy.

[1]time

FOR DISCUSSION

What ideas do you think Ms. Giovanni is expressing with these words?

6

A PARTNERSHIP OF MIRACLES

American Foundation for the Blind

Understanding Vocabulary in Context

Directions: *Read each group of sentences carefully. Then in the space provided, write a synonym or short definition for each boldface word. The boldface word in each sentence appears in the reading selection that follows this exercise.*

1. After the accident the doctor informed her that she would never walk again. Although it was difficult to accept at first, she learned to deal with her **handicap** and was eventually able to lead an active and interesting life.

   DISABILITY - IN ABILITY

   Definition or synonym: ~~HAVE A HANDICAP BE HANDICAPPED~~

2. During most of his life the author was unable to find a publisher willing to publish his work. Finally, after years of continued effort, his **perseverance** produced incredible results; not only was his book published, but it also won a major literary award, the Pulitzer Prize.

   CONTINUING EFFORT /

3. As she walked around the town she began to notice how strange her new **surroundings** were. The houses had no windows, and the door of every house was painted red and blue. All the men of the town wore blue, and the women were dressed only in red.

   EVERYTHING AROUND US / THE ENVIROMENT

4. His hate for the little man who smiled strangely at him was so **overwhelming**, so powerful and intense, that he took out his gun and threatened to kill him if he didn't get out of his sight immediately.

   POWER, AND INTENSE,

ODD=STRANGE, UNUSUAL.

5. Young boys growing up often dream about playing sports for both college and professional teams. Yet the chances of actually playing for a major university are not very great, and the **odds** of playing professionally are even smaller.

   CHANCES, POSSIBILITIES.

6. When the police officers asked the woman if they could enter her hotel room she hesitated momentarily. It was obvious that the woman was **reluctant** to allow them in, as if she had something to hide.

   UNWILLING

7. Three years ago, when that restaurant first opened, virtually no one ate there. Today, however, business is **flourishing**, and it's nearly impossible to eat dinner there without a reservation.

   DEVELOP / IMPROVE BUSSINESS / TO PROGRESS

8. When our uncle first began to complain of chest pains, we all tried to convince him to see a doctor. Of course, he reacted in his typically **stubborn** manner, refusing to listen to anyone and insisting that the pain was not all that serious.

   STRONG WILLED / HARD HEADED

9. What a temper that uncle of ours had! If he thought that people didn't believe him or simply doubted his words, he would throw a terrible **tan-**

trum, his anger exploding violently and uncontrollably, like a volcano erupting.

VIOLENTLY ANGRY / FULL OF RAGE

10. Although you can't expect to speak a foreign language after studying it for only a few months, you can **ultimately** speak it well if you persevere and continue practicing.

FINALLY / AT LAST / IN THE LONG RUN

A Partnership of Miracles: The Story of Helen Keller and Anne Sullivan Macy

HELEN'S HANDICAP

(1) One June day in 1880 a healthy baby girl was born to a white middle-class Southern family in the rural Alabama town of Tuscumbia. Her father was a newspaper editor and a former captain in the Confederate army during the U.S. Civil War. The little girl developed early and was making sounds similar to words by the time she was six months old. She was walking by the time she was a year. But when she was nineteen months old she developed an illness with a high fever that left her blind and deaf. The little girl's name was Helen Keller. Years later her name would symbolize incredible achievement over physical handicaps, monumental perseverance, and courage in the face of overwhelming odds. But for her parents at the time, her silence represented unbearable sadness and fear for her future.

(2) Helen Keller's parents felt very sorry for her. They knew that life was hard for the little girl, who could not see or hear. Because she could not hear people talking, she was also unable to speak. But she had a strong spirit and a desire to investigate the world, and she liked to experiment with her surroundings to learn the consequences. Many times her curiosity got her into trouble, but her parents were reluctant to discipline her. Even when she was eating dinner she was not controlled like most young children. She was allowed to walk around the table while her family was seated and take whatever food she wanted from their plates. When Helen was six years old she deliberately locked her mother in a room and then hid the key. Helen could feel her mother pounding on the door for three hours, but she refused to open it. It was Helen's way of asserting her power. When Helen was frustrated she would throw a temper tantrum. She would lose control of herself and scream and kick and hit. She was quickly becoming too strong and wild for her parents to control. They realized that they needed outside help.

HELEN'S TEACHER: THE ARRIVAL OF ANNE SULLIVAN

(3) The Kellers learned of a special school for the blind in Massachusetts, where another blind-deaf girl had been taught to understand words. Helen was too young to go away to school, but perhaps the school could find a teacher who would come to teach Helen at her home. Shortly before Helen turned seven, Anne Sullivan came to live with Helen's family in order to be Helen's teacher.

Anne Sullivan was a 21-year-old woman who had had an unfortunate childhood. She had lived with her poor parents for only a few years when her mother died. Her father then abandoned her to a poorhouse-infirmary in Tewksbury, Massachusetts. She was registered there as "virtually blind" because she had developed an eye infection called trachoma, a condition that flourished in unsanitary surroundings. As a child, Anne had several operations on her eyes, but even as an adult her sight remained poor. Anne Sullivan identified strongly with Helen, the sightless little deaf girl who stubbornly struggled to explore and understand her environment despite her great handicap.

(4) After Anne Sullivan came to live with the Kellers, Helen's life changed completely. When she first arrived, Anne was very warm and friendly toward Helen, but she was also very strict. She wanted Helen to be as normal as possible, and as a result she demanded more from Helen than Helen's parents had asked. The Kellers knew that Helen did not understand, so they had not disciplined her or taught her proper behavior. Anne saw it as her job to civilize this child and teach her to truly master her world. Anne spelled simple words into Helen's hand. She gave Helen a doll and then spelled the word d–o–l–l into her hand. But for several weeks Helen did not truly understand. She confused similar ideas such as *milk* and *mug* (the liquid and its container).

AN UNUSUAL EDUCATION

(5) Then one day, when Helen was feeling especially frustrated and angry with her new companion, they stopped their lesson and went outside to the water fountain and began to pump water from the well. As the water flowed out, the teacher spelled w–a–t–e–r into Helen's hand. And suddenly, like a light in the darkness, Helen understood that her new friend was giving a name to the cool liquid that flowed into her hand. Instantly she needed to know the name of everything, and before the day was over she had learned hundreds of names including her own, her teacher's, her mother's, her father's, and her sister's. Even more importantly, she had learned that everything has a name and every word corresponds to a thing. This revelation captivated young Helen. Years later she referred to this incident as the moment when she was reborn. From that time on, her energy was used to understand and master her world. She could not learn fast enough; she had to make up for lost time.

(6) It took a little longer for Helen to learn abstract ideas like *think* and *love*, but even these concepts became clear within the first year. She progressed from learning names and other nouns to verbs and simple sentences of position such as "the doll is on the bed." Eventually, Miss Sullivan was spelling the sentences of people who were talking near them. Helen even learned to understand idiomatic expressions. Before long Helen was receiving elementary instruction in arithmetic and science as well as English grammar.

(7) Helen quickly grew to love her teacher very dearly. Her teacher was the person who changed Helen from a primitive and ignorant being into a sensitive and masterful woman. Helen wrote two books about her own life. In her first book, entitled *The Story of My Life*, she wrote about her feelings for her teacher.

> My teacher is so near to me that I scarcely think of myself apart from her. How much of my delight in all beautiful things is innate and how much is due to her influence, I can never tell. I feel that her being is inseparable from my own, and that the footsteps of my life are in hers. All the best of me belongs to her—there is not a talent, or an inspiration or a joy in me that has not been awakened by her loving touch.

By all accounts, Helen's teacher was an incredible woman. She was born into poverty, the daughter of Irish Catholic immigrants who were always desperately poor and discriminated against by the Protestant population in New England. She had been orphaned and abandoned, blind and uneducated, but she had risen above these handicaps to make something of herself and her soon-to-be-famous pupil. It was Anne's own perseverance as well as her teaching techniques that enabled Helen to develop her potential.

(8) Most of Helen's knowledge of the world came through her fingertips. She learned shape and size and relationships because she could feel them with her hands. She also used her hands for speaking and conversation. She spoke of colors as feelings; yellow sunshine was warmth, blue sky was the freshness of the air, and gray was the feeling of an imminent storm. As an adult she wrote very beautifully, speaking of colors and situations together.

(9) But once, when she was twelve years old and attending the special school for the blind in Massachusetts that her teacher had also attended, Helen wrote a beautiful story as a birthday present for the director of the school. He was very pleased and published the story in the school newspaper. Someone claimed that Helen's story had been taken from a book by another author. It was true; the two stories were almost identical. Helen didn't know how to explain the stories' similarity. Maybe her teacher had read the story to her and she had unconsciously remembered it. However, the director believed he had been deceived by Helen, and the seriousness of her "crime" was impressed upon her. Thereafter, she felt inhibited in all her "creative writing," although ultimately she was able to write of her own life experiences.

HELEN'S DREAM

(10) As she grew older she recognized one ambition: to attend a regular college, not just a school for the blind. Before she could go on to college however, Helen needed proper preparation in many subjects. For more than a year she studied at a preparatory school in Boston, Massachusetts, and later received personal tutoring in French, German, Latin, and English (including their histories, philosophies, and literature) as well as mathematics. She also mastered three different systems of Braille, lipreading, and the manual alphabet of the deaf. After much practice she eventually mastered the pronunciation of some simple English sentences. This was enormously difficult for Helen because she could not remember human speech. She had to learn to put her hands on her teacher's throat and lips and even in her mouth in order to learn how to make comprehensible words. This Helen learned to do. However, most of Helen's speech was never perfectly pronounced and always sounded strange to other people.

(11) In the fall of 1900 Helen entered Radcliffe College (one of the most prestigious women's schools in the U.S.) and in June 1904, she was graduated *cum laude*. Helen overcame incredible obstacles within herself and outside her control. During all of the days and weeks and years of preparation, Anne Sullivan literally had held Helen's hand. Anne communicated the words from the classrooms into her hand, and she served as Helen's major translator to the world beyond. There were times when "Teacher's" eyes grew tired and weak (for she too had once been blind, and her sight was never perfectly restored). The work that Helen Keller and Anne Sullivan accomplished in four short years has rarely, if ever, been duplicated.

MORE STRUGGLES TO WIN

(12) Years later, Helen devoted much of her time and energy to the establishment of facilities for the handicapped. Both she and Anne Sullivan supported themselves by giving co-lectures in the U.S. and abroad. They talked with people in small towns as well as with high government officials. As a handicapped person, Helen was able to influence people of power because she herself was an inspiring example of the progress an individual can make if given the proper opportunity. Eventually a unified system of Braille was developed, in part through Helen's efforts. "Lighthouses" for the blind were also founded to help the blind to help themselves. Helen Keller died in 1968, just five years before the U.S. Congress established the Rehabilitation Act of 1973. This act prohibited discrimination on the basis of a handicap in programs or activities receiving federal financial assistance. Helen's work served to increase people's awareness of the needs and potential of handicapped people. The courage and spirit of Helen Keller in the face of tremendous obstacles will always remain an inspiration for everyone with a struggle to win.

Comprehension Questions

1. What difficult physical handicaps did Helen Keller have?
2. Why did Helen's parents have problems controlling her?
3. What did Helen's parents do when they realized they needed additional help for her?
4. Why do you think Anne Sullivan was so successful with Helen? What kind of person do you think Anne was? What qualities do you think she had?
5. What was the significance of Helen's experience with the water from the well pump?
6. What effect did this particular experience have on Helen's behavior?
7. What were Helen's feelings toward Anne Sullivan?
8. Why did Helen feel inhibited about writing creatively?
9. What different communication skills did Helen have to learn because of her special handicaps?
10. Why was Helen so successful in convincing the public of the need to help handicapped people?
11. Compare Helen Keller and Anne Sullivan. What qualities did these two women have in common?

Topics for Discussion and Composition

1. Anne Sullivan was a very special teacher. What do you think the qualities of a good teacher are?
2. Describe a special teacher that you have had. What made this teacher so special to you?

3. Helen's parents had many problems trying to raise her. Have you ever had a problem with a child? How did you deal with the situation?
4. Federal government regulations are requiring local governments to spend large amounts of money to provide special facilities for the handicapped such as special schools, buses, and elevators. Do you think the government should spend so much money for a small number of handicapped people when it doesn't have enough money to provide adequate services for its healthy citizens?
5. Do you think society has a responsibility to take care of handicapped persons?
6. Would you marry a blind person? Why or why not?
7. Have you known any people with physical handicaps? What did you learn from these people?
8. Try this experiment. Cover your eyes so that you cannot see at all. Sit quietly for five mintues. Then try to walk around your home. Describe how you felt and what happened to you. (Try to have another person present when you do this experiment.)
9. Do you think that parents should be especially demanding of young children who have a handicap? Why or why not?
10. Is it better to integrate severely handicapped individuals into a regular classroom, or is it better to provide them with special classes and teachers of their own? Give reasons to support your answer.
11. How do you define a social handicap? Give examples to support your definition.
12. Do you think there are similarities between people with physical handicaps and people with "social" handicaps? What are the similarities and what are the differences between these two groups of people?

Paragraph Analysis: Generating Unstated Main Ideas

Directions: *Refer to paragraphs 1–7 of the article "A Partnership of Miracles." In the spaces provided, use your own words to express the main idea of each of the seven paragraphs.*

Paragraph

1. ____

____

2. ____

____

3. ____

____

4. ______________________________

____

5. ______________________________

____

6. ______________________________

____

7. ______________________________

____

Vocabulary Development

Directions: *Refer to the paragraphs in the article that are indicated in this exercise. In each of the indicated paragraphs find a word or phrase that has the same meaning as the words listed. The first item has been done as an example.*

Paragraph 1

matured quickly	***developed early***
disease	______________
high temperature	______________
unable to hear	______________
physical disadvantages	______________
to represent	______________
an unbelievable accomplishment	______________
intolerable sorrow	______________

Paragraph 2

a need to explore	______________
environment	______________
hesitant	______________
permitted	______________
not able to see	______________
intentionally	______________
banging on the door	______________
to prove her strength	______________
yell, shout	______________

Paragraph 3

heard about	______________
almost unable to see	______________
unclean environment	______________
struggled obstinately	______________

Paragraph 5

a person who stays with another person	______________
a place (in) the ground where water is stored	______________
discovery	______________
event, occurrence	______________
to control her environment	______________
to compensate for wasted time	______________

Directions: *Use the letters in the spaces to help you complete the missing word in each sentence.*

1. As a child, Helen was a stubBERN little girl who would often throw a temper tantrum in order to get her own way.
2. During these tantrums, Helen would kick and scrEAM until her parents gave her what she wanted.
3. One day Helen deliBERATELY locked her mother in the bathroom and left her there for several hours.
4. Helen's parents felt very sorRY for their daughter because she was deaf and blind.
5. Anne Sullivan also had a difficult childhood, having grown up in depressing surrOUNDINGS. Like Helen, she had to overcome many obstacles and handICAPS.
6. Helen probably would have never overCOME her great handicaps without the support and assistance of her devoted teacher.
7. During her life Helen was able to masTER several languages including French, Latin, and German.
8. Despite her talent as a writer, Helen was relucTANT to write creatively because of a misunderstanding she had had with her headmaster when she was just twelve years old.
9. With Anne's help, Helen was able to achIEVE her dream of going to a real college.
10. Although Anne Sullivan later married, she continued to work with Helen. The two women were virtUALLY inseparable.
11. The work of these two women was truly a partNERSHIP of miracles.

Idiomatic Expressions

One of Helen Keller's most impressive achievements in learning to use language was her ability to understand idiomatic expressions so quickly. Idioms are phrases or groups of words that cannot be understood by analyzing each word separately for its literal meaning. Together, however, the words are used to convey a particular meaning or idea.

Directions: *Listed next are ten idiomatic expressions. Read the sentences that follow and try to write the meaning of each expression in the space provided. Check your answers by looking up the boldface words in a dictionary.*

at **odds** with	to **give** up
to **make** up for	to **feel** up to
as **well** as	out of **hand**
as **well**	on the **go**
to **give** in to	in a **class** by itself

1. It gradually became clear to Helen's parents that their child was getting **out of hand**. Because they could not control her behavior, they decided to send for professional help.

   Definition: OUT OF CONTROL

2. When Anne Sullivan first arrived at the Kellers' home, Helen's parents were shocked at the strict treatment and strong disciplining of their child. In fact, Helen's parents were so **at odds with** Anne's methods that Anne had to work with Helen in private.

   DISAGREE

3. At the beginning, Helen stubbornly resisted Anne's efforts to teach her. But Anne was just as stubborn and refused to **give in to** Helen whenever Helen threw a temper tantrum.

   TO ALLOW, ACCEPT.

4. Because Anne did not **give up** in her attempt to teach Helen, Helen was eventually able to achieve a great deal in life.

   RENDIRSE - SPANISH

5. When Helen finally understood that all objects had names, she wanted to learn the names of everything around her. She felt that she had to **make up for** all those lost years.

   TO WORK HARDER IN ORDER TO GET TO THE POINT.

6. It was Anne Sullivan's own perseverance, **as well as** her effective teaching methods, that enabled Helen to be so successful.

   TOO, ALSO

7. In addition to learning several foreign languages, Helen learned to read lips **as well**.

   TOO, ALSO

8. Because of Anne's poor eyesight, it was difficult for her to help Helen with her college studies. There were probably many times when Anne was tired and did not **feel up to** helping Helen study.

   TO HAVE ENERGY TO DO SOMETHING.

9. In later years, Anne and Helen were always extremely busy. They were always **on the go**, giving lectures all around the world in an effort to improve opportunities for handicapped people.

   BUSY

10. What Helen Keller and Anne Sullivan were able to achieve together is **in a class by itself**. Their partnership was truly something rare and special.

    THE BEST, TOPS, UNIQUE

Word Forms: -ed and -ing: Confusing EnD INGs

When the suffixes *-ed* and *-ing* are used to form an adjective, they also change the meaning of the root word. Can you explain the difference in meaning in these two sentences?

He's an interest*ed* teacher. He's an interest*ing* teacher.

An *interested* teacher *has* interest in someone or something. An *interesting* teacher *makes other people* have interest.

TWO GENERAL RULES TO FOLLOW

1. **-ed** indicates that someone *has* a particular quality or emotion.
2. **-ing** indicates that someone or something *causes others to have* a particular quality or emotion.

Examples:

She is a *bored* person. — She *has* a feeling of boredom.
She is a *boring* person. — She *causes* boredom in others.

He is a *frustrated* teacher. — He *has* a feeling of frustration.
He is a *frustrating* teacher. — He *causes* frustration in others.

USING -ED AND -ING AS ADJECTIVE SUFFIXES

Directions: *Refer to the following example. Then use the correct adjectival form to complete the sentences that follow.*

Example: The speaker **inspired** the crowd.

The crowd was ***inspired***. The speaker was ***inspiring***.
He was an ***inspiring*** speaker.

1. The speech **convinced** the group.

 The group was CONVINCED. The speech was CONVINCING.
 It was a CONVINCING speech.

2. The illness **threatened** his life.

 His life was THREATENED. The illness was life-THREATENING.
 It was a life-THREATENING illness.

3. The success **encouraged** the doctor.

 The doctor felt ENCOURAGED. The success was ENCOFAGING.
 It was an ENCORAGING success.

4. The lesson **confused** the student.

The student felt CONFUSED. The lesson was CONFUSING.

It was a CONFUSING lesson.

5. The team **overwhelmed** its oponent.

The opponent was OVERWHELMED. The team was OVERWHELMING.

6. The Constitution **unified** the nation.

The nation was UNIFIED. The Constitution was a UNIFYING document.

It was a UNIFIED nation.

Directions: *Complete each sentence by using the correct form of the words in parenthesis.*

Example: **(surprise, surprised, surprising)**

The party was a wonderful ***surprise***. I must have had a ***surprised*** expression on my face when I saw all my friends together.

1. **(depression, depressed, depressing)**

a. The Kellers experienced a period of great ____________ when their daughter first became deaf and blind.

b. At the time of her illness, Helen was probably too young to be ____________ about what happened to her.

c. Anne Sullivan grew up in an unhealthy and ____________ environment.

2. **(inspiration, inspired, inspiring)**

a. King gave an ____________ speech the night before he was assassinated.

b. Most people felt ____________ after they had listened to one of King's speeches.

c. Helen Keller's life serves as an ____________ to us all.

3. **(discouragement, discouraged, discouraging)**

a. I felt so ____________ when I learned that I had failed the course.

b. Everyone has some moments of ____________ at some time in life.

c. Remaining optimistic can sometimes help people overcome a ____________ experience.

4. **(reward, rewarding)**

a. I'm glad that I had an opportunity to take that course. It was a ____________ experience.

b. It's a ______________________ feeling when you accomplish something after you've worked hard to achieve it.

c. The only ______________________ that some parents want is to see their children grow up to be happy adults.

5. **(disappointment, disappointed, disappointing)**

a. She tried to console the ______________________ child.

b. Everyone has had a moment of ______________________ at some time in his or her life.

c. The results of the exam were very ______________________ .

6. **(excitement, excited, exciting)**

a. Helen was an ______________________ little girl when she discovered that the objects around her all had names.

b. This was probably one of the most ______________________ experiences of her life.

c. Anne probably felt a tremendous amount of ______________________ as she watched little Helen run around learning the names of things.

Outlining Activity

Directions: *Read the following paragraph carefully, then use the information in the paragraph to make a list of items that correspond to the title of the list. Be sure to use only brief phrases and to keep parallel form as indicated by the boldface word in the first line of the list.*

Helen Keller endures as a symbol for all people who have a handicap or an obstacle to overcome. During her life, Helen accomplished many incredible things. With the assistance of her talented teacher, Anne Sullivan, Helen learned to understand abstract ideas and idiomatic expressions, despite her blindness and deafness. Helen was able to read several other languages in addition to English such as French, German, and Latin. She also mastered three different systems of Braille. She was able to read lips (with her fingertips), and she knew how to communicate with the manual alphabet of the deaf. After much practice, she eventually mastered the pronunciation of simple English sentences, although her words were never perfectly formed and always sounded strange to other people. At the age of twenty-four, Helen graduated with honors from Radcliffe College, one of the most famous and prestigious schools in the United States. Helen's later work helped develop one common system of Braille, so that all blind people could use the same books. Finally, her influence and example were instrumental in helping pass the Rehabilitation At of 1973, which was enacted by Congress five years after her death.

What Helen Keller Was Able to Accomplish during Her Life

1. **To understand** abstract ideas and idiomatic expressions.
2.
3.

4.

5.

6.

7.

8.

9.

Comparison/Contrast

Compare and contrast the lives of Helen Keller and Martin Luther King, Jr. How were their lives similar? How were they different? Use the numbered categories as a basis for comparison. You may refer to the articles in chapters 5 and 6 to help you. The first category has been done for you as an example.

Martin Luther King, Jr.		Helen Keller
January 15, 1929	1. Date of birth	*June 1881*
	2. Year of death	
	3. Place of birth	
	4. Family heritage	
	5. Parents' social background	
	6. Physical characteristics	
	7. Personality	
	8. Personal dreams	
	9. Education (schools attended, academic achievement)	
	10. People who were important influences on them	
	11. Specific handicaps they overcame	
	12. Contributions to society	
	13. How society has recognized their achievements	

7

ANATOMY OF A MOVEMENT

Photograph by Ken Karp

Participants at the start of the New York City Marathon, a 26 mile 385 yard road race. The first N.Y.C. Marathon, organized in 1970, had 126 runners, including one woman; only one-half of the runners finished the race. By 1983, the race had more than 15,000 participants, including thousands of women, 4,671 foreign runners, and 209 people over the age of 60. That year, 14,458 persons completed the five-borough race, which attracted millions of spectators.

Understanding Vocabulary in Context

Use the context clues in each sentence to help you write a synonym or short definition for each of the boldface words. The boldface word in each sentence appears in the reading selection that follows this exercise.

1. In a nationally televised debate, one of the candidates **asserted** that he had a five-point plan for improving the nation's economy. He also stated that, if elected, he would change the nation's foreign policy toward Latin America.

   Definition or synonym: to affirm

2. Machines have changed society **irrevocably.** It's doubtful that we will voluntarily return to the days when we used human muscles to do most of our work. Machines are with us to stay!

   unwilling to go back. Not changeable back.

3. A hundred years ago, most people saw little probability in the idea that people would someday live in outer space. Today, however, the **likelihood** that people will someday live in space appears much greater.

   Posibilities, chances, Probabilities

4. Washington, D.C., is the capital of the U.S. However, it was not always the center of the country's national government. Both New York and Philadelphia were once the **seats** of the federal government.

   Home base / main office / capital

5. A man of tremendous physical strength, his muscles would **bulge** through his shirt, revealing a physique of powerful proportions.

6. The best way to know what something is like is to **undergo** the experience personally. For example, you can't really know what strawberry ice cream tastes like unless you experience it for yourself.

   to try / to experience / to do

7. Having a teen-ager in the house can be very **upsetting** at times. Teen-agers, in their effort to be independent, often insist on doing things their own way, refusing to listen to their parents' advice and wishes.

   Disappointed / mix with anger.

8. My friend is always so full of **vigor.** She is involved in countless activities, yet she still has enough energy to come home and take care of three children.

   Energy.

9. Daily life in today's world is filled with **stress.** Psychologists assert that overwhelming **pressure** can lead to illness and emotional problems.

   Stress (from inside), Pressure (from outside).

10. Statistics show that **strokes** (the paralysis that results from a sudden lack of oxygen flowing through the brain) occur today with less frequency than they did in the previous few decades.

    Big movement of the arm.

Anatomy of a Movement

TALKING TABOO

(1) Have you ever had the sudden desire to take off *all* your clothes and run naked down the street? Have you ever had the urge to push another person in front of an oncoming car or train? Maybe you have and maybe you haven't, but chances are that at some time in your life you've had a strong desire to do something strange or terrible. And chances are that you didn't act on your impulse, but let it pass instead. You knew that to commit the action was wrong in some way and that other people would not accept your behavior. Behavior that is considered "wrong" or "unacceptable" in society's eyes is often referred to as *taboo.*

(2) Sometimes even the mere mention of taboo behavior is considered a sin or violation of some kind. But perhaps the most interesting thing about the phenomenon of taboo behavior is how it can change over the years within the same society, how certain behavior and attitudes once considered taboo can become perfectly acceptable and natural at another point in time. Topics such as sex and death, for example, were once considered so upsetting and unpleasant that it was a taboo to even talk about them. Nowadays of course, sex is a popular topic in American society. And with the publication of important books such as *On Death and Dying* and *Learning to Say Goodbye,* people have become more aware of the importance of expressing feelings about death and, as a result, are more willing to talk about this taboo subject.

AMERICA'S NEW TABOO

(3) One of the newest taboos in American society is the topic of fat. Unlike many other taboos of the past, fat is a topic that Americans talk about constantly. It's not taboo to talk about fat; it's taboo to be fat. The "in" look is thin, not fat. You only need to look around you. Today's TV actors always seem to be successful, attractive, and, of course, thin. It's virtually impossible to find a TV news commentator or model who does not conform to this look. Tight-fitting jeans that accentuate a thin, youthful appearance are the fashion of the day. In the work world, most companies prefer youthful-looking, trim executives to sell their image as well as their products to the public. The thin look is associated with youth, vigor, and success. The fat person, on the other hand, is thought of as lazy and lacking in energy, self-discipline, and self-respect. After all, people think, how can people who care about themselves, and therefore the way they look, permit themselves to become fat? In an image-conscious society like the U.S., thin is "in," fat is "out."

(4) It's not surprising, then, that millions of Americans have become obsessed with staying slim and "in shape." One look at today's best-selling books and popular magazines will demonstrate America's preoccupation with physical appearance. Recent publications all claim to offer the latest and most effective recipes for losing weight. They tell us how to shape and trim our bodies to acquire that slim and healthy look. America's concern with keeping fit is so great that it has resulted in a multimillion dollar business for manufacturers of sportswear and athletic equipment.

IN PURSUIT OF THE FOUNTAIN OF YOUTH

(5) The pursuit of a youthful physical appearance is not, however, the sole season for America's obsession with diet and exercise. Recent research has clearly shown the critical importance of diet and exercise for personal health. As

in most technologically developed nations, the life-style of North Americans has changed dramatically and irrevocably during the course of the last century. Modern machines do all the physical labor that people were once forced to do by hand. Cars and buses transport us quickly from point to point. Elevators and escalators move us up and down in effortless fashion. As a result of inactivity and disuse, people's bodies can easily become weak and vulnerable to disease. People have seen too many friends and family members suffer fatal heart attacks and sudden strokes. Often the victims were people who ate too much and exercised too little. In an effort to avoid a similar fate, millions of Americans are spending more of their time exercising. The effect of this new appreciation of the importance of exercise is evident: parks are filled with joggers and bicyclists, health clubs are sprouting up everywhere, physical education programs are enjoying a newly found prestige, and many companies are providing special exercise facilities for their employees to use during the work day.

HOW IT WORKS: YOUR BODY, CAR(E), AND YOU

(6) To the person who has had little interest in or experience with physical exercise, this recent emphasis on physical activity can appear rather strange, even silly. Yet it's not so ridiculous if you stop to think about it. Compare the human body to a car. To function properly, both need fuel, rest, maintenance, and proper exercise. Take fuel, for example. Just as the automobile needs the proper amount of oil and gas to make it go, so our bodies need the right amount of food and water. If the car receives the wrong kind of fuel, too much oil, or not enough gas, it does not function properly. For the human body, proper nutrition and diet are also essential. Furthermore, just as the car cannot be driven indefinitely without eventually breaking down, so too the body requires adequate time to rest and sleep. If either the car or the body is abused by overwork, the consequences can be dangerous. The similarity doesn't stop there. Both the car and the body need to be maintained and cared for on a regular basis. Whereas human beings visit doctors for regular checkups, cars need mechanics for inspections and tune-ups. Both the doctor and the mechanic are consulted when physical problems arise; medicine and operations may be required for people in much the same way that new parts and repairs are sometimes needed for cars. Last of all, a car needs to be used regularly. Otherwise it will not run smoothly when it is finally called on to function. Our bodies are much the same way. A body that receives little exercise gradually becomes stiff and difficult to move. Like the car, the body will not function efficiently if it isn't used.

(7) Although most people have long been aware that exercise is beneficial to good health, many of them have had some misconceptions regarding health, exercise and physical appearance. For instance, they see a powerfully built man, his arms and chest bulging with muscles, and they automatically assume that this person is in excellent health. While the man may have great physical strength, he may actually be in poor physical condition and a likely candidate for a heart attack. How is this possible? you ask. The man must exercise every day to have such an impressive physique. However, exercise alone does not insure physical fitness; it is the *kind* of exercise that really matters. This relatively new understanding of the relationship between physical fitness and exercise is changing the way many people are exercising today.

WALKING THE AEROBIC WAY

(8) One of the people's most responsible for this new understanding of the correlation between good health and proper exercise is Dr. Kenneth Cooper. In 1968, Dr. Cooper, a medical doctor and researcher, wrote a book entitled *Aerobics,* which has since sold nearly 2 million copies. The title of the book means literally "with oxygen," and oxygen, you will see, is the key to it all.

(9) All physical activity requires energy. Our bodies produce energy by converting the food we eat. Like our relative, the car, our bodies mix oxygen with the food we ingest to make us go. There is, however, a significant difference in the way our bodies utilize food and oxygen. The body is able to digest food and then store it for future use. Thus we are able to go on living even if we do not eat for an entire day or more. With oxygen, this is not so. We must constantly breathe in order to maintain the body's supply of oxygen. If we stop the flow of oxygen into the body we will die within minutes, for unlike food, our bodies cannot store oxygen.

(10) What becomes critical for human health, then, is the ability of the body to utilize oxygen efficiently, since we need oxygen to produce energy every minute of our lives. Even when we sit or sleep, our bodies must produce energy to carry out basic biological functions: to keep the heart beating, to maintain body temperature, to digest food. When we stand up and begin to walk our bodies must increase their output of energy. When we run down the block, even more energy is required. However, the person in poor physical condition will soon begin to experience problems. The heart will start to beat extremely fast, the lungs will gasp for air. The body is now working overtime to supply enough oxygen to produce the energy to continue running. Because of its poor condition, the body is unable to work fast enough to process the oxygen. At this point the body sounds an alarm, and the person is forced to stop, heart racing madly, lungs calling desperately for more air.

(11) Situations such as the one just described arise from having a poor physical condition, the common result of inactivity. If the body is not used, it deteriorates. The lungs become inefficient. The blood vessels constrict, inhibiting or restricting the flow of blood. The muscles grow weak and flabby. And most significantly, the heart becomes weak as well. The whole body, in fact, is weak and extremely vulnerable to illness and disease.

THE HEART IS A LONELY MUSCLE

(12) Exercise, we all know, serves to strengthen the muscles of the body; different kinds of exercise help develop different muscles. Within the last fifteen years or so, physical fitness experts have been calling attention to the most vital of all muscles in the human body—the heart. We generally do not think of our hearts as muscles, but rather as the symbol or seat of our emotions. We never actually see our own hearts; we only know that the heart is there inside each of us and that without a heart we cannot go on living (unless, of course, someone has an artificial one). But the heart is a muscle, and like any other muscle of the body, it requires regular use to remain strong and healthy.

(13) Certain kinds of exercise are of more benefit to the heart than others. These are exercises that involve continual movement of the body. The heart is a pump, sending blood to all parts of the body. This pump, like any machine,

relies on various parts to function efficiently. The lungs take in the vital oxygen, which is carried in the blood to the cells of the body. It is this precious oxygen, combined with stored food, that produces the energy needed for physical activity. The greater the physical activity, the more oxygen required. As more oxygen is needed, more blood must be pumped by the heart, forcing the heart to pump faster. Thus, continued physical movement forces the heart to work harder and in the process makes the heart stronger and more efficient.

(14) A person in good physical condition has a heart that beats somewhere between sixty and eighty times per minute when he or she is at rest. A heart that beats less than sixty times per minute is unusually strong; such a heart is strong enough to pump the proper amount of blood required by the body with a minimum of effort. By contrast, a heart rate of ninety beats per minute indicates that the heart is weak; it has to work 50% percent harder to pump the same amount of blood. Compare the difference between a person with a heart rate of sixty beats per minute and a person with a rate of ninety.

Amount of time	60 beats per minute	90 beats per minute
1 minute	60	90
1 hour	3,600	5,400
1 day	50,400	75,600

(15) The person with a heart rate of ninety beats per minute is asking his, or her heart to pump 25,200 times more each day of his or her life than the person whose heart rate is sixty. Imagine how many more times that person's heart must work during a week, a year, a lifetime. People with very fast heart rates are overusing this vital part of the body. And like anything that is used too much, the heart can eventually break down from overwork.

AEROBIC EXERCISE HELPS BUILD STRONG BODIES TWELVE WAYS

(16) Dr. Cooper has studied the effects of exercise on the body's cardiovascular system. His research indicates that certain exercises, if done regularly and for a sufficient period of time, will result in a "*training effect.*" When the body achieves this *training effect,* it experiences a variety of specific physiological changes. First, the lungs are able to incorporate more air with less effort. Second, the heart is able to pump more blood further down the pipeline with each beat. In fact, when the body is at rest, the heart will actually beat more slowly, thus conserving energy and reducing the likelihood of heart problems. Third, the blood vessels of the body undergo change; the number of blood vessels and their size increase, permitting the blood to flow more freely and easily and helping to reduce high blood pressure. Since the blood vessels are now larger and more flexible, the total volume of blood in the body is increased. That is the fourth effect. More blood in the body means that the body is able to carry and use more oxygen, particularly in moments of high activity. Fifth, the muscles improve their tone, this means they become harder and stronger and help give the body a healthy, attractive appearance. As a result of all these changes, the overall health of the body is much improved, and the body is better equipped to fight off illness and disease.

(17) The physical benefits mentioned above are not the only benefits that are direct consequences of the *training effect.* Although more subjective and therefore more difficult to document scientifically, other positive changes are also believed to occur. People say they feel more relaxed and claim they are

better able to cope with the stress and pressure of daily life. (This assertion does have a strong scientific basis: The body produces *less* acid, which can cause ulcers and other stomach problems, when it performs aerobic exercise.) People also report that they feel better about themselves and that they have more self-confidence and self-esteem. Furthermore, they assert that they fall asleep more easily and enjoy a more restful sleep as well.

(18) All these benefits sound great, you say, but how do people actually achieve this "training effect"? Dr. Cooper's research has helped provide us with the answers. The benefits of the training effect occur, he states, if the exercise is vigorous enough to produce a heart rate of at least 150 beats per minute or more. The benefits begin approximately five minutes after you start to exercise and last as long as the exercise is done. If the exercise is *not* vigorous enough to make the heart rate reach 150 heart beats per minute, then the exercise must last much longer than five minutes. (The amount of time depends on how much oxygen is necessary to do the exercise.) To produce maximum results, the exercise should involve continuous movement of the body, thus forcing the body to process a certain quantity of oxygen. The best aerobic exercises are running, swimming, cycling and walking. Other exercises that involve stop-and-go movement, such as tennis and basketball, while helpful, are *not* as beneficial. To help people know just how much and how often they need to exercise, Dr. Cooper has developed a point system which, if followed, enables the exerciser to obtain the training effect, with all its positive results.

(19) It is little wonder then that so many Americans are doing aerobic exercises. They may all have their own reasons for doing them. But one thing is clear: It's important to take good care of your body. It may some day save your life.

Comprehension Questions

1. What is a taboo?
2. Based on the ideas presented in the first three paragraphs, what conclusion can you make about social taboos in general? Do you think "being fat" will always remain a taboo in American society? Explain your answer.
3. In what way is the taboo of "being fat" *different* from the taboos of sex and death?
4. How does American society tend to see fat people? Thin people? How does the article explain this difference in attitude?
5. What two main reasons does the article give for why so many Americans are exercising regularly?
6. Compare the human body's use of food with its use of oxygen. What is the significant difference in the body's ability to utilize these two sources of energy?
7. Refer to paragraph 5. What examples or illustrations does the paragraph give to show the different effects of society's interest in exercise?
8. What is meant by "aerobic" exercise?
9. What are the best kinds of aerobic exercise? Explain why these exercises are considered the most beneficial for a healthy cardiovascular system.

Drawing Conclusions

Directions: *Based on the information presented in the article, what do you think the author would say about each of the following statements? Put a circle around the one response you think the author would give.*

YES means the author would agree.
NO means the author would *not* agree.
MAYBE means there is not enough information in the article to know what the author would think.

1. A person who can lift 350 pounds has a stronger heart than a person who can lift only 150 pounds.	YES	NO	MAYBE
2. In the United States today, if a thin and fat person have the same qualifications, the fat person is more likely to get the job.	YES	NO	MAYBE
3. People will soon get tired of exercising, since it requires too much time and energy.	YES	NO	MAYBE
4. The widespread use of machines has contributed to the poor physical health of many Americans.	YES	NO	MAYBE
5. A person with a heart rate of only fifty beats per minute probably has a weaker heart than a person with a heart rate of eighty beats per minute.	YES	NO	MAYBE
6. The faster the heart beats during exercise, the more beneficial the exercise is for a person's heart and lungs.	YES	NO	MAYBE
7. Fat people have more difficulty talking about their health than thin people.	YES	NO	MAYBE
8. Playing baseball probably helps produce a more healthy cardiovascular system than playing soccer.	YES	NO	MAYBE

Topics for Discussion and Composition

1. Have you ever participated in a sport or physical activity on a regular basis? What did you enjoy most about the experience? How did the experience affect you?
2. At the present time, are you exercising on a regular basis? What exercises do you do? What benefits do you think you get from exercising?
3. What is your favorite sport? What is it that makes this sport so appealing to you?
4. Have you ever been seriously ill? Describe the experience. How did your illness affect your feelings about yourself and other people? How were you able to get better?
5. Describe your favorite food.

6. What do you think a healthy diet should consist of? Do you consider your diet to be a healthy one? Why or why not?
7. What are your feelings about the following: doctors, hospitals, dentists, walking, jogging, physical pain, sweating?
8. What do you think of the exercise craze in America? Do you think it's good? Do you think it will last?
9. "You can't judge a book by its cover." What do you think this expression means? Do you agree with this message?
10. A taboo is behavior that is considered "wrong" or "immoral" by most members of a society. What are some social taboos that exist in your culture? Do you think they will change someday?
11. Almost every person's body undergoes rapid changes during the period of adolescence. How did you react to these bodily changes?
12. What has been the most significant change to occur in your body in the last five years? In what ways has this change affected you?
13. Describe your own body. What is it that you like most about your body? What do you like the least?

Outlining Activity: Taking Notes from a Written Source

When a person does a sufficient amount of aerobic exercise on a regular basis, his or her body experiences many beneficial changes. (Dr. Cooper refers to this phenomenon as the "training effect.") In the space provided list the different benefits or effects of aerobic exercise on the human body. (To complete the outline, refer to the section of the article entitled "Aerobic Exercise Helps Build Strong Bodies Twelve Ways.")

I. Physiological Effects

A.

B.

C.

D.

E.

F.

G.

II. Psychological Effects

A.

B.

C.

D.

E.

PARAPHRASING ACTIVITY

Many elements are involved in the body's ability to produce energy. Using the information in the article, briefly tell what role each of the following elements has in the body's production of energy.

1. Cells:
2. Food:
3. Oxygen:
4. Lungs:
5. Heart:
6. Blood:
7. Blood vessels:

Seeing Relationships: Analogies

An analogy is used to show the similarity between two things that we ordinarily think of as dissimilar. The automobile and the human body are a good example of an analogy. At first glance, a car and a person's body seem to have very little in common. Yet, as the article "Anatomy of a Movement" showed, there are many similarities between a car and a human body. Here is an example of an analogous relationship:

Gas is the same thing to a **car** as **food** is to a **human body.**

Another way to write this analogy is as follows: **gas : car** AS **food : body.** Here are some other examples of analogous relationships:

mechanic : car AS **doctor : body**
garage : car AS **house : body**

Try to complete the following analogies:

wheels : car AS FEET : body
inspection: : car AS CHECK UP : body EXAMINATIONS
mechanical repairs : car AS OPERATION SURGERY : body
breakdown : car AS ILLNESS/INJURY : body
license plate : car AS ID : body

Class Activity: *What analogous relationships can you identify by comparing the following?*

1. A family to a business
2. Reading to physical exercise
3. A puppy to a child
4. The weather to a person's emotions
5. Life to a sport or game

What other analogies can you think of?

There are many kinds of analogies. Some of the ways analogous relationships can be used are as follows:

1. To compare a word to a synonym of itself
2. To compare a word to an antonym of itself
3. To compare a person or object to a characteristic of itself.
4. To compare something or someone to the function it performs

Directions: *Choose the one word in parentheses that correctly completes the analogy and write it in the appropriate blank space. The first item has been done for you as an example.*

1. ten : decade AS hundred: ***century***
(number, century, time, dollars)

2. bus : train AS elevator: ESCALATOR
(operator, floor, escalator, building)

3. weak : strong AS vulnerable: PROTECTED
(protected, acceptable, successful, impressive)

4. publish : book AS manufacture: CLOTHES
(factory, worker, fruit, clothes)

5. commentator : news AS model: FASHION
(fashion, beautiful, camera, photographer)

6. desire : urge AS topic: SUBJECT
(diet, subject, problem, interesting)

7. bright : mind AS healthy: BODY
(exercise, doctor, medicine, body)

8. virtually : almost AS completely: TOTALLY
(naturally, simply, totally, willingly)

9. tradition : continuous AS impulse: SUDDEN
(necessary, helpful, beneficial, sudden)

10. slim : fat AS thin: OVERWEIGHT
(attractive, overweight, healthy, shape)

11. actor : rehearse AS musician: PRACTICE
(instrument, practice, orchestra, music)

12. stomach : digestion AS heart: CIRCULATION
(health, circulation, blood, oxygen)

13. heart : pump AS blood vessels: ______PIPELINE______
(cells, narrow, blood, pipeline)

14. consequence : effect AS cause: ______REASON______
(problem, reason, result, pressure)

15. love : emotion AS heart: ______MUSCLE______
(beat, muscle, body, feeling)

Vocabulary Development

Directions: *Use these words to complete each of the sentences that follow: A word may be used more than once.*

to store	urge	efficient
to inhibit	taboo	subjective
to deteriorate	fitness	flexible
to convert	phenomenon	irrevocably

1. Publishing companies, health clubs, and sportswear manufacturers have all benefited from America's concern with physical ____________________ .

2. The muscles of the body gradually ____________________ if they're not used on a regular basis.

3. Aerobic exercise helps the blood vessels to become broader and more ____________________ , thus permitting blood to flow more easily throughout the body.

4. The cells of the body utilize oxygen to ____________________ stored food into energy.

5. People who exercise regularly claim that they feel more relaxed and self-confident. These are some of the ____________________ effects attributed to regular exercise.

6. In the United States, interest in health and physical fitness is one social ____________________ that seems to be more than just a passing fad.

7. Unlike with oxygen, the body is able to ____________________ food and then use it as a future source of energy.

8. Before the nineteenth century, when most Americans lived on farms, it was natural for people to watch their relatives die at home. However, as people moved to big cities and more people died in hospitals, it eventually became a ____________________ to talk openly about death.

9. The use of machines has become an essential part of daily life. Machines have changed our lives ____________________ .

10. Some pregnant women claim that they sometimes have a sudden _____________ to eat strange combinations of food, such as pickles with strawberry ice cream. This is one _____________ that is believed to be totally _____________, since it has not been scientifically proven.

11. World-class distance runners have exceptionally _____________ hearts; while at rest, their hearts usually beat fewer than fifty times per minute.

12. When a person's blood vessels are too narrow, they restrict and _____________ the flow of blood through the body.

Combined Activity: Vocabulary in Context/Dictionary Skills

Directions: *Read each sentence carefully. Try to identify how the boldface word is being used (as a noun, verb, or adjective) as well as the meaning of the word in each sentence. First write the part of speech in the parentheses, and then write the meaning on the blank line. After you complete the exercise, use an all-English dictionary to help you check your answers. The first item has been done for you as an example.*

1. A person who exercises regularly is more likely to have a **sound** body, one that is less vulnerable to disease and illness.
   [adjective] healthy

2. A person in poor physical condition cannot process oxygen efficiently. When such a person tries to run, his or her body soon **sounds** an alarm; the person is forced to stop, heart beating wildly, lungs calling desperately for air.
   [VERB] SIGNALS / SHOWS

3. Many people who exercise regularly claim that exercise helps them get a deeper and more restful sleep. However, scientists have not proved that regular exercise is directly responsible for **sound** sleep.
   [ADJECTIVE] GOOD SLEEP

4. In a close race, runners will sometimes make strange **sounds** as they push their bodies for that last burst of energy to get them to the finish line.
   [NOUN] NOISE

5. There have been many famous artists whose work did not **fit** society's idea of "good art." For example, the Dutch painter Vincent van Gogh died poor and unappreciated; it was only after his death that he was recognized as a great artistic genius.
   [VERB] MATCH

6. In general, Americans are very conscious of their physical appearance, and many work hard to keep their bodies **fit**.

   [ADJECTIVE] IN GOOD SHAPE

7. As a child, Helen Keller would throw temper tantrums to get what she wanted.. These wild **fits** made her parents realize that outside help was necessary.

   [NOUN] CONDUCT, BEHAVIOR

8. Cars and buses transport people from **point** to point.

   [NOUN] PLACE TO PLACE

9. One of the main **points** of the article was to show the many benefits aerobic exercise has on a person's health.

   [ADJECTIVE] SENSE, IDEA, EMPHASIS, TOPIC.

10. At this **point** in history, the possibility of nuclear war threatens the very future of life on Earth.

    [NOUN] TIME, PERIOD, MOMENT.

11. In many cultures, the human heart is viewed as the source of people's emotions. However, the article **points out** that the heart is really only a muscle that pumps blood throughout the body.

    [VERB] UNDERLINES, SHOWS, STRESSES. ASSERTS.

12. Children enjoy playing with **models** of cars and trains, imagining that these small-scale objects are actually real.

    [NOUN] MINIATURES COPIES.

13. In the clothing industry, **models** are used to show the latest styles and fashion. Most of today's **models** are invariably slim, attractive, and youthful looking.

    [ADJECTIVE] PEOPLE WHO DEMONSTRATE OR SHOW

14. Many great actors have successfully played the role of Shakespeare's Othello. However, many theater critics still claim that the **model** performance of Othello was given by Paul Robeson, the legendary actor and singer.

    [ADJECTIVE] BEST EXAMPLE

No matter how well we take care of ourselves, the time eventually comes when our bodies begin to lose their youthful tone and vigor; we begin to experience some of the physical limitations that old age inevitably brings. How we see "old" people and how we see ourselves as we grow older are an important part of the aging process. The two songs that follow reflect two different attitudes toward growing old. What feelings and concerns about growing old are expressed in each song? What images do the songwriters use to convey their attitudes about old age?

Old Friends

PAUL SIMON (1942–)

Paul Simon was born in Newark, New Jersey, in 1942. He is known for his collaboration with Art Garfunkel, whom he met in elementary school. Simon and Garfunkel were one of the most popular singing groups of the 1960s. During the 1970s and 1980s, Paul Simon has continued to write and perform his own songs to great critical acclaim. Simon and Garfunkel were reunited in 1981 in New York's Central Park, where they performed before half a million people. The song "Old Friends" was first recorded on the album Bookends, *and can also be found on the collection* Simon and Garfunkel's Greatest Hits.

Old friends,
Old friends
Sat on their park bench
Like bookends.

A newspaper blown through the grass
Falls on the round toes
On the high shoes
Of the old friends.

Old friends,
Winter companions,
The old men
Lost in their overcoats,
Waiting for the sunset.

The sounds of the city,
Sifting through the trees,
Settle like dust
On the shoulders
Of the old friends.

Can you imagine us
Years from today,
Sharing a park bench quietly?
How terribly strange
To be seventy.

Old friends,
Memory brushes the same years.
Silently sharing the same fear. . . .

QUESTIONS

1. With what does the songwriter compare the "old friends"? What is the singer trying to communicate about old people by making this comparison?
2. How do the "old friends" look in their clothes? What does their appearance suggest to you?
3. The songwriter speaks of the old friends "silently sharing the same fear." What do you think that fear is?
4. What is your reaction to the song's lyrics? How do the song's words make you feel about getting old?

When I'm Sixty-Four

JOHN LENNON (1940–1980) and PAUL MCCARTNEY (1942–)

John Lennon and Paul McCartney were born in Liverpool, England, in 1940 and 1942, respectively. As teenagers, they formed a local rock and roll group, The Quarrymen, which later became The Beatles, one of the most popular and influential musical groups of the 1960s. As members of The Beatles, Lennon and McCartney wrote some of the most memorable songs of their era. After the group disbanded in 1970, both continued performing on their own. John Lennon was fatally shot in 1980 in New York City. Paul McCartney remains active as a singer and songwriter.

In 1967 their song, "When I'm Sixty-Four," appeared on The Beatles album, Sergeant Pepper's Lonely Hearts Club Band, *one of the most musically innovative records of its time.*

When I get older losing my hair,
Many years from now,
Will you still be sending me a Valentine,
Birthday greetings, bottle of wine?
If I'd been out till quarter to three,
Would you lock the door?
Will you still need me, will you still feed me,
When I'm sixty-four?

You'll be older too,
And if you say the word,
I could stay with you,
I could be handy, mending a fuse
When your lights have gone.
You can knit a sweater by the fireside,
Sunday morning go for a ride.
Doing the garden, digging the weeds,
Who could ask for more?
Will you still need me, will you still feed me,
When I'm sixty-four?

Every summer we can rent a cottage
In the Isle of Wight, if it's not too dear.
We shall scrimp and save.
Grandchildren on your knee,
Vera, Chuck and Dave.
Send me a postcard, drop me a line,
Stating point of view.
Indicate precisely what you mean to say,
Yours sincerely, wasting away.
Give me your answer, fill in a form,
Mine forevermore.
Will you still need me, will you still feed me,
When I'm sixty-four?

QUESTIONS

1. What physical change does the songwriter expect to occur when he gets older?
2. The songwriter asks, "Will you still be sending me a Valentine, birthday greetings, bottle of wine?" What is the songwriter really concerned about when he asks this question?
3. How does the songwriter imagine himself spending time in the future? What different activities does he hope to have?
4. Compare the two songs "Old Friends" and "When I'm Sixty-Four" in terms of the following: the themes of each song, the songwriters' point of view, the images used in each song, your own reaction to the two songs.

8

ALL THE WORLD'S A STAGE

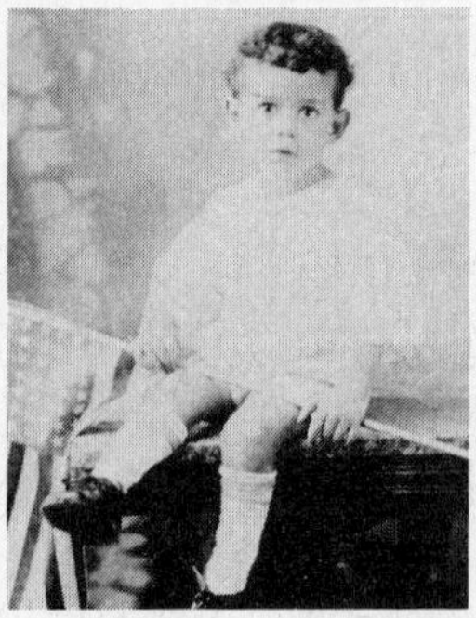

Understanding Vocabulary in Context

Use the context clues in each sentence to help you write a synonym or short definition for each of the boldface words. The boldface word in each sentence appears in the reading selection that follows this exercise.

1. A limited or narrow definition of the term "education" might be the formal training that a person receives in school. However, a **broader** definition would have to include all knowledge and abilities that a person develops in life, whether in or out of school.

   Definition or synonym:

2. Our mother likes to keep things she doesn't use, but even she had to admit that it was time to **discard** all those old magazines and newspapers that had been sitting in the corner collecting dust all those years.

3. As many people grow older they gradually feel less and less interested in their work. Some people, on the other hand, experience a **burst** of involvement and interest in their jobs.

4. For many years Juan had no contact or connection of any kind with his relatives in Mexico. Then, one day, he had a strong urge to reestablish **ties** with family members he hadn't seen in so long.

5. New York City has some famous **landmarks.** The Statue of Liberty, the Empire State Building, and the twin towers of the World Trade Center are places easily identified by most tourists.

6. In geometry one learns that there are different types of circles. **Tangential circles,** those whose lines touch each other but do not intersect, and **concentric circles,** those that have the same center but whose lines do not touch, are two kinds of circles that one studies.

   tangential circle:

   concentric circle:

8. As I looked ahead, I could see that the highway suddenly **diverged.** I wasn't sure which route to take at the point where the road divided.

9. After the operation the patient was in great pain, but she was soon given a drug to **alleviate** her discomfort.

10. It's not surprising that that couple feels "**out of synch.**" As soon as the husband comes home from work, the wife has to leave the house to go to her job. When she finally returns home, he's already getting ready to leave the house again.

11. The human body usually gives some kind of **warning** when something is wrong. There is often some symptom or indication that there is a problem developing.

---

12. Most cultures observe the death of a loved one in a particular way. Some families actually have a party to honor the dead person, while others **mourn** their loss quite differently, preferring to express their grief and sadness in private.

---

13. Although the man was still alive after he had jumped from a fourth floor window, his body was terribly **battered** and **bruised** from the impact of his fall.

All the World's a Stage

All the world's a stage, And all the men and women merely players: They have their exits and their entrances: And one man in his time plays many parts.—
WILLIAM SHAKESPEARE, (1564–1616), As You Like It

PART 1
SETTING THE STAGE

(1) It has become commonplace for people to refer to ages of child development as "stages," whether they be broadly or narrowly defined. Most cultures differentiate between infancy, childhood, and adolescence, and some even classify these stages in a more specific way. Early infancy, toddlers after the first year, "the terrible twos," preschoolers, grade schoolers, teen-agers and adolescents, and even "young adults," are some of the labels used. But what most of these models have in common is that they stop suddenly at the point of adulthood, as if developmental stages cease at the start of the third decade of life. Largely undifferentiated goes the time between twenty and sixty years of age, when suddenly a person is reclassified as "old," to be discarded like a wornout overcoat.

(2) Recent attempts to better understand adult development have produced some exciting results. One important researcher in this field is Gail Sheehy, a woman who has raised some challenging questions and come up with some provocative answers. When Sheehy undertook her project, entitled *Passages: Predictable Crises of Adult Life,* there were, essentially, three central issues she wished to investigate. They were, first, to locate and identify whatever patterns or stages might exist in adult development. Second, to compare the developmental rhythms of men and women in order to learn whether they generally coincided or conflicted in the overall life cycle: Do men and women change in similar ways or are they different? Third, she wished to examine whether or not couples, *as couples* (and not just as individuals), went through predictable changes. Are there specific times in a relationship when a couple can be expected to experience certain emotions: a burst of involvement, a lessening of interest, a deepening of ties?

(3) Since so much of adulthood is spent in coupled lives, Sheehy thought, it might be useful to examine these patterns to see if the difficulties and strains

of maintaining a relationship could be foretold. Anything would certainly be an improvement on the old refrain from childhood stories that "they lived happily ever after," a false and misleading message if there ever was one. Clearly, Sheehy reasoned, something needed to be learned from the alarming number of divorces: either something that would allow marriages to survive or something that would help lessen the trauma of divorce and separation. If people knew beforehand that problems and crises would occur at particular times in their lives, they might be better prepared to deal with them. To gain that knowledge was part of Sheehy's plan.

(4) Sheehy describes people as similar to crustaceans, such as lobsters or crabs, with their hard bony shells on the outside that serve as protective coats. Periodically, regularly, these animals shed their clothing in order to grow and expand their bodies. But in so doing they're left exposed for a time, vulnerable to the elements and possibly to attack. It takes some time to grow a new shell in which to house oneself. People too must grow and expand, discarding old "shells" or roles and persevering until new ones are built. During each transition we experience "crises," not necessarily outwardly for all to see like natural disasters, divorce, disease, or dying, but internal upheaval and unrest nonetheless. The insecurity we feel as we move from stage to stage in life makes us nervous, temperamental, and overly critical as we search for stability and safety during these vulnerable times of change and growth.

SPOTLIGHT ON GROWTH: THE PRODUCT AND THE PROCESS

(5) There are two basic ways to see growth: one as a product, the other as a process. People have generally viewed personal growth as an external result or product that can easily be identified and measured. The worker who gets a promotion, the student whose grades improve, the alcoholic who ends his addiction, the foreigner who learns a new language—all these are examples of people who have measurable results to show for their efforts.

(6) By contrast, the process of personal growth is much more difficult to determine, since by definition it is a journey and not the specific signposts or landmarks along the way. The process is not the road itself, but rather the attitudes and feelings people have, their caution or courage, as they encounter new experiences and unexpected obstacles. In this process, the journey never really ends; there are always new ways to experience the world, new ideas to try, new challenges to accept.

(7) In order to grow, to travel new roads, people need to have a willingness to take risks, to confront the unknown, and to accept the possibility that they may "fail" at first. How we see ourselves as we try a new way of being is crucial to our ability to grow. Do we perceive ourselves as quick and curious? If so, then we tend to take more chances and to be more open to unfamiliar experiences. Do we think we're shy and tentative? Then our sense of timidity can cause us to hesitate, to move slowly, and not to take a step until we know the ground is safe. Do we think we're slow to adapt to change or that we're not smart enough to cope with a new challenge? Then we are likely to take a more passive role or not try at all.

(8) Sheehy claims, however, that these "crises," these feelings of insecurity and self-doubt are both unavoidable and necessary if we are to change and grow. If we do not confront and overcome these internal fears and doubts, if we protect ourselves too much, then we cease to grow. We become trapped inside a shell of our own making.

COMPREHENSION QUESTIONS

1. What do you think is meant by the title "All the World's a Stage"? In what ways does the world resemble a stage?
2. Who is Gail Sheehy? What three basic questions did she want to answer when she began her work on adult development?
3. Why did Sheehy want to find out if there were specific and predictable changes in adult life?
4. Refer to paragraph 4. What analogy is used to describe people? In making this comparison, what are the different similarities that come out?
5. An earthquake, a flood, a fatal disease—these are all examples of crises. What does Sheehy mean by the word "crisis"?
6. In the article, human growth is described as a product and a process. What is the significant difference between product and process when used to talk about a person's growth or development?

PART 2
SHEEHY ON STAGE

(9) On the basis of extensive research, original insights, and exhaustive interviews, Sheehy has been able to map out five periods that adults predictably encounter as they age from eighteen to about fifty-five. These stages, or "passages" as she calls them, do not nearly fit into equal chronological divisions. Some, like doorways, are brief and quickly crossed; others, like hallways, are longer and take more time to travel through. Sheehy claims that no passage can be bypassed or avoided in order to get to the next stage, although some of us arrive more battered and bruised from having stumbled and fallen along the way. Some of us, by contrast, seem to make the transition from one stage to the next relatively smoothly and with little apparent effort.

"PULLING UP ROOTS"

(10) Sheehy's "passages" have interesting names that describe their primary characteristics. The first, as one might expect with an eighteen- or twenty-year-old, is called "Pulling up Roots." This passage, as its name suggests, describes a time of breaking away from the family fold and physically departing to be on one's own. This is a typical American pattern. Whether this physical departure from the family involves college, the armed services, travel, or simply a separate apartment, this initial uprooting generally corresponds to an internal emotional separation from parents, as the younger generation go off to test their competency in a truly independent role. Young people need to ask themselves "Who am I?" "What do I want?" "How do I know if it's right?" All the ideas about independence absorbed to this point must be practiced and perfected in the coming years.

"THE TRYING TWENTIES"

(11) Usually by age twenty-two, the passage known as the "Trying Twenties" begins. This stage involves a concerted effort to take on the roles of adult life. Fresh out of college or the service, people make their first serious attempt to act the part of a professional, whether salesperson, secretary, homemaker, or government employee. Much of the time these young adults are preoccu-

pied with trying to master specific techniques. The questions they now ask themselves and older adults are: "How can I get what I want?" "What is the best way to start?" "Where should I go?" "Who can help me?" and, "How did *you* do it?"

(12) All of these questions presuppose that there is only one correct answer and that the technique, like learning to read, can be mastered with the proper guidance. Young people at this stage usually believe that there is a preestablished path to follow, and most are concerned with trying to fit into these trying and difficult roles, whether they be career hunting, spousehunting, or sight-seeing the world. Whatever their choice, or path, it always appears fixed and irrevocable, permitting little room for innovation and change.

(13) Even at this early adult stage men's and women's lives are beginning the divergence that will characterize their typical patterns until old age sets in. If marriages are begun now, they rarely occupy the same position in the partner's lives. Men often run right down the career racetrack, trying to gain a place of importance in the competition. Women traditionally have concentrated much more of their time and energy on running a house and caring for a family, even when they assume outside responsibilities such as school or another job. Most women still try to play the traditionally prescribed female role, although they're free to take on a second or third role if they can manage it all.

(14) As men and women in their twenties assume their different responsibilities, they begin the long years of separate paths, moving in concentric and even tangential circles. Is it any wonder that men and women often find these separate orbits problematic? Sheehy found that large differences do exist between the life problems of most men and women. The evidence shows that the timing of women's and men's experiences is not synchronized to create a team; the teammates are pursuing opposite goals on the field. Only the women who choose *not* to take partners resemble the standard male pattern of career involvement, but usually at the exclusion of close personal relationships.

"CATCH 30"

(15) Sheehy observed that no matter what life-style was established in the twenties, the majority of adults were ready for a change by the time "Catch 30" arrived. "Catch 30" occurs sometime between ages twenty-eight and thirty-five and has been so named in order to remind the reader of the familiar phrase, "Catch 22."* It also reminds the reader that the life cycle is like a game, and that anyone can be "caught" in it. Sheehy describes this passage as a time of resistance to the prescribed and limiting life-styles embraced with such vigor during the "Trying Twenties." The roles so carefully cultivated and rehearsed are now thrown off like worn-out clothing. Dissatisfaction and frustration with preestablished roles manifest themselves in the form of divorce, separation, and extramarital affairs. People often reevaluate career positions and change directions without warning, tearing up the grounds so laboriously laid before. Single people take on partners, childless couples start a family. Stabilizing and rooting or rerooting activities are the rule. But whereas previously couples may have had a sense of having a common cause, "their family," there is now a sense

***Catch 22* is the title of a book written by Joseph Heller in 1955. The phrase became a symbol of circular reasoning whereby the solution to a problem is impossible to obtain because of the nature of the problem. The expression is typically used to illustrate a certain kind of bureaucratic thinking or military logic with which it is impossible to argue. Here's an example of a "Catch 22" situation. A person needs a pass to enter a room. However, the only way he can obtain the pass is if he enters the room. But he can't enter the room because he doesn't have the pass. The person is caught in a "Catch 22."

of separation and compartmentalization. The sense of unity seems to disappear as men and women specialize in their separate domains. Both partners may have the sense that something is missing in their respective lives. However, because they have gained confidence in their own abilities and expertise, they are not yet ready to recognize that trying to fit a preestablished model is inherently problematic. People tend to blame their spouses for their own dissatisfaction.

(16) People can recognize that there is a problem, but their attempted solutions often miss the mark. They may imagine that another child would reproduce the early intimacy and closeness of their relationship and alleviate their discontent. In fact, it would probably do just the reverse. Another baby is not really a change but more of the same. The image of a new baby, and the harmony and intimacy it represents, does not correspond to the reality of added responsibilities. With another mouth to feed, men feel the pressure to get ahead in their jobs and thus spend more time away from home. Women either stay home and continue in the same role as before, or they take a job away from home, with little pay and less fulfillment. Often at this point, marriage is not viewed as the unity once hoped for and the sanctuary from loneliness, but rather as a solitary prison that keeps the inmates jailed.

THE "DEADLINE DECADE"

(17) By the middle of people's thirties, the start of the "Deadline Decade," the need for change becomes imperative. Time is running out! Women who have postponed motherhood now can think of little else. As they count down on the biological clock, they are aware that the possibility of retardation among babies of first-time mothers rises sharply after the age of thirty-five. Likewise, women who have stayed at home know the tyranny of biology too. They become consumed with the concept of beauty-gone or about-to-go and the need for alternative skills in life's marketplace. Weary of demanding children who cling to their skirts for attention and care, women march back to school in droves, consuming course catalogs in an effort to return to circulation and civilization once again.

(18) Men who have concentrated on their work begin to realize that the last opportunity to pull ahead of the competition is now, if they want to distinguish themselves in the rat race of the business world. Men in their thirties need promotions by this decade if they expect to reach the upper levels of management by age fifty. This is the time for the final push along the road to success; "it's now or never," and the drive for power can be fierce. As age fifty fast approaches and options become foreclosed, a new self-awareness takes shape. We begin to realize that we are the designers and directors of our own lives. We are not the actors in a play with a preestablished script to follow; we are not the victims of some prearranged plot. It is *we* who decide the courses that our lives take. We may mourn for the selves we can no longer be and for the plans we had hoped to fulfill but never did. We begin to accept ourselves for who we *are* and not for what we thought we *should be.*

THE "COMEBACK DECADE"

(19) After age forty-five, the start of the "Comeback Decade" (ages forty-five to fifty-five), people are ready to try new activities and take on new roles. As men receive their "final grades" in the business world, they often come to appreciate that there's more to life than just money and business. Fathers who had previously devoted little time to family are now more interested in spending time with their families. But this new desire comes at a bad time. Their

adolescent-aged children are now getting ready to go off on their own and are demanding more independence. Mothers too, if not already out of the home, are set to go out and try their wings in the outside world. Once again men's and women's lives are "out of synch" and dissatisfaction and conflict can often be the result.

SUCCESSFUL STAGE CHARACTERS: "PATHFINDERS"

(20) In her subsequent study, *Pathfinders,* Sheehy describes the passages that occur after age fifty-five. She has named these later stages "The Free-style Fifties," "The Selective Sixties," "The Thoughtful Seventies," and "The Proud-To-Be-Eighties." Each has its time and characteristic qualities. According to Sheehy, the attitude a person has while passing from one stage to the next is one of the critical factors for life-satisfaction. By the time she undertook this study, Sheehy was no longer satisfied with merely mapping out the life stages; she also wanted to learn the characteristics of the people who traversed them optimally. She termed such people "pathfinders." Sheehy discovered that many people who turned out to be "pathfinders" also had had at least one unhappy period in their lives, many times in childhood. Sheehy concluded that because they have not had "the easy life," the pathfinders have had to learn to value their inner achievements as much as their outer rewards.

(21) Perhaps the most significant point Sheehy learned is that "pathfinders" have the "capacity to draw from the environment what they need even when it is not readily available." They are able to find other people who can help guide and support them emotionally. They seem to have the ability or foresight to anticipate what their needs will be in the future, and thus they appear to have a good sense of timing. They're also not afraid of their true strengths and weaknesses, accepting both without regard to their "male" or "female" qualities. They've learned that there's a time to be gentle and a time to be tough, and they're not ashamed to be either. And last of all, they've come to discover a purpose larger than themselves around which to focus their lives. The people most satisfied with their lives know why they're living; they have a value worth pursuing. These people have not been afraid to pursue their own route into and out of the wilderness. These are the people who pass through the passages of life to become "pathfinders," people who have found happiness in growing and getting older.

CHARTING SHEEHY'S PASSAGES

	PULLING UP ROOTS	TRYING TWENTIES	CATCH 30	DEADLINE DECADE	COMEBACK DECADE
Approximate Age Stage Occurs	18–22	22–28	28–33	33–45	45–55
Principal Characteristics of Stage	Physical and emotional separation from parents Desire to test one's competency Need for independence	First serious attempt to take on adult role Attempt to follow preestablished roles Concentration on mastering specific techniques	Resistance to lifestyle chosen in previous stage Dissatisfaction and frustration with preestablished roles	Need for change intensified Time for final push along road to success—"It's now or never" Realization that all plans and dreams will not be realized	Readiness to take on new roles and try new activities
Some Ways that Characteristics Manifest Themselves	Young adults go off to college, armed forces, travel, separate apartment. People need to ask themselves: Who am I? What do I want? How do I know it's right?	People try to act the parts of housewife, secretary, professional, etc. People need to ask themselves: How can I get what I want? Where do I start? Who can help me? People assume there is *one* correct way.	Divorce, separation, and extramarital affairs are common. Single people get married. People often change careers. People tend to blame their spouses for their dissatisfaction.	People compete harder to distinguish themselves in careers. People begin to accept themselves for who they are, *not* for what they thought they should be.	Businessmen often want more involvement in family life. Housewives want new experiences away from home.

Drawing Conclusions

Directions: *Based on the information presented in the second part of the article, what do you think the author would say about each of the following statements? Put a circle around the one response you think the author would give.*

YES means the author would agree.
NO means the author would not agree.
MAYBE means there is not enough information in the article to know what the author would think.

1. All five stages of adult development described in the article last the same period of time. YES NO MAYBE
2. In the life cycle, it is possible to bypass a stage, that is, to jump from one stage to another without completing an in-between stage. YES NO MAYBE
3. In most cultures around the world, young people leave their parents between the ages of eighteen and twenty-two. YES NO MAYBE
4. People in their twenties often feel that once they have chosen a career it is an irrevocable decision. YES NO MAYBE
5. At around the age of thirty, most North Americans feel that they are ready for some kind of change. YES NO MAYBE
6. The need for change among married couples is one of the main reasons for divorce and extramarital affairs. YES NO MAYBE
7. Older adults who have successfully passed through the five stages are generally more content with their lives than young adults. YES NO MAYBE
8. Most married men in their fifties are more concerned with making a lot of money than spending time with their families. YES NO MAYBE
9. In general, people who have had happy childhoods are also happier adults. YES NO MAYBE
10. The emotional needs of men and women are generally in conflict during the course of the life cycle. YES NO MAYBE

Understanding Figurative Language

An author often uses words to help create a picture in the reader's mind. In trying to create this imaginary picture, the author usually tells what he or she is actually talking about and compares it to something else.

Example: After the snow had stopped, the park looked like it was covered in a blanket of white.

To what does the blanket of white refer? What associations or characteristics does a blanket of white have for you? Warm, soft, easily dirtied—these are some of the qualities or characteristics often associated with a blanket of white. However, *soft* is really the quality that applies to the "blanket of white," given the context of the sentence. Thus the blanket of white represents the snow, which appears *soft* and white as it covers the park. By making this comparison, the author creates an image or picture in the reader's mind so that the reader can *visualize* the author's idea, and thus understand the idea more clearly.

Directions: *The following sentences have been paraphrased from the indicated paragraphs in the article. In each sentence, try to identify the following:*

(1) Who or what is the author literally talking about?

(2) What other words are used to give you a picture of what is being talked about? (What comparison is the author making?)

(3) What idea is the author trying to communicate by making this comparison?

Paragraph

9 These stages, or "passages" as she calls them, do not fit into equal chronological divisions. Some, like doorways, are brief and quickly crossed; others, like hallways, are longer and take more time to travel through.

13 Men often run right down the career racetrack, trying to gain a place of importance in the competition.

14 As men and women in their twenties assume their different responsibilities, they begin the long years of separate paths, moving in concentric and tangential circles.

14 The evidence shows that the timing of women's and men's experiences is not synchronized to create a team; the teammates are pursuing opposite goals on the field.

15 People often reevaluate career positions and change directions without warning, tearing up the grounds so laboriously laid before.

16 Often at this point, marriage is not viewed as the unity once hoped for and the sanctuary from loneliness, but rather as a solitary prison that keeps the inmates jailed.

17 Women who have stayed at home know the tyranny of biology too. They become consumed with the concept of beauty-gone or about-to-go.

18 For men in their thirties, this is the time for the final push along the road to success if they expect to reach the upper levels of management by age fifty.

18 We begin to realize that we are the designers and directors of our own lives. We are not the actors in a play with a preestablished script to follow; we are not the victims of some prearranged plot.

21 Pathfinders are people who have not been afraid to pursue their own route into and out of the wilderness.

Seeing Relationships: Extended Definitions

Often, an author uses a word to mean something different from the way the word is commonly used or thought of. Take the word "crisis" as an example. We generally think of "crisis" as a difficult situation that may lead to a dangerous or disastrous result. But Sheehy uses the word "crisis" to mean something quite different. She refers to "crisis" as a time of internal upheaval and unrest.

When using a word in a different way, authors attempt to *define* the word so that its meaning is clear to the reader. The definition of a word or a concept may require a short sentence, a paragraph, a chapter, or sometimes even an entire book. To define a particular word or idea, authors may use the following techniques:

1. **comparing** one idea to another to show how the author's meaning is different from most people's understanding of the word
2. **giving examples** of the idea

Directions: *Look at the following words. Notice how the dictionary defines each word. Then refer to the indicated paragraphs. What definitions or meaning is given each word? What different techniques does the author use in defining each word? In the space provided, try to write some of the specific comparisons and examples that are used.*

Paragraph 4, **crisis:**

____

____

____

Paragraphs 5–8, **growth:**

____

____

____

____

____

Paragraph 9, **passage:**

____

____

Paragraphs 20–21, **pathfinder:**

____

____

____

____

____

____

____

Outlining Activity

Directions: *In the space provided, list the five different stages that Sheehy identifies in her book* Passages. *Next to each stage, write the age at which this stage is believed to occur. Then, under the title of each stage, list the important characteristics that are commonly found during each stage or "passage." Also, under the subtitle "Potential Conflict," list the reasons why problems may occur between couples at each stage.*

1. ______________________________

   a. Characteristics

   b. Potential Conflict

2. ______________________________

   a. Characteristics

   b. Potential Conflict

3. ______________________________

   a. Characteristics

   b. Potential Conflict

4. ______________________________

   a. Characteristics

   b. Potential Conflict

5. ______________________________

   a. Characteristics

   b. Potential Conflict

Literal and Figurative Meanings

Most of the titles Sheehy has given to the various stages or "passages" of adult development have both a literal and a figurative meaning. What images can be associated with each title? How do the images relate to the events that occur at each stage?

1. "Pulling Up Roots" ______________________________

____

____

2. "The Trying Twenties": ______________________________

____

____

3. "Catch 30": ______________________________

____

____

4. "The Deadline Decade": ______________________________

____

5. "The Comeback Decade": ______________________________

____

Your Turn on Stage

1. In the spaces provided, write as many of the important events of *your* life as best you remember them. These events can be both *positive* and *negative* moments or periods in your life.

2. Refer to your list. Next to each event, write your age at the time it occurred.

3. Evaluate each event that you listed, that is, decide whether the event was *fantastic, good, difficult,* or *extremely difficult.* Then refer to the charts that follow. Write each event of your life in the appropriate space on the chart. When you have completed the first chart, you may be able to see the different stages of your own life more clearly.

	0–10 YEARS	11–20 YEARS	21–30 YEARS	31–40 YEARS	41–50 YEARS
Fantastic Events					
Good Events					
Difficult Events					
Extremely Difficult Events					

Directions: *Now recopy the events of your life from the chart above onto the chart below, making sure that each event is recorded in the appropriate box. Compare the two charts. In what ways are the patterns of your life similar? In what ways are they different? Does looking at your life in chart form reveal anything new to you about yourself? Explain.*

	0–17 YEARS	18–22 YEARS	23–28 YEARS	29–33 YEARS	34–45 YEARS
Fantastic Events					
Good Events					
Difficult Events					
Extremely Difficult Events					

Topics for Discussion and Composition

1. Describe your own life in terms of stages. What are the different passages of your life? Be sure to describe both your "internal" feelings and the "external" circumstances of each passage. Do your life stages correspond in any way to the stages Sheehy has identified? What similarities or differences do you see? (Choose another person whose life you know very well. Describe his or her life in terms of "passages.")
2. What feelings and reactions do you usually have in the following situations?

   a. A change of job
   b. A change of residence

c. Going to a class where you don't know the other students or the teacher
d. Meeting another person for the first time
e. Going to a party where you don't know most of the people

3. Describe the most significant change in your life. How did the change affect you? What did you do to help you deal with the change?
4. Do you think men and women develop differently as adults? Give reasons for your answer.
5. What period of your life was the happiest?
6. What period of your life was the most difficult?
7. In Sheehy's use of the term "pathfinders," she describes the qualities a person needs to successfully pass through the different stages of life. Do you agree with the qualities she identifies? What other qualities do you think are important in order for a person to deal with change?
8. Many children's stories end with the characters "living happily ever after." What idea does this ending communicate about life in general? Do you think it's a good message to give to children? Why or why not?
9. Refer to the stories "Linda's Home and Garden" and "The Importance of Being Ernest" (pages 31 and 32). Based on the themes of the two stories, what passage do you think Linda and Ernest are going through? Explain.

Seeing Relationships: Analogies

Directions: *Choose the one word in parentheses that correctly completes the analogy and write it in the appropriate blank space. (For an explanation of analogies, please refer to page 132).*

1. hard : shell AS soft : ______________________
   (bone, eye, skin, stomach)
2. natural : hurricane AS man-made : ______________________
   (factory, pollution, building, product)
3. marriage : spouse As sports : ______________________
   (exercise, teammate, victory, baseball)
4. together : apart AS synchronize : ______________________
   (diverge, time, cultivate, communicate)
5. succeed : fail AS reluctance : ______________________
   (fear, security, willingness, hesitance)
6. child : adolescent AS elementary school: ______________________
   (college, teen-ager, high school, book)

7. confront : avoid AS imperative : ______________________
(simple, lonely, demanding, unnecessary)

8. synchronize : time AS concentrate : ______________________
(threat, energy, stage, divorce)

9. lobster : crustacean AS human being: ______________________
(woman, sex, land, mammal)

10. director : play AS writer : ______________________
(pencil, script, promotion, designer)

11. marks : school AS salary : ______________________
(business, opportunity, option, money)

Vocabulary Development

Directions: *Use the words to complete the sentences that follow. Change the form of the verb when necessary.*

to undertake	cycle	predictable
crises	stage	synchronized
willingness	vulnerable	insecurity

1. When Gail Sheehy first ______________ her study of adults, she was interested in comparing the development of men and women through the life ______________ .
2. She discovered that the needs of men and women are often not ______________ ; this is one reason, she feels, why so many marriages end in divorce.
3. Sheehy also believes that there are ______________ stages in adult life when people begin to reevaluate their lives.
4. Sheehy also claims that in order for people to change and grow, they must experience feelings of doubt and ______________ .
5. Sheehy refers to these periods of internal upheaval as ______________ .
6. People must overcome these feelings of self-doubt and anxiety if they are going to move to the next ______________ .
7. In order to grow and change, however, people need to have the ______________ to take chances, to risk failure in their efforts to improve themselves.
8. During periods of personal change, it's natural for adults to feel ______________ and unprotected.

to blame	to mourn	patterns
to presuppose	to face up to	fierce
to accept	retardation	

9. As a result, many adults try to protect themselves by returning to previous _________________ of behavior, since their old habits make them feel more comfortable and secure.
10. During their twenties, many young adults assume or _________________ that there is one clear road or path to success and that their job is to find it.
11. Between the ages of twenty-eight and thirty-three, many adults begin to feel unhappy with their lives, and married couples tend to _________________ their spouses for their dissatisfaction and frustration.
12. After the age of thirty-five, it becomes more dangerous for a woman to have her first child, since the possibility of _________________ increases sharply for newborn babies.
13. In the business world, competition is very _________________, with each person trying to get ahead of everyone else.
14. Between the ages of forty and fifty, it's common for people to _________________ their lost dreams and hopes.
15. People must _________________ the fact that they are probably never going to be rich or famous. Adults who successfully pass this stage begin to _________________ themselves for who they are, not for what they hoped to be.

Dictionary Skills: Multiple Definitions and Parts of Speech

Directions: *This exercise combines two skills: identifying a word's part of speech (whether a word is a noun, verb, adjective, or adverb) and identifying its meaning. First, read the dictionary definition of the word. Then in the space provided after each sentence, write the part of speech and the meaning of the boldface word in each sentence. The first one has been done as an example.*

set (set) *v.* 1. To put in a particular place. 2. To determine or fix the amount. 3. To begin to move; travel (used with out, forth), off. 4. To pass below the horizon, as in *The sun sets in the west.* 5. In theater or works of literature: to place (a scene) in a particular location. *adj.* 1. Fixed or determined in advance. *n.* A group or collection of things belonging together. 2. Specialized equipment for radio or television assembled for use, as in *TV set.* 3. The background scenery assembled for a play, movie, or opera.

1. As young adults **set** out to begin a life of their own, it's common for them to experience an emotional separation from their parents.
   v.-3. begin to move; travel

2. Although there is no **set** time for this separation to occur, most young adults in the U.S. leave home between eighteen and twenty years of age.

3. The story of "Mr. Know-All" was **set** on an ocean liner that was on its way from San Francisco to Japan right after the first world war.

4. When Gail Sheehy undertook her study of adult development, she had a **set** of topics and issues that she wanted to investigate.

5. In the past, the **sets** for most films were quite simple. Today, however, movie **sets** are so elaborate and detailed that their cost often runs into millions of dollars.

draw (drô) *v.,* **drew, drawn. 1.** To cause to follow by use of physical force; pull; drag. **2.** To attract; charm. **3.** To get or receive from a source. **4.** To extract (a conclusion or inference); to deduce. **5.** To make lines, as with a pencil, pen, or brush. **6.** To come; move; approach.

6. According to Sheehy, "pathfinders" are people who have an ability to **draw** what they need from their environment, especially during trying times.

7. Sheehy was able to **draw** several important conclusions about adult development as a result of extensive interviews with hundreds of adults.

8. As young adults, people are often **drawn** to glamorous professions, only to find out that these careers do not satisfy or fulfill them.

9. As old age **draws** near, many people learn to accept themselves for who they are and not for what they thought they should be.

regard (ri gärd) *v.* **1.** To view or consider in a particular way. *n.* **1.** Attention; concern; consideration. **2.** Esteem or respect. **3.** Reference; relation.

10. "Pathfinders" are not afraid of their true strengths and weaknesses, accepting both without **regard** to their "male" or "female" qualities.

11. Some people **regard** Gail Sheehy's *Passages* and *Pathfinders* as significant contributions to the understanding of adult development.

12. The work of the psychologist Erik Erikson is also held in high **regard** by those involved in the study of adult behavior and growth.

____

13. In **regard** to the subject of adult development, it's important that more research be done on this challenging and provocative topic.

____

The Road Not Taken

ROBERT FROST (1874–1963)

Robert Frost was born in San Francisco, California, in 1874. When his father died ten years later, he and his mother returned to New England, where his parents had previously lived. Even as a teenager, Frost showed a talent for poetry. Although his mother, a schoolteacher, was proud of his writing, the rest of the family was very upset. His grandfather told him, "No one can make a living at poetry." His grandfather's words were, for a time, prophetic. To earn a living, Frost worked as a shoemaker, farmer, and English teacher. Yet the urge to write poetry never left him.

When success finally came, it reached unprecedented proportions. He is the only American poet to have been awarded the Pulitzer Prize for the best poetry book of the year four times—in 1924 for New Hampshire; *in 1931 for* Collected Poems; *in 1937 for* A Further Range; *and in 1943 for* A Witness Tree. *He also received numerous degrees from this country's most prestigious universities.*

Frost's poetry speaks to all people of life's ordinary concerns. His verse has a special intimacy and wisdom to which one returns like an old friend. Robert Frost died in 1963, three weeks before his eighty-ninth birthday. He remains one of North America's best-loved poets.

Two roads diverged in a yellow wood,
And sorry I could not travel both
And be one traveler, long I stood
And looked down one as far as I could
To where it bent in the undergrowth;

Then took the other, as just as fair,
And having perhaps the better claim,
Because it was grassy and wanted wear;
Though as for that the passing there
Had worn them really about the same,

And both that morning equally lay
In leaves no step had trodden back.
Oh, I kept the first for another day!
Yet knowing how way leads on to way,
I doubted if I should ever come back.

I shall be telling this with a sigh
Somewhere ages and ages hence;
Two roads diverged in a wood, and I—
I took the one less traveled by,
And that has made all the difference.

QUESTIONS

1. Describe the two roads mentioned in the poem. How are they different?
2. What do you think the roads represent?
3. Which road did the poet take? How does he feel about his choice?
4. How do you think the poet views his life?
5. What similarity do you see between the themes of this poem and some of the themes in the article "All the World's a Stage"?
6. Have you ever had to choose between "two roads"? Which one did you take? How do you now feel about the choice you made?

9

THE MYSTERY OF DREAMS

Photograph by Ken Karp

Understanding Vocabulary in Context

Directions: *Use the context clues in each sentence to help you write a synonym or brief definition for each boldface word. The boldface word in each sentence appears in the reading selection that follows this exercise.*

1. My friend has an incredible memory. He can **recall** events that occurred years ago, remembering who was there and what they were all wearing.
   Definition or synonym: ________________
2. Upon awakening, the poet Coleridge began to **record** the wonderful imagery he had dreamt—now not composing poetry but merely writing it from memory.
   WRITE DOWN
3. When our family first moved to California, everything seemed strange and different. Gradually, however, as I became **acquainted** with my surroundings and made new friends, California began to feel familiar, like home.
   BECOME ACCOSTUM TO / TO FAMILIARIZE WITH
4. Our minds reflect the memories of things unseen but seen, unknown but known; and somehow we are struck momentarily with a **fleeting** sense of the eternal.
   MOMENTARALY / FOR A MOMENT
5. I remember a student telling me of a recurrent, serial-story dream, with each chapter of the experience connected to the last **installment.**
   LAST PART OF THE WHOLE EVENT
6. She and Anne would chat at the corner for a moment and then **stroll** a hundred yards to a large old house with a huge veranda.
   WALK
7. She walked up the steps and **peered** into the empty building. She looked in through the bay window, past the window seat where she had sat in so many of her dreams.
   TO LOOK INTO A ROOM? THROUGH THE WINDOW
8. They lost control of the canoe, and, in spite of their desperate attempt to get to shore, they were **drawn** to the edge of the falls.
   PULL TO / TO ATTRACT TO
9. At this point she woke, her hands clenched, her breathing heavy, her nightclothing **damp** with perspiration.
   WET / MOIST
10. Before he died, he made one last **request** of his family. He asked that his valuable art collection be given to a local museum.
    WISH WISH
11. The area around the house had been carefully planned. In the back there were many types of trees, including **birches** and **beeches,** and a variety of colorful flowers, especially **lilacs** and **forsythia.**

birch: ______________________________

beech: ______________________________

lilac: ______________________________

forsythia: ______________________________

12. The **lawn** in front of the house resembled a bright green blanket that invited you to lie down on it.

GRASS THAT GROWS IN THE YARD.

13. Although it was difficult to see because of the huge crowds of people, I was able to catch a **glimpse** of the President as he passed in his limousine.

SHORT LOOK, FAST LOOK.

14. She dislikes going to loud, crowded parties, but she **is fond of** eating out in small, intimate restaurants.

TO LIKE

15. Although only twenty-two at the time of her husband's death, she never remarried. She remained a **widow** for the rest of her life.

WOMAN WHOSE HUSBAND HAS DIED.

16. In the past, women were usually made to stay in the hospital for at least five to seven days after giving birth. Today, however, many hospitals **discharge** women after only a day or two if everything has gone well.

LET GO, RELEASE, ALLOW TO GO

The Mystery of Dreams

S. RALPH HARLOW

People in ancient times—perhaps because they were more superstitious and ignorant, perhaps because their simple lives were much closer to the verities—placed far more importance on dreams than we do today.

True, our modern world has its volumes of dream interpretation by modern soothsayer and modern psychiatrist alike; it has its scientists probing into the mechanics of dreams; it has its psychologists connecting dreams to the subconscious mind. But it is a rare modern man who seriously wonders if some dreams might not be simple, uncluttered communications with the psychic world.

Are not some dreams psychic experiences in themselves? Few Americans are unfamiliar with the death dreams of Abraham Lincoln. This realistic, practical American repeatedly dreamed of attending his own funeral, the last time only a few days before his tragic assassination. In early April of 1865 the tall, bearded President told guests at a White House party of his previous night's dream. He was walking in the White House, he said, and suddenly became aware of the sound of weeping. He traced the voice to the East Room, where he saw mourners and guards surrounding a casket.

"Who is dead?" Lincoln asked a soldier. "The President is dead," the soldier replied. "Killed by an assassin."

A few days later, on Good Friday, April 14, the President and Mrs. Lincoln sat in a private box in Ford's Theater in Washington watching *Our American Cousin.* And it was then, during intermission, that John Wilkes Booth made Lincoln's dream of death come true.

Benjamin Franklin told friends that often his dreams had foretold the outcome of events that were of great concern to him. And Samuel Taylor Coleridge, the great English poet, composed several hundred lines of his famous poem "Kubla Khan" while dreaming during an afternoon nap. Upon awakening he immediately began to record the wonderful imagery—now not composing poetry but merely writing it from memory. He was interrupted in this task, and when he returned, the unrecorded verses had vanished, as had his dream.

If dreams, or at least some of them, are indeed psychic experiences, perhaps we approach an explanation to the "I've been here before" experience that almost all of us have felt at one time or another in our lives. You are exploring a wooded path on a gentle slope in New Hampshire, and you have never been to New Hampshire before. It is pleasant and quiet, and a sense of peace lulls you into wonderful tranquility. Your senses somehow seem sharpened, and although there is not the excitement of new awareness you begin to feel that you can see more and feel more in a new perspective. Then, dimly, you begin to know that this path, this forest, this day is a timeless place and a timeless time; that you have been here before. Do all forest paths have split birches or smooth-skinned beeches? you ask yourself in some elated confusion. And you answer: Perhaps, only perhaps, and if they do, are they always in this precise position, and would I know the pattern of the ancient lichen spattered green on the glacial boulder to my right? Yet I do; for these things I know: I have been here before, I have walked this path; yet I know that I have not. A tiny, shining facet of our minds reflects the memories of things unseen but seen, unknown but known; and somehow we are struck momentarily with a fleeting sense of the eternal.

It goes quickly, this glimpse of greater glory, but most of us have had it, regretting when it is taken back from us—sometimes snatched suddenly as if the giver changed his mind; sometimes drained slowly from our senses and leaving us again with unsatisfying reality.

Have we dreamed these experiences, these times when we recognize rooms and faces and strange places which we have never seen before, and then stored them into our subconscious for later recall? And if we have indeed dreamed them just how can we explain the precise accuracy of our dreams in foretelling what we are yet to see?

I remember a student—let's call her Anne—telling me of such a dream, a recurrent, serial-story dream, with each chapter of the experience connected to the last installment. Always the scene opened on a street corner in a small New England town. There were white-painted clapboard houses with shutters the color of ancient weathered copper. There were green lawns and lilacs and forsythia. And in each dream a young girl was waiting for her. She and Anne would chat on the corner for a moment and then stroll a hundred yards to a large old house with a huge veranda. Inside, in the big living room, a group of young people would already be gathered, and Anne and her dream companion would join them, singing around the piano, playing parlor games, and spending endless hours in young people's discussions.

Each dream was essentially a repetition of the first one; the circumstances of meeting were identical—always on the same street corner—and the stroll to the house, up the long walk to the veranda and into the living room to see the same young people gather. As the dream sequence progressed, Anne became acquainted with the other youth in the house, learned their names and characteristics, their likes and dislikes, and she became very fond of them.

And then one night, when the dream had run for perhaps a dozen nights, Anne met her friend on the corner and found her depressed and sad. "This is our last meeting," her dream friend said. "I will see you but you will not see me." Anne brushed aside the words of her friend, saying, "Of course we shall meet again," But they never did; the dreams stopped suddenly and never recurred.

A few months later, with her father and sister, who had come from Michigan for her graduation, Anne was driving up the New England coast. None of the family had ever seen the Atlantic shore, and they toured from Boston into Maine, enjoying the early summer beauty and exploring the small seacoast colonial towns.

Then suddenly in one small coastal village Anne recognized the street corner where she had met her dream friend so many times. Excitedly she said, "Father, turn left here. Turn left at this corner." And her father was obedient to his daughter's request.

"Four more houses," Anne said as they drove slowly up the street. "Three more. It's on the right just on the other side of that lilac hedge. Now. Stop here, Father. Right here. In front of this house."

Anne got out of the car. It was the house. Identical with that in her dreams. The same lilac hedge, the same four wide wooden steps to the veranda, the same huge door with tarnished brass knocker and with small rectangular panes set on each side of it. But now the lawn needed mowing and a black and white sign near the walk said "For Rent." She walked up the steps and peered into the empty building. She looked in through the bay window, past the window seat where she had sat in so many of her dreams; she saw the fireplace, empty and black now instead of dancing with flames as she had known it; and the staircase once used in her dreams as a sort of choir loft for singing youngsters. It was the house she had known, but it was empty now, its furniture gone, its floors bare and dusty, its youthful voices transferred to some other place—or to some other dreams.

In one definition of the word, Anne's dreams were consecutive; but a series of dreams would be a more accurate description, because in the literature of psychic phenomena there is a consecutive dream that involves two or more persons. In such dreams one person experiences the first part of the incident, and another takes up the dream where the first leaves off. One example of this was supplied by a former student of mine who frequently shared consecutive dreams with her mother.

The daughter reported that she dreamed she and her mother were canoeing in a swift river above a waterfall. They lost control of the canoe, and in spite of their desperate paddling they were drawn to the edge of the falls. The canoe teetered and they were swept away into the rapids below. At this point she woke, her hands clenched, her breathing heavy, her nightclothing damp with perspiration. Then she returned to sleep and spent the rest of the night in peaceful, dreamless sleep.

Next morning she told her mother, who slept in the adjoining bedroom, about her dream and was told that her mother had continued the event. Her dream had begun as she and her daughter struggled in the water at the foot of the falls, and had continued until they reached the shore, bedraggled and exhausted.

Some people have identical dreams during the same night and apparently at the same time. Dr. Hornell Hart, formerly a member of the Duke University faculty and a man who has made an exhaustive study of dreams, records one identical dream he shared with his wife. Both dreamed they walked together in the garden; he discovered their dreams were the same while describing his dream to her. He incorrectly named a flower in the dream garden, and she corrected him; then they knew that they were sharing not only their waking lives but also their dream world.

There is always the possibility that a dream can be a psychic communication with someone we have known in this life and who has gone on to the next one. Only recently my wife Marion reported to me an experience that strengthens this possibility. Marion, recovering from a broken hip, shared her hospital room with Ruth, the elderly widow of a musician.

One morning after their early hospital breakfast Ruth said, "Marion, last night I saw my husband." Marion was immediately alert because of her interest in psychic phenomena.

"It was a dream," Ruth said, "but it was so vivid. He was carrying his cornet and he played for me." Her voice softened and grew lower. "I've heard him play it many times. I recognized it. It was Chopin's 'Funeral March.' And when he'd finished he said, 'Ruth, I need you over here. Come to me.' "

And that evening Ruth, who was expected to be discharged from the hospital in a few days, did go over to her husband. She died quietly in her sleep.

I was attending a meeting in a neighboring town when I was informed of her death, and on the way home I thought of her previous night's dream and of the request made by her dead husband. At home I switched on the hall light; it burned steadily for a few minutes and then suddenly went out. It was a fairly new bulb and I remembered inserting it only a short time before. Therefore I tested it in a floor lamp. It burned brightly, and I knew I would need to call an electrician the next day to repair the hall switch, for there, obviously, was the trouble.

Then I thought of Ruth's death and our previous flashlights experience after the death of Helen,* and I returned the bulb to its socket in the hall ceiling. It burned brightly and steadily. Only six hours previously I had held Ruth's hand and she had said to me in a strong voice, "I will be all right." Was the erratic light bulb just that—a manufacturer's error that escaped detection and was brought back to life by my handling of it? Or was its behavior some signal from Ruth that there is life after death— that there is survival of personality?

Comprehension Questions

1. What do you think is the purpose of the article? What basic idea is the author trying to communicate?
2. The author refers to the personal experiences of such famous people as Abraham Lincoln, Benjamin Franklin, and Samuel Taylor Coleridge. Why do you think the author mentions them in this article?
3. Compare the experiences of the three men. How were they different? How were they similar?
4. The author states that almost all people have had the feeling of "I've been here before," even though they know their bodies are really there for the first time. How does the author attempt to explain this phenomenon?
5. Describe the dream of the author's student, Anne. What did she see? What happened to her?

*This is a reference to an event *not* previously mentioned in this particular article. To what do you think it refers?

6. What real-life experience did Anne later have that was related to her dreams? What things did she see that she had seen before? What things were different? How do you explain these differences?
7. List three other dreams mentioned in the article. How are the dreams different from each other?
8. At the end of the article, the author describes his own experiences involving a new light bulb that goes out suddenly but then works again only hours later. Why do you think he includes this experience in the article? What idea is he suggesting by mentioning this experience?

Topics for Discussion and Composition

1. Tell about a dream you have had recently. Describe what you saw and what happened. Give as many details as you can. How do you interpret the events of your dream?
2. Have you ever had any one of the following experiences? Describe what happened.
   a. You have a dream that something will happen in the future and then that dream actually comes true.
   b. You dream about a place you have never been to. Then you actually visit the place you had seen in your dream.
   c. You and another person have exactly the same dream at the same time.
   d. In the same night, you experience the first part of a dream, and someone else completes the rest of the dream.
3. Have you ever had a recurring dream the way Anne did? Describe these dreams. Did these dreams vary in any way? If yes, how so?
4. What strange and unusual experience have you had in your life that seems to have no logical scientific explanation? What was your reaction to your experience?
5. Do you think there is life after death? What reasons do you have for your belief?
6. People claim that while they have been awake they have communicated their thoughts and feelings to another person who was very far away. Do you know of any such experiences? Has this ever happened to you?

Determining Significant Details

Directions: *In a story or article, an author often includes many specific details. Some of the information may be essential to the development of the author's idea, while other facts may be less important. Listed here are a set of statements related to the story of Anne and her dream experience. Put an* **"S"** *next to each statement that you think is significant or essential to her story. Put an* **"X"** *next to each statement that you think is insignificant, that is, not very important to the story's main idea.*

_____ 1. Anne had a recurrent, serial-story dream, with each new dream connected to the previous dream.

_____ 2. The scene in the dream always began on the same street corner of a small town in New England.

_____ 3. Anne was able to remember the exact appearance of the house.

_____ 4. Anne's father lived in Michigan.

_____ 5. One summer Anne and her family took a vacation up the New England coast.

_____ 6. Boston and Maine are both located on the coast of New England.

_____ 7. Anne's sister had recently graduated from school.

_____ 8. It was the first time Anne had ever visited New England.

_____ 9. The New England seacoast had many small colonial towns.

_____ 10. It was early summer and a good time to enjoy a vacation.

_____ 11. During the trip Anne suddenly recognized the street corner that had appeared in her dreams.

_____ 12. Anne was able to direct her father to the house.

_____ 13. It was the same house she had seen in her dreams, only now it was abandoned.

Vocabulary Development Puzzle: Einstein's Message

Directions: *Complete each missing word in the following sentences, using only one letter for each blank space. Rewrite each numbered letter in the corresponding space of the two sentences marked "Einstein's Message." When you have completed all the letters of these two sentences, you will have a message from the great scientist, Albert Einstein.*

Einstein's Message:

T h e   _ _ _ t   _ _ _ _ _ _ f _ _   _ _ _ _ g   _ e
1 2 3   4 5 6 7 8 9 10 11   12 13 14 15   16

_ _ n   _ _ _ _ _ _ _ _ _ e   _ s   t h e
17 18   19 20 21 22 23 24 25 26 27   28

_ _ _ _ _ _ _ _ _ s.   I t   _ _   t h e
29 30 31 32 33 34 35 36 37   38 39

_ _ _ _ _ e   o f   _ _ l   _ _ _ e   _ _ t
40 41 42 43 44   45 46   47 48 49   50 51

a n d   _ _ _ _ _ _ e.
52 53 54 55 56 57

1. In general, people in ancient times were more s _(42) p e _(51) s _(47) _(14) _(47) _(14) o _(42) s than the average person is today, probably because they didn't understand the reasons why things happened.
2. In a dream just before he was assassinated, President Lincoln saw guards and m _(2) _(49) _(23) n e _(23) _(3) surrounding his own c a _(52) k _(5) _(12).
3. Benjamin Franklin claimed that in his dreams he could f o _(43) e _(12) e _(46) _(46) the outcome of future events.
4. Franklin often dreamed of things that were of great c _(2) _(15) c _(25) r _(15) to him.
5. The great English poet, Samuel Taylor Coleridge, c o _(1) _(21) o _(31) _(55) _ several hundred lines of his poem "Kubla Khan" while he was d _(23) _(22) a _(29) _(24) n g one afternoon.
6. It's easier to take a stroll in a forest when there is a p _(45) t _(13) to walk on.
7. Some people have had i d _ _(15) t i _(44) a _(11) dreams in the same night; that is, they dream exactly the same thing.
8. When visiting a foreign country, some people prefer to take a guided t _(36) _(7) _(51) of the places they want to see.
9. A dream that happens again and again is referred to as a r _(19) _(57) _(10) r r i n g dream.
10. Some people claim that during a dream they have actually heard the v _(41) _(9) _(57) _(5) of a person who is dead.
11. Hospitals usually do not d i s c h _(50) _(34) _ _(19) a patient until the doctors feel the person is ready to go home.
12. A w _(35) _ _(41) w is a person whose husband has died.
13. In order for a light bulb to work, you first have to turn on the light s _(16) i _(8) _(17) h.
14. Some people have been able to accurately predict the future because of a dream which they've had. This is one example of a p s _(30) _(17) h _(54) _(17) phenomenon.

15. Everyone dreams while sleeping. However, many people are unable to r _ _ a _ _ (55 53, 11 11) their dreams when they wake up.

16. There are some events for which there seem to be no acceptable scientific e _ p l _ _ _ _ _ _ o _ (20, 6 56 6, 28, 56).

17. The states of Maine and Massachusetts are both located on the Atlantic c _ _ _ _ t (18 40) of the United States.

18. People sometimes r _ _ o g _ _ z _ (19 27, 26, 19) a place which they've never visited because they have seen the place in their dreams.

19. Some people have been able to give a precise and a c c _ _ _ a _ _ (37 51, 47 33) description of a place before they have ever been there.

20. People need a _ _ _ g h _ (4 51 38, 32) light in order to read in the dark.

21. Personality, dreams, the subconscious mind—these phenomena are all part of life's m _ _ _ t e _ _ (30 39, 48 30).

Dictionary Skills: People and Places

In the article "The Mystery of Dreams," the author mentions the names of some famous people (Lincoln, Franklin, Coleridge, Chopin) and places (Boston, Maine, New Hampshire, New England). When reading, it is not uncommon to encounter the names of people and places that you may not know. One convenient source for learning about unfamiliar people and places is the dictionary.

Directions: *Here are the names of people and places you will encounter in the supplementary reading that follows ("Examining Psychic Phenomena"). Use an all-English dictionary to look up the names of each person and place; write the information you find in the space provided.*

PEOPLE

1. Churchill, Winston ________________
2. Faust ________________
3. Mozart ________________
4. Napoleon ________________
5. Ottoman ________________
6. Voltaire ________________

PLACES

1. Beárn (bearnaise) ______________________
2. Cleveland ______________________
3. Düsseldorf ______________________
4. Istanbul ______________________
5. New World ______________________
6. Rhode Island ______________________
7. Vienna ______________________

Examining Psychic Phenomena

WOODY ALLEN (1935-   )

Woody Allen was born in 1935 in New York City. After leaving both New York University and City College without having graduated from either, Allen began writing for television and for professional comedians. In 1964 he became a stand-up comic himself, later recording three albums of live concert performances. He is also the creator of two Broadway plays, Don't Drink the Water *and* Play It Again, Sam.

He is perhaps best known for his work in the film world, where he has written, directed, and acted in numerous movies. Among them are Take the Money and Run, Bananas, Everything You've Always Wanted to Know about Sex, Sleeper, Love and Death, Annie Hall, Manhattan, *and* Zelig. *His stories, many of which first appeared in* The New Yorker *magazine, can be found in three books —* Side Effects, Getting Even, *and* Without Feathers, *where the story, "Examining Psychic Phenomena," appears.*

It has often been said that Mr. Allen is obsessed with the themes of death, sex, identity, and romantic relationships. In this story, however, Mr. Allen turns his considerable creative talents to the subject of psychic phenomena. The results are . . . well, you decide for yourself.

There is no question that there is an unseen world. The problem is, how far is it from midtown and how late is it open? Unexplainable events occur constantly. One man will see spirits. Another will hear voices. A third will wake up and find himself running in the Preakness[1]. How many of us have not at one time or another felt an ice-cold hand on the back of our neck while we were home alone? (Not me, thank God, but some have.) What is behind these experiences? Or in front of them, for that matter? Is it true that some men can foresee the future or communicate with ghosts? And after death is it still possible to take showers?

Fortunately, these questions about psychic phenomena are answered in a soon-to-be-published book, Boo!, by Dr. Osgood Mulford Twelge, the noted para-psychologist and professor of ectoplasm at Columbia University. Dr. Twelge has assembled a remarkable history of supernatural incidents that covers the whole range of psychic phenomena, from thought transference to the bizarre[2] experience of two brothers on opposite parts of the globe, one of whom took a bath while the other suddenly got clean. What follows is but a sampling of Dr. Twelge's most celebrated cases, with his comments.

[1]**the Preakness:** a famous horse race
[2]**bizarre:** strange; weird; unbelievable

APPARITIONS

On March 16, 1992, Mr. J.C. Dubbs awoke in the middle of the night and saw his brother Amos, who had been dead for fourteen years, sitting at the foot of the bed flicking[3] chickens. Dubbs asked his brother what he was doing there, and his brother said not to worry, he was dead and was only in town for the weekend. Dubbs asked his brother what it was like in "the other world," and his brother said it was not unlike Cleveland. He said he had returned to give Dubbs a message, which was that a dark-blue suit and Argyle socks are a big mistake.

At that point, Dubb's servant girl entered and saw Dubbs talking to "a shapeless, milky haze,"[4] which she said reminded her of Amos Dubbs but was a little better-looking. Finally, the ghost asked Dubbs to join him in an aria from *Faust,* which the two sang with great fervor. As dawn rose, the ghost walked through the wall, and Dubbs, trying to follow, broke his nose.

This appears to be a classic case of the apparition phenomenon, and if Dubbs is to be believed, the ghost returned again and caused Mrs. Dubbs to rise out of a chair and hover over the dinner table for twenty minutes until she dropped into some gravy. It is interesting to note that spirits have a tenency to be mischievous[5], which A.F. Childe, the British mystic, attributes to a marked feeling of inferiority they have over being dead. "Apparitions" are often associated with individuals who have suffered an unusual demise[6]. Amos Dubbs, for instance, had died under mysterious circumstances when a farmer accidentally planted him along with some turnips[7].

SPIRIT DEPARTURE

Mr. Albert Sykes reports the following experience: "I was sitting having biscuits with some friends when I felt my spirit leave my body and go make a telephone call. For some reason, it called the Moscowitz Fiber Glass Company. My spirit then returned to my body and sat for another twenty minutes or so, hoping nobody would suggest charades[8]. When the conversation turned to mutual funds, it left again and began wandering around the city. I am convinced that it visited the Statue of Liberty and then saw the stage show at Radio City Music Hall. Following that, it went to Benny's Steak House and ran up a tab[9] of sixty-eight dollars. My spirit then decided to return to my body, but it was impossible to get a cab[10]. Finally, it walked up Fifth Avenue and rejoined me just in time to catch the late news. I could tell that it was reentering my body, because I felt a sudden chill[11] and a voice said. 'I'm back. You want to pass me those raisins?'

"This phenomenon has happened to me several times since. Once, my spirit went to Miami for a week-end and once it was arrested for trying to leave Macy's without paying for a tie. The fourth time, it was actually my body that left my spirit, although all it did was get a rubdown[12] and come right back."

Spirit departure was very common around 1910, when many "spirits" were reported wandering aimlessly around India searching for the American Consulate. The phenomenon is quite similar to transubstantiation, the process whereby a person will suddenly dematerialize and rematerialize somewhere else

[3]**flicking:** removing the feathers from
[4]**haze:** vapor; cloud; fog
[5]**mischievous:** full of tricks
[6]**demise:** death
[7]**turnips:** a plant of the mustard family
[8]**charades:** a type of game
[9]**tab:** bill
[10]**cab:** taxi
[11]**chill:** coldness
[12]**rubdown:** massage

in the world. This is not a bad way to travel, although there is usually a half-hour wait for luggage. The most astonishing case of transubstantiation was that of Sir Arthur Nurney, who vanished with an audible pop while he was taking a bath and suddenly appeared in the string section of the Vienna Symphony Orchestra. He stayed on as the first violinist for twenty-seven years, although he could only play "Three Blind Mice,"[13] and vanished abruptly one day during Mozart's Jupiter Symphony, turning up[14] in bed with Winston Churchill.

PRECOGNITION

Mr. Fenton Allentuck describes the following precognitive dream: "I went to sleep at midnight and dreamed that I was playing whist[15] with a plate of chives.[16] Suddenly the dream shifted, and I saw my grandfather about to be run over by a truck in the middle of the street, where he was waltzing[17] with a clothing dummy.[18] I tried to scream, but when I opened my mouth the only sound that came out was chimes,[19] and my grandfather was run over.

"I woke in a sweat[20] and ran to my grandfather's house and asked him if he had plans to go waltzing with a clothing dummy. He said of course not, although he had comtemplated posing as a shepherd to fool his enemies. Relieved, I walked home, but learned later that the old man had slipped on a chicken-salad sandwich and fallen off the Chrysler Building."

Precognitive dreams are too common to be dismissed[21] as pure coincidence. Here a man dreams of a relative's death, and it occurs. Not everyone is so lucky. J. Martinez, of Kennebunkport, Maine, dreamed he won the Irish Sweepstakes.[22] When he awoke, his bed had floated out to sea.

TRANCES

Sir Hugh Swiggles, the skeptic, reports an interesting séance experience:

We attended the home of Madame Reynaud, the noted medium where we were all told to sit around the table and join hands. Mr. Weeks couldn't stop giggling[23] and Madame Reynaud smashed him on the head with a Ouija board. The lights were turned out, and Madame Reynaud attempted to contact Mrs. Marple's husband, who had died at the opera when his beard caught fire. The following is an exact transcript:

MRS. MARPLE: What do you see?

MEDIUM: I see a man with blue eyes and a pinwheel hat.

MRS. MARPLE: That's my husband!

MEDIUM: His name is . . . Robert. No . . . Richard . . .

MRS. MARPLE: Quincy.

MEDIUM: Quincy! Yes, that's it!

MRS. MARPLE: What else about him?

MEDIUM: He is bald but usually keeps some leaves on his head so nobody will notice.

[13]**Three Blind Mice:** a popular children's song
[14]**turning up:** reappearing
[15]**whist:** a card game
[16]**chives:** a plant with an onion-like odor
[17]**waltzing:** dancing
[18]**dummy:** mannequin
[19]**chimes:** bell-like sounds
[20]**in a sweat:** perspiring
[21]**dismissed:** rejected
[22]**sweepstakes:** lottery
[23]**giggling:** laughing

MRS. MARPLE: Yes! Exactly!

MEDIUM: For some reason, he has an object . . . a loin of pork.

MRS. MARPLE: My anniversary present to him! Can you make him speak?

MEDIUM: Speak, spirit. Speak.

QUINCY: Claire, this is Quincy.

MRS. MARPLE: Oh, Quincy! Quincy!

QUINCY: How long do you keep the chicken in when you're trying to broil it?

MRS. MARPLE: That voice! It's him!

MEDIUM: Everybody concentrate.

MRS. MARPLE: Quincy, are they treating you okay?

QUINCY: Not bad, except it takes four days to get your cleaning back.

MRS. MARPLE: Quincy, do you miss me?

QUINCY: Huh? Oh, er, sure. Sure, kid. I got to be going . . .

MEDIUM: I'm losing it. He's fading . . .

I found this séance to pass the most stringent[24] tests of credulity with the minor exception of a phonograph, which was found under Madame Reynaud's dress.

There is no doubt that certain events recorded as séances are genuine. Who does not recall the famous incident at Sybil Seretsky's, when her goldfish sang "I Got Rhythm" — a favorite tune of her recently deceased nephew? But contacting the dead is at best difficult, since most deceased are reluctant to speak up and those that do seem to hem and haw[25] before getting to the point. The author has actually seen a table rise, and Dr. Joshua Fleagle, of Harvard, attended a séance in which a table not only rose but excused itself and went upstairs to sleep.

CLAIRVOYANCE

One of the most astounding cases of clairvoyance is that of the noted Greek psychic, Achille Londos. Londos realized he had "unusual powers" by the age of ten, when he could lie in bed and, by concentrating, make his father's false teeth jump out of his mouth. After a neighbor's husband had been missing for three weeks, Londos told them to look in the stove, where the man was found knitting. Londos could concentrate on a person's face and force the image to come out on a roll of ordinary Kodak film, although he could never seem to get anybody to smile.

In 1964, he was called in to aid police in capturing the Düsseldorf Strangler, a fiend[26] who always left a baked Alaska on the chests of his victims. Merely by sniffing[27] a handkerchief, Londos led police to Siegfried Lenz, handyman at a school for deaf turkeys, who said he was the strangler and could he please have his handkerchief back.

Londos is just one of many people with psychic powers. C.N. Jerome, the psychic, of Newport, Rhode Island, claims he can guess any card being thought of by a squirrel.

[24]**stringent:** difficult; strict
[25]**to hem and haw:** to hesitate; to pause
[26]**fiend:** cruel, evil person
[27]**sniffing:** smelling

PROGNOSTICATION

Finally, we come to Aristonidis, the sixteenth-century count whose predictions continue to dazzle[28] and perplex[29] even the most skeptical.[30] Typical examples are:

"Two nations will go to war, but only one will win."

(Experts feel this probably refers to the Russo-Japanese War of 1904–05—an astounding feat of prognostication,[31] considering the fact that it was made in 1540.)

"A man in Istanbul will have his hat blocked,[32] and it will be ruined."

(In 1860, Abu Hamid, Ottoman warrior, sent his cap out to be cleaned, and it came back with spots.)

"I see a great person, who one day will invent for mankind a garment to be worn over his trousers[33] for protection while cooking. It will be called an 'abron' or 'aprone.' "

(Aristonidis meant the apron, of course.)

"A leader will emerge in France. He will be very short and will cause great calamity."[34]

(This is a reference either to Napolean or to Marcel Lumet, an eighteenth-century midget[35] who instigated a plot[36] to rub bearnaise sauce on Voltaire.)

"In the New World, there will be a place named California, and a man named Joseph Cotten[37] will become famous."

(No explanation necessary.)

QUESTIONS

1. What point do you think the author, Woody Allen, was trying to make when he wrote the article "Examining Psychic Phenomena"?
2. At what point in the article did you begin to realize what the author's real purpose or objective was?
3. Who is Dr. Osgood Mulford Twelge? Do you think he really exists? What function does he serve in the article?
4. Describe in your own words what happened to the following people. What explanation does Dr. Twelge offer for each case?

   a. Mr. Amos Dubbs
   b. Mr. Albert Sykes
   c. Sir Arthur Nurney
   d. Mr. Fenton Allentuck
   e. Achille Londos

5. Who is Aristonidis? What great predictions did he make?
6. Which case in the article did you enjoy the most?

[28]**dazzle:** amaze; surprise
[29]**perplex:** confuse
[30]**skeptical:** suspicious; unbelieving
[31]**prognostication:** prediction
[32]**blocked:** cleaned
[33]**trousers:** pants
[34]**calamity:** trouble; disaster
[35]**midget:** an unusually short person
[36]**plot:** conspiracy; plan
[37]**Joseph Cotton:** a well known movie actor of the 1940s and 1950s

Directions: *Write the one word or phrase from the right in the space provided, that has the same meaning as the boldface word on the left.*

1.	a **bizarre** experience	______________	unbelieving, suspicious
2.	a supernatural **incident**	______________	predict, know in advance
3.	a sudden **demise**	______________	without purpose
4.	to wander **aimlessly**	______________	death
5.	a **noted** scientist	______________	strange, unusual
6.	to remain **skeptical**	______________	event
7.	to **foresee** the future	______________	reject
8.	to **assemble** a group	______________	gather
9.	to **emerge** in France	______________	famous, well-known
10.	to **dismiss** a reply	______________	appear

10

AHEAD IN REVERSE: IN SEARCH OF THE REVOLUTION

United Nations/Photo by J. Foxx

Photograph by Marc Anderson

Understanding Vocabulary in Context

Directions: *Use the context clues in each sentence to help you write a synonym or brief definition for each boldface word. The boldface word in each sentence appears in the reading selection that follows this exercise.*

1. Before people learned to grow their own food, they spent much of their time **foraging** for food. In order to survive, they were forced to search for plants, berries, and animals to eat.

   Definition or synonym:

2. Only a few centuries ago, most people used their hands to produce the things they needed, and as a result, the process was slow and time-consuming. Later, however, with the creation of machines, the production of goods became more **swift** and efficient.

3. As fast as factories were built, people moved from their farms to live in towns and cities. This mass migration accelerated the development of large urban areas and also **hastened** the process of industrialization.

4. Large quantities of finished products are often sent from the factory to huge **warehouses.** Here the products are kept until they can be distributed directly to stores.

5. The life of a farmer is more **intertwined** with nature than that of most city residents. A farmer tends to be more respectful and protective of the environment because he relies on the land and weather to grow his crops.

6. Unlike oil and gas, which require millions of years to be created, wind, water, and sun are regarded as excellent potential sources of energy, since they are all **renewable.**

7. During an economic depression, millions of people lose their jobs and their families struggle to survive. People everywhere fear for their very future; it's a period of tremendous upheaval and **turmoil.**

8. In some cultures, it is common for people to live together as **extended families,** which include parents, children, and other relatives such as grandparents, uncles, and aunts. In other societies, however, the **nuclear family,** which is only the children and parents, is the rule.

   extended family:

   nuclear family:

10. **Teachers impart** information in various ways, such as by the presentation of lectures, the assignment of readings, and the showing of films.

Ahead in Reverse: In Search of the Revolution

Revolutions are not made; they come. A revolution is as natural a growth as an oak. It comes out of the past. Its foundations are laid far back.
—WENDELL PHILLIPS (1811–1884)
American orator and abolitionist

(1) News from the front arrives faster now. The first lines of defense have been broken. The sounds of gunfire are becoming louder. A bomb explodes. Bullets pierce the air around you. The revolution is fast approaching.

(2) The revolution is, in fact, already here. It has been with us for more than a generation, but it has only just begun. It is not a revolution of guns and bombs, although violence is likely to be part of it. It is a revolution so vast and powerful that it will change what we do, where we live, and how we think. The changes will be so profound, so dramatic, and so rapid that they will change our entire concept of time, space, and civilization.

(3) To understand just how this revolution will affect all of us, it's useful to go back in time, back to the two other great revolutions of human history.

STALKING THE AGRICULTURAL REVOLUTION

(4) Imagine for a moment that you are living 10,000 years ago. The year is approximately 8000 B.C. It's summer now. You and your family have spent the year moving from place to place, hunting animals for your food, and searching the land for plants and berries to eat. It's been a struggle just to survive. You return to a place you had visited the year before. There, you discover that some of the seeds you had left behind have now grown into young plants that you can use for food. You and your family remain. You learn that on this land it is possible to grow enough food to permit you to survive another year. You no longer need to hunt and forage for all your food. You are a farmer; your entire way of life has changed.

(5) As you come to depend on the crops you grow, you become more and more tied to the land. Your life is intertwined with nature, whose forceful presence provides you with an abundance of renewable energy—sun, wind, wood, and water. Your family is large, with several generations living together under one roof. The workday is long; it begins as soon as the sun rises and ends only when the sun goes down. Your children, those who were fortunate enough to survive infancy, help with the work at an early age. From the youngest to the eldest, everyone lives together and shares the work load until death calls.

(6) As time passes, communities form. These are small villages that are largely self-sufficient. What people need to survive they produce themselves, and what is produced is always used; whatever little is left over can be exchanged for some other needed item. Most people's time is so occupied by the daily labor necessary for survival that the opportunity for any formal education is virtually nonexistent. Consequently none but a chosen few, maybe only one or two, are able to read and write.

(7) The clothes, blankets, furniture, and other objects that people produce are made by hand, thus giving each product its own individual quality and originality. From time to time, new inventions are introduced into the society, but most of these inventions are merely substitutes for the muscle power of animals and people. People's concept of time is governed by the rising and set-

ting of the sun and the change of seasons. The people of the earth are separated by great distances, by uncrossable mountains and oceans, or by dense, dangerous forests. News of far away events comes as fast as it takes someone to bring it. Often there is no news at all. Life in one century is very similar to life several centuries later. The success of an individual can be measured by one word: survival.

UNLOCKING THE KEYS TO THE INDUSTRIAL AGE

(8) By the end of the 1600s, however, the world began to experience the effects of a second revolution, a revolution so powerful that, as it spread, it changed the very concept of civilization. The causes and results of the revolution are both numerous and complex, but the roots of the revolution can perhaps be traced to a single source: machines. Machines appeared with powers and abilities that far exceeded anything any human or animal could do. These machines could perform the work of people more swiftly and efficiently than anyone had imagined possible. They permitted people to accomplish more with less time and effort. The desire to exploit the machine's power for profit quickly led to the construction of factories, where goods and materials could be produced in large quantities at an astounding rate. Everything, from guns and clothes to furniture and soap, came rapidly off the assembly line. In Europe and North America, the process of mass production further accelerated change.

(9) The wheels of this mass-production system were turned by new forms of energy. No longer able to rely on sun, wood, wind, and water to meet their energy needs, people began to extract huge amounts of coal, gas, and oil from the earth. These resources were cheap and plentiful, and they greatly hastened the process of industrialization. Although these energy sources were irreplaceable, they existed in such abundance as to seem limitless. Nature was merely an object to be exploited and conquered.

(10) Mass production not only affected people's relationship with nature; it had a tremendous impact on their use and concept of time, space, and objects as well. As the influence of mass production grew, a whole new set of characteristics emerged. These characteristics became the foundation on which an industrial society was built. In his book *The Third Wave* social observer Alvin Toffler analyzes such characteristics as *standardization, specialization, concentration,* and *synchronization,* claiming that the understanding of each is essential to understanding the changes of both the past and the future.

DISASSEMBLING THE ASSEMBLY LINE

(11) Let's begin with the notion of *standardization.* Objects and products could now be made at tremendously fast speeds, each one identical to the next. The pressure to sell these identical products for profit resulted in a vast and sophisticated distribution network as finished products were quickly sent from factory to warehouse to store to home. By the year 1871, the ability to produce and distribute large quantities of identical goods culminated in the United States in an impressive achievement; that year the first giant chain-store system in the world, the Great Atlantic and Pacific Tea Company (A&P), was established by George Huntington Hartford. The production and sale of standard goods soon spread quickly across an entire continent, from small towns to big cities.

(12) As the Industrial Revolution grew in size and scope, the phenomenon of *standardization* spread into other areas of life. Taking the factory as a model, nations of the world created huge school systems to educate their young and

to prepare them to assume adult roles in the new industrialized world. Teachers resembled workers on an assembly line, students the finished product. Uniform textbooks, curricula, and standardized tests became the accepted way to impart information and measure success.

(13) *Standardization* spread even further; time and units of measure became standard. International time zones were established. Entire systems of mass communication were developed by government and business, from national postal services to national telephone systems. The speed with which communication began to occur was astounding. In 1865, the year President Lincoln was assassinated, it took twelve days for news of the event to reach London, England. By the next century, news could travel almost anywhere across the globe instantly. In industrial nations, the daily influx of information served to create a more uniform view of the world. Nationally distributed movies and magazines, news service agencies, and national TV networks all contributed to standardizing the information people received. Through this extensive mass communication, even language became standardized. Many regional dialects disappeared, replaced by a standard form of speech.

WHAT'S SPECIAL IN THE INDUSTRIAL REVOLUTION

(14) With standardization came a second feature of industrial society: *specialization.* As the products of factories became more refined and sophisticated, the tasks involved to produce them also became more specialized and diverse. The construction of Henry Ford's *Model T* automobile in 1908 is a good case in point; it requires 7,882 separate operations to build. Too often, however, specialized roles that improved production also resulted in dehumanizing work conditions, as factory workers were forced to perform the same task in the same place, day after day, year after year.

(15) *Specialization* caused great upheaval in family life as well. As people moved away from the land to the factory, the division of labor was altered. Men worked away from the home, children went off to school, and women stayed home and took care of the housework. Both the young and the elderly were segregated from the rest of society, and the large, extended family, so much a necessary part of farm life, became smaller in industrial society. The modern nuclear family of two parents and two or three children soon became the ideal.

CONCENTRATING THE WORLD'S RESOURCES

(16) The change in family life was also accelerated by another phenomenon of industrialization: the mass migration of people away from the farm to the city. Huge urban centers began to dot the globe. These giant metropolises housed the great factories and industries of the world as well as the marketplaces for the exchange of goods and ideas. In 1850, there were but 4 cities in the world with populations of over 1 million. By 1900 the number had increased to 19. By 1960, 141 cities around the planet had more than a million inhabitants. The concentration of large numbers of people to serve the needs of a growing industrial society became commonplace: in cities, factories, and schools. In fact, society began to concentrate all people of similar circumstances in the same place. The result: prisons for criminals, hospitals for the sick, asylums for the mentally ill.

(17) This tendency toward *concentration* is not limited solely to people. Energy can also be included in this category. Energy sources that helped give rise to the Industrial Revolution are found in large concentrated amounts in certain areas of the earth. Possession or control of these resources has been

a critical factor in industrial development. The theme of *concentration* can be extended to include another product of industrial society: the giant corporation. The economy of the world is dominated by the operations of these giant "immortal" creatures, for it is with these institutions that great concentrations of the world's capital or money are now to be found. These corporations monopolize and dominate the world market for many products. In the U.S. in the mid-1960s, for example, only three companies, General Motors, Ford, and Chrysler, manufactured 94 percent of all American cars. Over 80 percent of all the aluminum, beer, cigarettes, and breakfast cereals were made in the U.S. by only four or five companies in each field. In short, industrial society put everything together in a concentrated form: people, energy, and money.

SYNCHRONIZING SOCIETY'S CLOCKS

(18) Even our concept of time has been affected by the industrial wave, as the need for *synchronization* has become essential. Synchronized time became necessary as each person assumed a specialized role in the complex system of production and distribution. Each person became dependent on others in order to do his or her job. The efficiency of the system depends on people performing their parts at the appropriate time, much like the interlocking parts of a complex machine. Failure to perform a job on time has a negative impact on the rest of the system. Production and profit are lost whenever there is any delay. It's hardly surprising then that industrial societies place such emphasis on punctuality and efficient use of time. After all, they claim, "Time is money." To synchronize their efforts, most members of an industrial society wake up, go to work, come home, go to sleep, even make love, all at approximately the same time.

(19) These foundations of industrial society, *standardization, specialization, concentration,* and *synchronization,* have all combined to make each individual person and each separate nation dependent on a larger whole. Unlike the small but self-sufficient village of a previous age, members of industrial society no longer produce what they consume. There is a strong and clear separation between production and consumption. The change from independent self-sufficiency to dependent consumerism is best reflected by people's use of language. The United States is often referred to today as the "consumer society." In the societies of ancient Greece and Rome and medieval Europe the term "consumer" did not even exist. Today most of us have become consumers, dependent on others for our own survival. It is this interconnectedness of the earth's people that is perhaps the single greatest achievement of the Industrial Revolution.

WHEN WORLDS COLLIDE

(20) "No civilization spreads without conflict." This maxim of history was shown to be true on countless occasions as the Industrial Revolution collided with the forces of agricultural society. The causes of the U.S. Civil War (1861–1865) and the Russian Revolution (1917) were in large part related to economic and social tensions that resulted from the conflict between industry and agriculture. As the industrial world became more developed, it could no longer exist in isolation. The need for cheap raw materials extended beyond national borders. The world quickly became divided into nation states, with each state trying to protect its own special interests. The industrial world saw itself as "developed" and "civilized" and viewed agriculturally based societies as "backward" and "primitive." This view of the world helped industrial na-

tions to justify their actions as they exploited and sometimes destroyed the peoples of "less developed" lands in the name of "progress."

(21) But in industrial societies the second revolution is ending. It has lasted only 300 years, a mere step along the path of history. Of course industrialization has not taken hold in all parts of the world. It has spread around the world at different speeds. Many societies are still struggling with the transition between the first and second revolutions. There are even some peoples who have yet to experience the first revolution: Some tribal groups in South America or Papua, New Guinea, for example, continue to hunt and forage for food. But in the United States, Japan, and parts of western Europe, the second global revolution has spent itself. It is dying around us. The signs are everywhere.

(22) The social, economic, and political institutions that grew out of the Industrial Revolution are in turmoil. As one looks around the industrial world, one finds abundant examples of a society in crisis. Vandalism, crime, and juvenile delinquency, plus the widespread use of drugs and alcohol among both young and old, only begin to point up the problem. The annual rise in the separation and divorce rate, with all its human pain and trauma, is additional proof. The constant search for new life-styles and the rapid emergence and disappearance of cults, fads, and other assorted movements also reflect the malaise of the times. Psychologists estimate that one out of four citizens in the United States now suffers from severe emotional stress. Inflation, unemployment, energy shortages, terrorism, war, and the prospect of nuclear annihilation dominate today's headlines. The whole world seems to be in the throes of conflict, instability, and violent change.

(23) It is inevitable that conflict and turmoil will continue as the powers of a dying industrial society fight to preserve their familiar world. Efforts to resist change will slow down the new revolution now in progress, but they will not stop it. For the next revolution is upon us, bringing with it tales of extraordinary challenge and adventure.

Comprehension Questions

1. What do you think caused people to change from hunting and foraging for food to farming as a way of life?
2. In the transition from an agricultural society to an industrial society, people also changed in the way they saw nature. In what way did people's attitudes change? Why do you think people changed their view of nature?
3. What prompted huge transportation systems to develop so rapidly in industrial societies?
4. What is the significance of the Great Atlantic and Pacific Tea Company (A&P)? How did it change society?
5. How did family life change in industrial society?
6. In American business, people like to say that "time is money." Explain what is meant by this expression. Do you agree with this philosophy?
7. The author refers to large corporations as "giant, immortal creatures." Why do you think corporations are called "immortal"?
8. During the agricultural revolution, how did most people get what they needed for survival? How has this way of life changed for most members of an industrial society?

9. According to the author, what happens when an industrial society begins to spread? What can happen to agricultural societies? How do industrial societies tend to view agricultural societies?
10. According to the author, what is now happening to industrial societies? What examples are given to support the author's point of view?
11. The author claims that a new revolution is coming. Does the author tell what this new revolution is?
12. According to the author, how will many people react to the coming revolution? Why will they react this way?
13. What do you think the general purpose of the article is?

Drawing Conclusions

Directions: *Based on the information presented in the article, what do you think the author would say about each of the following ten statements? Put a circle around the one response you think the author would give.*

YES means that the author would agree.
NO means that the author would *not* agree.
MAYBE means that there is not enough information in the article to know what the author would think.

1. Revolutions always involve violence and destruction.	YES	NO	MAYBE
2. People probably began to grow their own crops when they discovered that it was easier than hunting and foraging for food.	YES	NO	MAYBE
3. Most products made by hand are superior to machine-made products.	YES	NO	MAYBE
4. Television and radio helped to eliminate many regional dialects.	YES	NO	MAYBE
5. Throughout much of history, people were not careful in their use of natural resources because they thought the supply was limitless.	YES	NO	MAYBE
6. The most important reason behind industrial growth is that governments wanted their people to have more comfortable lives.	YES	NO	MAYBE
7. The U.S. Civil War was primarily the result of a conflict between industry and agriculture, and *not,* as presented in chapter 4, a moral conflict about slavery and civil rights.	YES	NO	MAYBE
8. The emotional stress that most people feel today is the direct result of energy shortages and terrorism.	YES	NO	MAYBE

9. The 300-year process of industrialization was relatively brief.	YES	NO	MAYBE
10. Instability and conflict are an inevitable part of any major social change.	YES	NO	MAYBE

Topics for Discussion and Composition

1. Did you grow up in an agricultural or industrial community? How do you think your environment influenced your view of nature?
2. What do you think was the most important invention of the last century? Give reasons for your choice.
3. Where would you prefer to live, in a rural, urban, or suburban society? What are the advantages and disadvantages of each kind of life?
4. Try this experiment for one day: Do not use any machines or electricity. Describe your feelings. What modern convenience or invention did you miss the most?
5. Do you think children should take care of their parents when their parents get old? Should elderly parents live with children?
6. Have you ever worked in a factory? Describe your experience.
7. Have you ever worked on a farm? Tell about your experience.
8. Are there different dialects or accents in your country? In what way are they different? What attitudes do people have about each dialect or accent?
9. Do you prefer to have one teacher for all your subjects or a different teacher for each subject? What advantages and disadvantages do you see in each case?
10. Which of the following problems do you consider to be the most serious at the present time: crime, juvenile delinquency, use of drugs, divorce, inflation, unemployment, stress, energy shortage, terrorism, possibility of nuclear war. Give reasons for your choice.
11. Refer to the topics just listed. Have you ever experienced a personal problem related to one of these topics? Tell about your experience. How did it affect you? How did you deal with your problem?
12. Choose a revolution you know a lot about. What were the important events of the revolution? What different factors do you think were responsible for this revolution? What effects did it have?
13. If you could choose any past period of history in which to live, which one would you select? What appeals to you about this particular time in history?
14. A fad is a fashion or custom that is very popular, but only for a short period of time. Have you ever participated in a fad? What attracted you to this activity or fashion? What feelings and experiences did you have?
15. What other examples of fads can you name? What do you think caused each fad? Why do you think each fad ended?

16. Do you think high school or college students should specialize in a particular career or do you think they should receive a general education first before specializing in a specific subject? What benefits and limitations do you see for each kind of preparation?

17. Do you prefer to have a specific routine to follow every day, or do you prefer to organize your time each day in your own way? What are the problems and benefits of each life-style?

18. Compare social change with personal change. What similarities do you see between the process of change in a person and the process of change in a society? Are there predictable crises or stages that each goes through? Also, how do individuals and societies tend to react to change?

Seeing Relationships: Extended Definitions

In the explanation of what happened to societies during the Industrial Revolution, four important terms or concepts were used. What were these four words? List them in the space provided. Give your own definition or explanation of each of the four terms. Then list some of the specific examples given in the article that helped to illustrate each concept.

1.

2.

3.

4.

Applying Previously Learned Concepts to New Situations

Directions: *Listed next are ten sets of statements. Each set describes a particular aspect of industrial society. In the space provided, indicate whether each situation is an example of* **standardization, specialization, concentration,** *or* **synchronization.** *(In some cases more than one term may apply.)*

__________ 1. Between 1790 and 1850, the population of New York City went from 49,000 to more than 696,000 (in just 60 years). By 1970, the city's population had reached almost 8 million.

__________ 2. In big cities across the United States, there is a tremendous amount of traffic during the early morning and late afternoon "rush hours."

__________ 3. In the field of medicine it's difficult to find doctors nowadays who treat all types of illnesses and medical problems. Most doctors today have a very restricted area of expertise.

__________ 4. It's possible to drive a car three thousand miles from New York to Los Angeles and still eat at McDonald's or Burger King in hundreds of places along the way.

__________ 5. During the 1950s and 1960s one of the most popular TV programs was the "Ed Sullivan Show." Every Sunday at 7:00 P.M. millions of Americans would turn on their TV sets to watch this variety show.

__________ 6. During the 1970s the price of oil increased dramatically. The United States and Europe experienced great economic problems because they were dependent on large quantities of oil located in the Middle East.

__________ 7. Cigarette smokers can go to almost any store in the United States and buy a package of any known brand of cigarettes.

__________ 8. During summers and at Christmastime, millions of schoolchildren have vacation.

__________ 9. Most large companies have a different person in charge of every aspect of their business, from advertising and distributing their products to hiring employees and supervising production.

__________ 10. Millions of Americans interested in current events read *Time* or *Newsweek* magazine every week.

For Class Discussion: How many other examples of *standardization, specialization, concentration* and *synchronization* can you name?

Vocabulary Development Puzzle: Santayana's Message

Directions: *Complete each missing word in the sentences that follow, using one letter for each blank space. Rewrite each numbered letter in the corresponding space of the sentence marked "Santayana's Message" that appears at the end of this exercise. When you have completed all the letters of this sentence, you will have a famous quotation about the importance of the past by the Spanish philosopher and writer George Santayana.*

Santayana's Message:

___ ___ ___ ___ ___   ___ ___ ___   ___ ___ ___ ___ ___ ___   ___ ___ ___ ___ ___ ___ ___ ___
1 2 3 4 5   6 7 8   9 10 11 12 13 14   15 16 17 18 19 20 21 22

___ ___ ___   ___ ___ ___ ___   ___ ___ ___   ___ ___ ___ ___ ___ ___ ___ ___ ___   ___ ___
23 24 25   26 27 28 29   30 31 32   33 34 35 36 37 38 39 40 41   42 43

___ ___ ___ ___ ___ ___   ___ ___.
44 45 46 47 48 49   50 51

1. The Agricultural Revolution began ___ ___ ___ r ___ x ___ ___ ___ ___ ___ l y ten thousand years ago.
   (10 26 26 8 50 17 10 45)

2. People who cultivate the land as a way of life tend to have more r e s ___ e ___ ___ and concern for ___ ___ ___ u r ___.
   (46 9 51; 11 10 1 21)

3. In agricultural societies of the past, people relied on ___ ___ n ___ ___ ___ a ___ ___ l ___ sources of energy, such as sun, wind, wood, and water.
   (44 5 5 6 20 5)

4. With the development of industrial society, people began to ___ x ___ r ___ c ___ huge amounts of coal and oil from the ground.
   (5 1 48 1)

5. At first, coal and oil seemed so plentiful and abundant that most people thought their supply was l ___ m ___ ___ l ___ ___ ___.
   (50 50 14 32 4 4)

6. The origin of the Industrial Revolution can perhaps be ___ r ___ c ___ ___ to a single source: the machine.
   (14 30 5 36)

7. Machines began to produce goods and objects at an ___ s ___ ___ u ___ ___ ___ i ___ g speed.
   (10 1 8 11 36 11)

8. One major disadvantage of factory work is that workers are forced to perform the same ___ a ___ k or work every day without much variation or change.
   (29 28)

9. Faster forms of communication and transportation helped to a ___ ___ ___ l ___ ___ a ___ ___ or speed up the process of industrialization.
   (33 33 25 25 44 42 25)

10. In most industrial societies, the modern ___(12) u ___(33) l ___(40) a ___(15) family of two parents and two or three children soon became the model.

11. The A&P was first established in the U.S. in 1871. It was the first example of a ___(9) ___(7) ___(48) i ___(35) store. It sold the same products across the entire ___(9) ___(3) ___(35) ___(51) i ___(35) e ___(35) ___(51), from the Atlantic to the Pacific coast.

12. The process of industrialization helped to change people's concepts of time, space, and ___(9) i v i ___ i ___ ___(48) ___(51) i ___(13) ___(39).

13. During the nineteenth century, industrial societies began to create ___(2) u g ___(16) school systems in order to prepare their young for adult roles later in life.

14. In these enormous school systems, teachers resembled factory workers, students the f i ___(39) i s ___(24) ___ ___(41) product.

15. During the Industrial Revolution there was a mass ___(19) i g ___(31) ___(27) t i ___(3) ___(13) of people away from the farm to the city. Gradually, more and more urban centers began to ___(36) ___(3) ___(23) the globe.

16. Machines serve as a ___(4) u b ___(4) ___(49) i ___(49) u ___(49) ___(37) for the muscle power of people and animals.

17. Today many people tend to measure their success by how much money they have. Thousands of years ago people were considered lucky if they were able to ___(28) u ___(22) v ___(50) v ___(37) infancy.

18. The United States has often been referred to as the ___(33) ___(43) n s u ___(38) ___(18) r society, since most people do not produce or make the things they use in daily life.

19. Not all societies have made the ___(1) r ___(30) ___(39) s i ___(1) i ___(34) ___(39) from an agricultural to an industrial economy. In fact, there are still some people who ___(24) u ___(39) ___(1) and forage for food.

20. Industrial societies seem to be in the throes of tremendous upheaval and ___(29) u r ___(19) ___(34) i l.

21. Psychologists estimate that approximately one out of every four persons in the United States suffers from severe emotional ___(28) ___(23) r ___(47) ___(28) ___(28).

Word Forms/Sequencing Ideas

Directions: *(1) Complete each group of sentences by writing in the appropriate blank space the correct word from those in parentheses. Change the form of the verb or noun when necessary.*

(2) After completing all the sentences, put the sentences in order so that each group of sentences forms a well-organized pararaph. Write its number in the blank space at the left of each sentence.

1. **(to develop, development, developing)**

_____ Another significant factor in industrial ____________________ was the construction of a transcontinental railroad in the mid-1880s, enabling factory products to be distributed from coast to coast.

_____ As a young and ____________________ nation, the United States possessed the vast amounts of coal and wood needed to make its factories run.

_____ Last but not least, new inventions such as steel, telephones, and telegraphs were ____________________ , and this further accelerated industrial growth and ____________________ .

_____ The industrial ____________________ of the United States was accelerated by many factors.

_____ One important factor in the ____________________ of United States industry was the abundance of cheap energy on the North American continent.

2. **(to abound, abundance, abundant)**

_____ For the peoples of the Agricultural Revolution, there existed an ____________________ of renewable energy: sun, wind, wood, and water.

_____ Even in the Middle East, where oil still ____________________ , the time will eventually come when this precious energy source will disappear.

_____ For people at the start of the Industrial Age, coal and oil seemed to exist in unlimited ____________________ .

_____ Agricultural peoples relied on these ____________________ sources of energy to provide them with both heat and transportation.

_____ In recent times, however, these once ____________________ amounts of nonrenewable energy have begun to run out.

3. **(to produce, product, production, productive)**

_____ These factories began to ____________________ goods at an astonishing rate.

_____ As a result, most people depend on others to
__________________ the material goods needed for survival.

_____ However, with the rise of industrial society, the
__________________ of goods moved out of people's homes into giant factories.

_____ From children to grandparents, all worked togeher to help make the various __________________ necessary for survival.

_____ Thousands of years ago, long before the Industrial Age began, both young and old were __________________ members of society.

4. **(to standardize, standardization, standard)**

_____ For example, in an industrial society, products come off factory assembly lines at astounding speeds, all in
__________________ sizes and styles.

_____ These forms of mass media all serve __________________ the information we receive, and thus influence our entire view of the world.

_____ People then consume these __________________ products every day of their lives, from toothpaste to soap.

_____ Another example of __________________ can be seen in the way national TV networks and magazines inform us about the world.

_____ One of the main features of industrial society is the element of
__________________ .

Seeing Relationships: Analogies

Directions: *Choose the one word in parentheses that correctly completes the analogy and write it in the appropriate blank space. (For an explanation of analogies, please refer to page 132.)*

1. automobile : horse AS : telephone : __________________
(newspaper, television, messenger, invention)

2. dense : forest AS deep : __________________
(mountain, ocean, village, distance)

3. giant : huge AS urban center : __________________
(metropolis, village, community, population)

4. extended family : agricultural revolution AS nuclear family : ____________ (Civil War, Russian Revolution, atomic energy, Industrial Revolution)

5. plentiful : abundant AS self-sufficient : ____________ (inevitable, limitless, independent, immortal)

6. summer : season AS Earth : ____________ (sun, planet, oil, resource)

7. juvenile delinquency : crime AS oil : ____________ (nonrenewable, earth, natural resource, Middle East)

8. telephone : communication AS automobile : ____________ (speed, car, gasoline, transportation)

9. factories : industry AS farms : ____________ (seeds, tractors, primitive, agriculture)

10. resist : accept AS emerge : ____________ (struggle, disappear, preserve, develop)

Generating a Basis for Comparison

It's possible to compare any two people, any two objects, any two ideas to see how they are similar or different. However, in making any kind of comparison, it's necessary to identify what it is you're comparing. Take people as an example. You can compare any two people in many different ways: by sex, age, their physical features, their personalities, their family heritage, their personal interests. The list could go on and on. By identifying these different categories you are establishing a *basis for comparison.* In comparing two people you would not say "John is a mechanic, but Richard has a wife and three children." There is no uniform basis of comparison; John's *work* and Richard's *family* are two totally different things.

Directions: *It's extremely important to establish a clear and uniform basis for comparison when comparing two people, objects, or ideas. In this exercise, try to find as many different categories as you can that will serve as a basis for comparison between the Agricultural and Industrial Revolutions. To help you think of possible categories, you may want to refer to paragraphs 4–7 of the article. Almost every sentence introduces a new topic or category that can be used as a* ***basis for comparison.*** *Write each category in the space located in the middle of the page, under "Basis for Comparison." Then, in the space on the right and left, write the specific information about each Revolution that corresponds to the categories you have chosen. Two categories are provided as examples. You may want to do this activity in small groups.*

The Agricultural Revolution	Basis for Comparison	The Industrial Revolution
People learn that it's easier to grow crops than to hunt and forage for food.	1. *Principal cause*	*People discover the usefulness of machines.*
	2. *Energy sources*	
	3.	
	4.	
	5.	
	6.	
	7.	
	8.	
	9.	
	10.	
	11.	
	12.	
	13.	

Living as a Navajo

GRACE HALSELL

Grace Halsell was born in West Texas. From an early age she was encouraged by her father to travel and to learn about the world and its people. She apparently took this advice to heart. At one time or another, she has made Paris, London, Tokyo, Berlin, and Seoul her home. Her interest in travel and people has led her to have many unique experiences, among them, living on a fishing junk in Hong Kong with a Chinese family of twenty-eight people, crossing the Andes Mountains by jeep, and journeying two thousand miles down the Amazon River by tug boat.

Perhaps her most unique adventure began in 1968 when she changed her skin color from white to black. Her experiences as a "black" woman living in Harlem and the South of the United States are chronicled in her book Soul Sister.

The article presented here tells of her experience among the Navajo Indians of the North American Southwest, and captures the spirit of a way of life that has all but disappeared from the modern, industrialized world. Ms. Halsell now makes her home in Washington, D.C.

(1) I grew up hearing about Indians from my father, who was born in 1860, when we still called some of the United States "Indian territory." My father fought and killed Indians; he thought it was his duty[1] to win the West. He later told me: It was their land. We took it. We gave the Indian a choice: be bleached white—or die.

(2) The Navajos were pushed back and put on a reservation (another word for prison) on lands that the whites deemed[2] worthless. And there they have remained, until now quite isolated.

(3) I went to live with the Navajos in early 1972. The reservation is a vast land, stretching[3] west out from Albuquerque to the Grand Canyon and from near Tucson and Phoenix on the south to near Salt Lake City on the North. Once you are on the reservation, you are at least 200 miles from any place you've ever heard of.

(4) I became acquainted[4] with a young woman, Bessie Yellowhair, and I lived with her family, in a hogan—shaped like an igloo and made of mud and sticks. Bahe Yellowhair, the father, and the entire family are shepherds. The Navajos build their entire way of life around sheep: they eat the meat from sheep, they make their clothes and their beautiful Navajos rugs from sheep. The land, however, is spectacularly beautiful. It is not land so much as high mountain ranges, canyons, gorges, all rock and sand. Seeing it, you feel awed, shocked by its magnitude. It is like being alone in a small boat on a vast ocean: It is a spiritual experience.

(5) When I lived with the Yellowhair family, I was one of the 14 people living in an area about the size of your bedroom. There is no furniture in the hogan: only one stove used for cooking, for heating.

(6) You sleep on dirt floors, on sheepskins. When you wake up, you don't need to get dressed, because you have slept in your clothes. There are no windows in the hogan: it's dark as a dungeon.[5]

(7) When you wake up, you want to start turning things on: You want

[1]**duty:** responsibility

[2]**deemed:** considered

[3]**stretching:** extending

[4]**acquainted:** familiar

[5]**dungeon:** underground prison

to turn on some lights, you want to turn on some heat. But there is nothing to turn on: no gas, no electricity, no phones, no running water. To get water, you go by horsedrawn wagon 30 miles to the nearest windmill.

(8) Suppose you are Bahe Yellowhair, a man, or Bessie Yellowhair, a young woman, and you get sick. You never say: my head hurts, my feet hurt, my stomach hurts. The Navajo never separates the mind from the body. He says: "I feel bad all over."

(9) First you call in a Hand Trembler. He puts himself in a trance, his arm shakes uncontrollably—and he diagnoses your case. Maybe you've stepped on a snake or got too close to a tree struck by lightning. He prescribes a certain healing ceremony.

(10) Then you call in a Medicine Man, who is priest, psychologist, doctor. Your family sits in a circle inside the hogan. The Medicine Man prays, chants—he partially undresses you, smears your face with paint, he paints snakes on your feet. A chorus of old men chant, sing, rattle[6] gourds[7]—and this can go on for nine days. The visitor feels mesmerized,[8] taken back a thousand years in time.

(11) The Medicine Man prays to the Holy people—the good and the evil—that you will be put back in harmony with nature. The Medicine Man knows that he must cure the whole person—mentally, spiritually, physically.

(12) Being an Indian is not having a certain skin color: It is not anything on the outside, but rather a way of viewing life.

(13) Bessie Yellowhair told me she had gone to work for a white family in California. It had been difficult for her: She missed the birds, the plants, the animals of Navajoland. City noises and dirt and smog and pollution assailed her. I wanted to understand what it means for an Indian, who is quiet, passive, peaceful, to enter into our aggressive, loud, materialistic world. One day I saw an ad,[9] such as the one Bessie Yellowhair had answered.

(14) "WANTED," the ad said, "loving Navajo babysitter for three children, six, four and two."

(15) I asked Bessie Yellowhair if I might borrow some of her clothes—even her name. I rode a bus to Irvine, California, and the woman who hired me met me. When we arrived at her large home she gave me her first rule: The children, she said, are never allowed in her bedroom.

(16) On the reservation I had seen an almost complete absence of things. But in that large house I saw an abundance of things, an absence of love.

(17) Sometimes people ask, what was more difficult—living for a moment in time as a "black" woman or as Bessie Yellowhair? The Indian experience was more difficult. For my "Soul Sister" experience, I had changed myself cosmetically. I had changed the color of my eyes, the color of my hair, the color of my skin. But I was always me, raised with the same values and judgements all of us—black and white—have grown to share in this country. We've been taught the work ethic; we've been taught to want the good things in life, as we define them: good salary, good house, good car, a good carpet on the floor. None of us really wants to go back to sleeping on dirt floors.

(18) But the Indian, if he remains Indian, is tied to the land. He worships the land, which he calls his mother Earth. He never attempts to conquer nature, but to live in harmony with it. He wishes to be like a fish in a sea, a bird on the wind: to pass by without leaving a trace[10] of his existence. Being, not achieving, is important.

[6]**rattle:** shake

[7]**gourds:** cups

[8]**mesmerized:** fascinated, hypnotized

[9]**ad:** advertisement

[10]**trace:** sign; mark

(19) The Indians have not lost what is basic: They have a "connection" to all of life. They see, smell, hear, taste—with a directness of perception.

(20) Many young people are saying: Let's learn from the Indians, let's look at their values, let's respect nature. They see that in our attempt to conquer nature, we have polluted our streams, our air.

(21) The Indians have stressed[11] cooperation, and we have stressed competition and look at our waste: those sent to insane asylums, those sent to prisons, the old who are sent to nursing homes.

(22) Should you ask Bessie Yellowhair, What is your religion? that would be the same as asking, What is your life? Religion is all of life. Religion is being in harmony with nature. A church, then, can be as little as you want it or as big as all humanity.

(23) Let me share with you My Truth. It is this: I try to abandon myself—to my life. I know that no one—no one church, no one creed, no one government—has Truth for me. I have to find my own. I do not assume that Life has a meaning. Already written out. For all of us. I do not ask: What is the meaning of life? Rather, what is the meaning of my life?

(24) Out in the vastness of land and sky, you can look out infinitely, into space, and somehow you can see so far that you begin to see—inside of you. And there is your happiness.

QUESTIONS

1. How does the author describe the life of Navajo Indians? What impressed you most about the Navajo's way of life?
2. What are some of the main differences between the Navajo life-style and the kind of life-style found in large cities?
3. According to the author, how do Navajos view religion? How do their religious beliefs influence their view of the world?
4. What is your reaction to "Living as a Navajo"?

[11]**stressed:** emphasized

11

CLOSE ENCOUNTERS WITH THE THIRD WAVE

Photograph courtesy of the Ford Motor Company

Robots at work on an automobile assembly line

Photograph courtesy of NASA

The planet Earth as seen from the moon

Understanding Vocabulary in Context

Directions: *Use the context clues in each sentence to help you write a synonym or brief definition for each boldface word. The boldface word in each sentence appears in the reading selection that follows this exercise.*

1. Life in modern times seems to have a more **transient** quality; people change jobs and addresses with greater frequency, old buildings are torn down and new ones are quickly built in their place, and new scientific discoveries are made almost every day.

   Definition or synonym: ______________________

2. Some people don't like to travel to foreign countries. They prefer the comforts and familiarity of home instead of the strangeness of an **alien** environment.

   ____

3. In ancient times it was customary for people to watch the stars and think about what might exist up there in space. Thousands of years later, scientists continue to **speculate** about the nature of the universe.

   ____

4. Only a century ago most people thought that it was impossible for human beings to live in outer space. Today, however, some scientists believe that it will soon be **feasible** for large numbers of people to live in space.

   ____

5. During the past century there have been many important discoveries in the field of medical science. One important **breakthrough** occurred in the 1950s when Dr. Jonas Salk developed a vaccine to prevent polio, a disease that had killed or crippled many infants and children.

   ____

6. Biologists generally agree that **heredity**, the transmission of genetic characteristics from parents to their children, is the essential factor in determining a person's physical appearance.

   ____

7. Young children who go to the beach for the first time are often **startled** to discover that ocean water is full of salt.

   ____

8. One of the most amazing achievements in flight history took place in 1927 when Charles Lindbergh first crossed the Atlantic Ocean, flying from New York to Paris in just under 33½ hours. Another incredible **feat** occurred in 1969 when Neil Armstrong became the first man to set foot on the moon.

   ____

9. Unlike the first computers, which were relatively large in size, today's computers have such **miniature** parts that it's possible to store much more information in them and still use much less space.

---

10. The search for a cure to an illness or disease is usually a long, laborious, and expensive process. Millions of dollars are often needed for researchers to continue in their **quest** for a cure.

Close Encounters with the Third Wave

PART I

"STOP THE WORLD, I WANT TO GET OFF"— PLANNING FOR THE SHOCK OF CHANGE

Anyone who has ever visited a foreign country probably remembers the shock of that initial contact with a new culture. People, places, customs, and even time seem completely different and strange. The stimulation of so many new things all at once produces a feeling of disorientation or fatigue, a phenomenon often referred to as "culture shock." It takes time for people to accustom themselves to a new environment.

The concept of "culture shock" can also be applied to the future. Today's world seems to be moving so fast, changing so quickly in so many ways, that we sometimes find ourselves wanting to shout, in the words of an old Broadway musical, "Stop the World, I Want to Get Off!" People seem to move out of our lives as quickly as they came in.* We live in a society where people change jobs so frequently that the feeling is "Here today, gone tomorrow." (Just ask any baseball manager!) At the IBM Corporation (*I*nternational *B*usiness *M*achines) employees like to say the letters "IBM" really mean "*I*'ve *B*een *M*oved."

Changes in residence and jobs place a tremendous amount of stress and pressure on people as they try to reorient and adjust themselves to new people and places. Yet transient relationships are not limited only to people and places. Objects move in and out of our lives at an astonishing rate. America, the "consumer society," has also earned the name "the throwaway society." Every year we throw away incredible quantities of bottles, cans, razors, paper, and on and on. The average car owner in this country keeps a car only 3½ years. Nowadays, it's possible to rent almost any object, from cars to furniture, from flowers to art. Buildings are torn down around us, and new ones take their place; they're cheaper to replace than to repair. With every major change, our neighborhoods feel alien, our places less familiar. Our lives become filled with a sense of impermanence and uncertainty.

The rate at which new and sometimes contradictory information comes at us further contributes to our feelings of instability and transience. It's estimated that 90 percent of all scientists who ever lived are alive today. New scientific discoveries are being made every day of the week, but unlike in other ages,

*In major United States cities the average time a person remains in the same residence is less than four years.

new ideas are quickly applied in practical ways. The influence of new technology on our lives is felt almost immediately. The English philosopher Francis Bacon once said, "Knowledge is power." In today's world "knowledge is change."

As we look back on history, we think in terms of large periods of time, from the ten thousand years of the Agricultural Revolution to the three hundred years of the Industrial Age. Today, time feels like it's accelerating. We no longer tend to think of change in terms of centuries but rather in terms of decades: the 1950s, 1960s, 1970s, and 1980s. These ten-year periods of change will shrink even more as the rate of change continues to accelerate. The day may come when we think of great periods of historical change in terms of years, even months.

As our sense of time and change continues to accelerate, we begin to feel lost and disoriented, like "strangers in a strange land." If we are to maintain a sense of stability and well-being, we must be able to cope with rapid change. One way to prepare for "future shock" is to try to anticipate what may lie ahead, for it is in thinking and speculating about the future that we prepare ourselves for the challenge and change of tomorrow.

THE "PROFIT IN PROPHECY"

People's need to know and talk about the future is of course nothing new. Throughout history, gypsies, palm readers, doomsayers, and prophets have all come forth to offer their opinions and predictions about what lay ahead. However, in today's rapidly changing world, the need to anticipate the future in a more systematic way has brought forth a new kind of prophet: the think tank. A think tank is a group of experts from different fields of study who come together to scientifically analyze past and present trends. By analyzing tremendous quantities of available information, think tanks are often able to predict events and trends that are likely to occur. Previous periods of unemployment, labor strikes, economic crises, revolutions, and wars have all been predicted by think tanks. In fact, the "findings" of think tanks are often sought by governments and business, and many times they form the basis of future policy decisions.

One such think tank is Forecasting, International, located just outside Washington, D.C., in Arlington, Virginia. Its president, Dr. Marvin Cetron, has written a book entitled *Encounters with the Future: A Forecast of Life into the 21st Century.* In attempting to forecast change, Dr. Cetron states that he relies on the answers to three fundamental questions: (1) Is the change technically feasible? (2) Is it economically feasible? (3) Is it socially acceptable? In other words, what Dr. Cetron is asking is the following: Do we have the knowledge and ability to bring about the change? Is the change now or can it soon be cheap enough to carry out? Will most people accept the change, or does the change go against people's morals, values, or ability to adapt?

Most people, however, find it difficult to envision the future. When asked to talk about the future, people tend to describe a world that is more or less a continuation of the present one. Others, greatly troubled by the grave threats of nuclear war and global pollution, have difficulty seeing any future at all. While these threats to people's survival on Earth certainly are very real and frightening, there are those who feel that these threats can and will be overcome. These are people who have a strong faith in humanity's ability to survive and who share a positive and hopeful view of the future. Many of the views and predictions that follow are based on such a hopeful view of the human future.

Class Activity: *Before reading the rest of the article, try forming your own think tanks in class. Divide into small groups and discuss your own ideas about the future.*

1. What changes do you think will occur before the year 2000?
2. What changes do you predict will occur during the next one hundred years?
3. What changes would you like to see occur during your lifetime?

After writing down your group's predictions, compare them with the predictions of the other "think tanks" in your class.

PART 2

YOUNG AT 85

Why do people grow old? No one really knows for sure. What we do know, however, is that people born in the United States today can be expected to live longer and healthier lives than previous generations. In fact, the change in life expectancy since the turn of the century is nothing short of astounding! In 1900, the average American was expected to live not much more than 40 years. Compare that with the average American born in 1980, who is expected to live close to 80 years of age; that's almost double the number of years! However, today's biologists are on the verge of a new scientific breakthrough: understanding the biological causes of old age. When that happens, anti-aging drugs will be developed to slow down the aging process. As childhood diseases are eliminated, as people learn to take better care of themselves, anti-aging drugs will help people born in the next century to live between 150 and 200 years. Imagine what effects that will have on people's decisions to get married or pursue careers. Some people may prefer to have several marriages and several careers during their lifetimes. After all, they'll have plenty of time in which to do it.

THE GENIUS OF THE GENE

One of the great achievements in medical science has already taken place, however. It occurred in 1952, the year James D. Watson and Francis H. C. Crick identified the molecular structure DNA (deoxyribonucleic acid), the molecular source of heredity. The field of genetic engineering will soon produce some of the most incredible developments the world has ever witnessed.

People suffering from hereditary diseases will soon be helped by a process known as *gene splicing.* This process will permit doctors to replace abnormal, unhealthy genes with normal, healthy ones. Today some 12 million Americans suffer from some form of genetic disorder. Such tragic diseases as sickle-cell anemia, hemophilia, and Down's syndrome (mongolism) will someday be greatly reduced by gene splicing techniques.

Geneticists are also experimenting with, and developing new forms of life. The implications and consequences of these developments are both staggering and frightening. Some of the results promise to be of great benefit: new forms of life that can protect plants from harmful insects, new forms of natural food that can be grown in places as diverse as a laboratory, a desert, or an ocean.

But what will happen if a company can create a new and terrible disease for which only it has the cure? And what will happen to the human species if geneticists can produce a bigger, stronger, more intelligent person?

WHO SAID THERE CAN NEVER BE ANOTHER YOU?

Another outgrowth of the genetic revolution is a phenomenon called cloning. Cloning is a process by which the genes of a person are used to make an identical physical copy of that person. In theory, then, there can be two yous, or three, or more. As of yet, geneticists cannot recreate people. But they're working on it. In laboratories researchers have already "cloned" frogs and other forms of life. Can our turn be that far off?

What is a human being? What is life? Advances in medical science are forcing us to ask these kinds of questions. We have already seen heart transplants, in which the heart of a recently dead patient is used to replace the sick heart of another person. The procedure astounded the world when it was first performed in 1967 by Dr. Christiaan Barnard. Today, of course, a heart transplant is no longer a newsworthy item. In 1982 yet another incredible medical achievement startled the world, when an artificial heart made of plastic and aluminum was implanted in the body of a Utah dentist. Like the heart transplant of fifteen years before, this amazing feat is only a first step. Medical researchers are already in the process of developing artificial blood and other artificial organs. It's only a matter of time before the implementation of artificial organs will be a routine form of surgery.

FROM REPLACING PARTS TO REPLACING PEOPLE: R-2 D-2 WHERE ARE YOU?

The science fiction movie *Star Wars* created a sensation when it first came out. Both children and adults were charmed and fascinated by the characters in the movie, particularly R-2 D-2 and C-3P-O. These characters were not people but robots. The appearance of these robots, with their humanlike qualities, excited the imagination. Robots as "intelligent" and "human" as R-2 D-2 are still a long way off, but robots are already here. Approximately 14,000, to be more specific, were in use in Japan, the United States, Sweden, France, and Germany at the end of 1981. By 1990, it is projected that as many as 200,000 robots may be in existence in the United States alone.

Of course, the robots in use today do not yet resemble the robots of *Star Wars,* where cinematic special effects and sound-track recording created the illusion of intelligent, sentient beings. Today's robots, however, do possess some human features. They have miniature, high-speed computers for "brains," TV cameras for "eyes," hydraulic and pneumatic-powered parts for "arms," and special gripping devices for "hands." Although still in a relatively primitive stage of development, these robots can successfully perform many assembly-line functions. Robots have already demonstrated their value in increasing production and lowering labor costs. The Chrysler automobile company claims that robots have improved the quality of welding. General Electric states that robot painters save the company thousands of dollars each year, since robots do not waste as much paint as people do. General Motors already employs 300 robots, and they plan to spend $1 billion to include 14,000 more by the year 1990; they're already designing new factories to make use of their new "employees."

At the present time Japan is the world leader in robot technology. Having begun to develop robots in the mid-1960s, Japan is now exporting them at the rate of 100 per month, and it already has a factory where robots are used to manufacture other robots!

What about robots to help with the housework? The Nieman-Marcus Company has made a domestic robot. The company claims its 4½ foot tall robot can dust and vacuum a house, open doors, serve guests, and walk the dog. If you want to find out how well the robot can do all these things, you can buy one. It only costs about $15,000!

PART 3

THE DAWN OF THE COMPUTER AGE

The progress of computer technology during the past two decades has been nothing short of staggering. Today's computers play an essential role in many areas of daily life: they help universities to register students, meteorologists to forecast weather, business and government to maintain records. These are but a few examples. As the years pass, as computer technology continues to improve and costs to decrease, computers will be an integral part of daily life for the average citizen, the way telephones are today. The computer industry already enjoys sales of $1 billion per year. It is estimated that that figure will reach $4 billion by the late 1980s. Computers in the home will be as common as TV sets are today (they will also cost about the same). The computer will assist the human mind the way the machine aided the human muscle. The computer will be to the third revolution what the machine was to the Industrial Age; it will have a tremendous impact on almost every aspect of daily life, from work, family life, and education to energy, transportation, and communication.

It is virtually impossible for us to comprehend and appreciate the abilities of tomorrow's computers. By 1990, it is projected that computers will be able to perform 200 million operations per second. By the year 2000, that number is expected to jump to 8 billion operations a second. Someday soon a computer the size of a 2″ x 3″ business card will store all the information contained in a large library. Imagine being able to walk around with the Library of Congress in your pocket. With computer technology at such an advanced level the potential effects on society are practically limitless.

"THE CITI NEVER SLEEPS"

We have already witnessed the effects of computers on banking. In the late 1970s Citibank instituted a 24-hour banking service, permitting people to make almost any banking transaction by machine at any time of the day. Almost instantly other banks followed Citibank's example. Today, 24-hour banking machines can be found everywhere in the average American city. Soon people will pay all their bills by a home computer connected to a cable TV set. Don't laugh! Citibank has already been experimenting with this system with several hundred customers. This service is expected to be available sometime before 1990.

But this is only a beginning. People will eventually do most of their shopping by home computer and cable TV. Pictures of products with their descriptions and prices will appear on your TV screen. You will place your order from your home and your purchase will be charged to your account, then sent to your home. It's only a matter of time.

LIVING IN "THE ELECTRONIC COTTAGE"

Alvin Toffler, author of *Future Shock* and *The Third Wave,* two influential books that attempt to describe life in the future, sees tomorrow's home as an "electronic cottage" where people will make use of computers and more sophisticated communications technology in order to work at home. Instead of traveling to offices for business meetings and conferences, people in different towns and cities will be able to confer with each other by means of a video screen in their own homes. Businesses are already adopting teleconferencing systems to cut down on business trips. Although this technology is still rather expensive, the day will soon come when we can talk to each other on "TV" as easily as we now talk by phone.

Toffler sees many benefits to working at home: It will save time, energy, and money. It will cost individuals much less money to operate home computers and video screens than to travel to and from an office. It will cost businesses much less to own or rent centrally located space in cities if many of their employees choose to work at home. Fewer cars taking people in and out of cities to work will also mean less pollution, traffic, and overcrowding for everyone. With computers in the home, people will also have much more freedom in choosing the hours they want to work. The need to live in cities will also decrease as more people start to communicate through home computers and home TVs.

"FROM ONE SIZE FOR ALL TO YOUR SIZE FOR YOU"

Today items of clothing, hundreds at a time, all the same size, style, and color, come off the assembly line in rapid succession. Soon new technology will change all that. New laser machines will produce any item of clothing one at a time more cheaply and quickly than the old mass-production methods. The day will come when you will be able to contact a clothing manufacturer by phone and give your personal measurements and preferences to a computer. A laser machine will produce exactly the kind of clothing you want for little or no extra cost. The days of standardized sizes of clothing will someday belong to the past. In fact, factories may be able to produce many products, such as cars and furniture, with the style, size, and color you prefer, just by your calling up the factory computer.

"WIRING UP FOR CABLE"

TV, the invention most responsible for standardizing the images and information we receive, is also experiencing the greatest change. Since its beginnings in the late 1940s, American TV has been dominated by three major commercial networks: ABC, NBC, and CBS. Most American TV viewers have been limited to watching whatever programs these networks offered, whenever they offered them. This situation is changing incredibly fast. "Video cassettes" now permit TV viewers to record programs while they are away from the TV and then watch them at a more convenient time. Cable TV programming is expanding rapidly across the country as more and more people choose to pay for access to cable TV stations. Cable TV offers people more freedom of choice in the programs they watch. Programs related to one specific subject such as news, weather, sports, or movies can be seen almost twenty-four hours a day.

But cable TV is only in an infant stage. The combination of computers and TV will soon offer a staggering number of possibilities. The Warner Amex Corporation has already developed a cable system called QUBE that not only provides access to sixty different channels, but also allows QUBE owners to interact with their TVs by using a special control connected to a home computer. The home computer permits them to talk into the TV for two-way communication. A town meeting can be shown and issues can be discussed, and then viewers can vote directly through their television screens. When this capability is found in most homes, what will be its effects on government and politics? Will we still need senators and representatives to vote for us in Congress if we can directly use our televisions to vote on important matters? This may very well be one of the major political issues of the future.

Some futurists foresee the day when children will receive many of their classes through computerized TV screens. (Children are already interacting with their TVs on a regular basis by means of video games, and others are even spending their summer vacations at computer camps where they are taught the basics of computer science.) Students will someday be able to interact with the TV "teacher," ask questions, and receive answers on an individualized basis. Children of the future will go to school more for social contact with other children than for actual academic instruction. Children who know how to operate computers may even be able to assist their parents with work, since many parents will also be working at home, much like the days during the Agricultural Era when children watched their parents work and even helped them.

Although such a day is still quite a few years away, it's evident that a new age of telecommunications is already with us. The tremendous variety of newspapers, magazines, and radio and TV programs is reducing the power and control that national magazines and network TV have over us. As a consequence, the images and information we receive are less standard and uniform. People not only have access to more kinds of information more quickly and easily, but they also have more freedom in choosing what they want, when they want it. As futurist Alvin Toffler puts it, the mass media has been "demassified."

PART 4

THE PATH TO HIGHER GROUND

During the 1700s and 1800s a human movement of dramatic proportions took place as millions of people left their homes in Europe to make the long voyage to North America. One important factor in this mass migration was the need for more space. The land in Europe was controlled by wealthy landowners; most people, the poor, had little or no opportunity to own land. The availability of abundant, cheap land in North America attracted millions of immigrants in search of their own property. Today, of course, land in the New World is no longer available in such cheap abundance. As the world rapidly becomes more and more overcrowded, a new wave of human migration is likely to take place. The day is fast approaching when we will choose to live in a farther frontier: outer space.

Looking back at the development of flight technology, one can see that our ability to fly has improved at an almost frightening pace. From ancient times, people watched birds move across the sky with the dream that some day they too might fly. In 1903, that dream finally came true when a plane built by two brothers, Wilbur and Orville Wright, stayed aloft for 59 seconds. (It had traveled only 852 feet, less than the length of three football fields.) In 1927, Charles Lindbergh made the first trans-Atlantic flight, flying from New York to Paris in 33 hours 29½ minutes. Today, the Concorde covers the same distance in 3 hours, almost a day and a half less. In 1961 Cosmonaut Yuri Gagarin of the Soviet Union circled the Earth in 1 hour 48 minutes, reaching speeds of up to 18,000 miles per hour. Only eight years later, on July 20, 1969, the United States added another remarkable page to flight history when astronaut Neil Armstrong stepped foot on the moon's surface with the words, "That's one small step for man, one giant leap for mankind." In just sixty-six years humanity had progressed from a brief, crude, one-minute flight to the actual landing of a man on the moon!

During the 1970s, space technology overcame yet another important barrier; it developed the ability to go up in space and return with the *same* space vehicle. Previously, the destruction of a rocket as it left the Earth's atmosphere was an inevitable part of all space travel. With the creation of the Columbia space shuttle, it became possible to use the same space vehicle repeatedly, thus saving millions of dollars. This achievement will further help to accelerate man's exploration of space.

Dr. Gerard O'Neill, professor of physics at Princeton University and head of the Space Studies Institute there, predicts that space travel will be comparable in the next century to what the automobile has been in this century. Dr. O'Neill claims that we already have the existing technology to enable us to live in outer space. In fact, NASA (National Aeronautics and Space Administration) has already designed "Island One," a space habitat in which 10,000 people can live. Dr. O'Neill believes that within a hundred years "there may be more Americans in space colonies than there are in the United States." That view may seem a bit too optimistic to even the most adventurous. What is "a certainty," Dr. O'Neill states, is that a "breakout into space" will occur "within the next decade." By 2081, he adds, we will be able to "provide transport into space and back again for several hundred million people per year." Of course not everyone will want to live in space, "but," Dr. O'Neill asserts, "a voyage of a few days to space colony will be as commonplace in 2081 as a Caribbean cruise is to us today."

RESOURCEFUL ALTERNATIVES

New energy sources represent the key to many of the changes we are about to experience. There are several reasons for this. Most of the energy sources we now depend on, such as oil and natural gas, exist on the Earth in limited supply and thus have become terribly expensive. Today's energy sources have also been the cause of much of the pollution that increasingly threatens the health of human beings, wildlife, and the environment. Until now, the technology of industrial society has been based on these nonrenewable forms of energy. The high cost, limited supply, and harmful environmental effects of these traditional energy sources are forcing the industrial world to develop alternate sources of energy.

During the Agricultural Revolution, people relied on renewable sources of energy provided by the natural environment such as sun, wind, and water. Ironically, societies of the coming era will be returning to nature's renewable sources to obtain cheap, abundant, and unharmful energy. New technology is being developed to take advantage of nature's gifts. In the quest for cheaper, more efficient energy, we will be moving in several directions. Satellite stations will someday be able to collect solar energy in space and transmit it back to Earth. It is believed that thermal energy, produced by changes in temperature made by the currents of the ocean, will be another energy source. Nuclear energy is yet another alternative. However, there will be one major difference: The nuclear energy will come mostly by means of fusion, not fission. In simple terms, this means that atom particles will be combined instead of split or divided. The fusion method will be much safer and less costly.

The principal fuel for fusion is deuterium, a material that can be obtained from sea water. When processed through a fusion reactor, the deuterium in one gallon of sea water is the energy equivalent of 300 gallons of gasoline, enough gas to power the average car from New York to Argentina. A few pounds of deuterium can provide enough energy for a large city to function for several weeks. A $1 billion experimental fusion plant is already in an early stage of operation at Princeton University and is expected to be in full operation in 1990. Dr. Cetron believes that by the year 2010, the time when the world's supply will finally begin to run out, fusion power will be a major source of abundant and cheap electricity. By then, Dr. Cetron predicts, most automobiles will be powered by electricity. Cars on highways may operate by means of electrified rails in much the same way that subway cars run today.

WHAT'S IN A NAME?

Many people have been struggling to find the words to describe the incredible transformation that has been taking place around us. It has been referred to as the Computer Age, the Information Age, the Space Age, the Global Village. Daniel Bell, professor of sociology at Harvard University, simply calls it "Post-Industrial Society." But perhaps the most expressive term has been the one coined by Alvin Toffler as the title for his highly successful book, *The Third Wave.* The phrase "third wave" brings to mind the notion of two previous waves and the sea. Like the powerful waves of a sea, the "Third Wave" is colliding, clashing, and overlapping with the waves of the past, creating a turbulent and constantly changing environment. All of us are living in this sea of change that we are only beginning to fathom. We are passengers embarking on a voyage powered by the new technology. Or, as Toffler would have us see ourselves, "We are the children of the next transformation, the Third Wave."

Riding the Third Wave

Directions: *This exercise has two parts. First, identify the different predictions or possibilities that the article presents concerning each topic listed here. Second, try to list some of the effects that these changes may have on society. (These effects may be mentioned in the article or they may be your own interpretation.)*

1. Life Expectancy
2. Hereditary Disease
3. New Forms of Life
4. Cloning
5. Artificial Organs
6. Robots
7. Computers
8. Cable TV
9. Manufacturing of Products
10. Space Travel
11. Energy Sources

For Class Discussion: *Evaluate each of the previous predictions using Dr. Cetron's three questions for forecasting change:*

(1) Is the change technologically feasible?
(2) Is the change economically feasible?
(3) Is the change socially acceptable?

What problems and benefits do you envision if these predictions were to come true?

Time Line

Directions: *Scan the article (parts 2, 3, and 4) to identify the important events that occurred or will occur in the years listed next. Write each event in the appropriate space next to each year or years. The first event mentioned in the article has been written in for you as an example.*

Year	Event
1700s and 1800s	______
1903	______
1927	______
1952	***Watson and Crick identify molecular structure of DNA.***
1961	______
mid-1960s	______
1967	______
1969	______
1970s	______
late 1970s	______
1982	______

Predictions

1990 Computer technology: ______

1990 Banking: ______

1990 Energy: ______

2010 Energy: ______

2081 Space travel: ______

Future Test

How ready are you for life in the twenty-first century?

Directions: *Read the statements in each category listed next. Then put a check next to the one statement that best expresses your own opinion. After indicating your personal preference in all ten categories, consult the chart on page 211 to find out your score on the Future Test.*

1. SPACE TRAVEL

_____ a. I refuse to fly, even in an airplane.

_____ b. Although I ride in an airplane, I have no interest in flying in outer space.
_____ c. I would like to take a two-week vacation in outer space.
_____ d. I would like to live in a space colony if I could return to Earth once a year to visit my family and friends.
_____ e. I would leave the Earth with my family and friends in a spaceship and never return to this planet.

2. ANTI-AGING DRUGS
_____ a. I have no interest in taking an anti-aging drug.
_____ b. I would take an anti-aging drug if I could live to be 100 years old.
_____ c. I would agree to have only *one* child during my life if I could take an anti-aging drug that permitted me to live 150 years.
_____ d. I would take an anti-aging drug that prevented me from having children if this drug permitted me to live 200 years.

3. ROBOTS
_____ a. I don't think robots should be used at all.
_____ b. I think robots should be used only for factory work.
_____ c. I think robots should be used as much as possible. I would like to have a robot at home to help me with the housework.
_____ e. I would like to marry a robot.

4. FAMILY LIFE
If I lived 150 years and my marriage was a happy one,
_____ a. I would prefer to keep the same family and the same profession for my entire life.
_____ b. I would prefer to keep the same family but try a second profession.
_____ c. I would prefer to start another family and have at least two professions.
_____ e. I would prefer to have several marriages and several professions during my life.

5. HAPPINESS DRUGS (These are drugs that make you feel positive and happy about everything, regardless of what happens.)
_____ a. I would never use these drugs.
_____ b. I would use these drugs infrequently (about once a year).
_____ c. I would use these drugs often (at least once a month).
_____ d. I would use these drugs every day so that I would feel happy all the time.

6. CHILDREN
_____ a. I don't want to be able to determine my child's sex.
_____ b. I would like to be able to choose my child's sex.
_____ c. I would like to choose all of my child's physical characteristics.
_____ e. I would like my child to be a clone (an exact duplicate) of me.

7. ARTIFICIAL ORGANS AND BODY PARTS
_____ a. I would never accept an organ from another person's body.
_____ b. I would never accept an artificial organ under any circumstances.
_____ c. I would accept an artificial organ only in a life-and-death emergency.
_____ d. I would like to replace my body parts as I get older with artificial parts to make sure my body stays healthy.
_____ e. I would replace my body parts at an early age if this gave me super powers, such as incredible strength or the ability to fly.

8. WORK SCHEDULE

_____ a. I would prefer to begin work when the sun comes up and only stop at the end of the day.

_____ b. I would prefer to work eight hours a day, Monday through Friday.

_____ c. I would prefer to go to work ten hours a day for four days or twelve hours a day for three days each week.

_____ d. I would prefer to work twenty-five hours a week. I would be happy to divide these hours between work in an office and work at home.

_____ e. I would prefer to work twenty-five hours a week at the times I choose. I would like to use home computers and video telephones to communicate with my co-workers.

9. TELEPHONES

_____ a. I prefer not to use telephones at all.

_____ b. I use telephones, but I would prefer not to see other people while I'm talking to them by telephone.

_____ c. I would like to have either a telephone in my car or a video telephone, not both.

_____ d. I would like to have both a telephone in my car and a telephone that permits me to see the other person I'm talking to.

10. MONEY AND CREDIT

_____ a. I prefer to use only cash when I buy something.

_____ b. I prefer to buy things by cash or check.

_____ c. I prefer to pay for most things by credit card.

_____ d. I would prefer to pay for everything by credit card and never use cash, even for purchases of ten cents.

FUTURE TEST: HOW TO DETERMINE YOUR SCORE

Directions: *Count how many times you put a check next to each letter in the preceding questionnaire. In the appropriate space that follows, write the number of times you checked each letter. Then multiply that number by the number of marked points. To get your total score, add all the numbers in the spaces on the right. To interpret your score, consult the chart that follows.*

	Number of Times Each Letter Was Checked		Points		Total Points
a.	__________	×	2	=	__________
b.	__________	×	4	=	__________
c.	__________	×	6	=	__________
d.	__________	×	8	=	__________
e.	__________	×	10	=	__________
			Total score		__________

INTERPRETING YOUR SCORE

Points		
Less than 25	=	You're living in the wrong century. You would probably have been much happier living 500 years ago.
25–44	=	Try to remain in the present. You probably have little interest in living in the next century.

45–64	=	You're not yet ready for life in the twenty-first century, but you might enjoy it if you keep an open mind.
65–80	=	You're almost ready for the next century right now.
81–100	=	No doubt about it. You would be very happy living 100 years from now. (Don't forget to send a postcard from outer space to your family and friends!)

Seeing Relationships: Analogies

Directions: *Choose the one word or phrase in parentheses that correctly completes the analogy and write it in the appropriate blank space.* *(For an explanation of analogies, please refer to page 132.)*

1. breakthrough : discovery AS quest : ______________________
(travel, search, shuttle, barrier)

2. meteorologist : weather AS prophet : ______________________
(future, think tank, government, experts)

3. abnormal : healthy AS startling : ______________________
(astonishing, astounding, expected, limitless)

4. machine : muscle AS computer : ______________________
(library, mind, speed, human being)

5. fusion : fission AS combine : ______________________
(forecast, develop, deuterium, divide)

6. think : speculate AS foretell : ______________________
(astound, predict, experiment, resemble)

7. Wright brothers : airplane AS Dr. Christiaan Barnard :
____
(film industry, banking, Princeton University, heart transplants)

8. witness : observe AS accelerate : ______________________
(eliminate, produce, slow down, speed up)

9. Charles Lindbergh : 1927 AS Neil Armstrong : ______________________
(1903, 1961, 1969, 1982)

10. Down's syndrome : genetic disorder AS television :
____
(science fiction, flight history, special effects, mass media)

11. achievement : feat AS cloning : ______________________
(genetic disorder, certainty, genetic duplication, DNA)

12. New World : Europe AS outer space : ______________________
(Concorde, Japan, Earth, think tank)

Vocabulary Development Puzzle: Kettering's Message

Directions: *Complete each missing word in the sentences using only one letter for each blank space. Rewrite each numbered letter in the corresponding space of the sentence marked "Kettering's Message." When you have completed all the letters of this sentence, you will have a message from the American inventor Charles Franklin Kettering (1867–1958).*

Kettering's Message:

W_ s____d a__ b_
1 2 3 4 5 6 7 8

c________ ab___ the
9 10 11 12 13 14 15 16 17 18 19

f____e b_____e w_ w__l
20 21 22 23 24 25 26 27 28 29 30 31

h___ t_ s____ the r___
32 33 34 35 36 37 38 39 40 41 42

of our l____ t____.
43 44 45 46 47 48 49 50

1. People generally feel **d___r___t_d** when they are forced to deal with too much change too quickly.
   30 46 3 30 1 14 1
2. In order to predict whether an idea will become part of our daily lives, it's important to know if the idea is technologically and economically **f__s_b__**.
   45 43 5 45
3. As our planet becomes more and more **ov____ow___**, people may choose to live in outer space.
   1 13 13 16 1 16
4. The energy sources of the future will resemble the primary energy sources of many centuries ago; people will eventually depend on **r___w_bl_** sources of energy such as sun and water for most of their energy needs.
   29 14 29 32 29
5. The Columbia space **s_____e** was an important breakthrough in space technology; it allows people to leave the Earth's **a_m__ph_r_** and then return to the Earth in the same vehicle.
   2 4 42 42 5 — 42 35 28 8 49 8
6. The life **ex_e_____y** of the average person in the U.S. will increase as soon as new drugs are developed to help people live longer.
   36 11 10 11
7. Oil and natural gas exist on this planet in a limited **s____y**. Therefore it's essential for us to develop **a_t___at____** to these nonrenewable energy sources.
   27 36 36 6 — 6 12 10 43 44 12 28

8. The ability of human beings to fly has progressed at an almost frightening **p** ___ **c** ___ since 1903, the year the first airplane stayed aloft for fifty-nine seconds.
   (26 40)

9. Another incredible achievement in **f** ___ **i** **g** ___ ___ history took place in 1927 when Charles Lindbergh flew from New York to Paris in approximately 33½ hours.
   (7 47 21)

10. Computers have already had a tremendous **i** **m** ___ ___ **c** ___ on our daily lives.
   (36 32 21)

11. Some Scientists predict that during the next century people will be able to take a vacation **c** ___ ___ **i** ___ ___ in outer space.
   (49 20 41 48)

12. James Watson and Francis Crick received a Nobel Prize for their work in identifying the molecular structure of deoxyribonucleic acid (DNA), the basic source of **h** ___ ___ ___ **d** ___ ___ **y** .
   (29 49 29 21)

13. Today people's relationships are often very **t** ___ ___ **n** ___ ___ ___ **n** **t** because so many people change residences and jobs with great frequency.
   (13 26 41 48)

14. For many people it helps to try to **a** **n** ___ ___ **c** ___ ___ **a** ___ **e** the future. Knowing what to expect helps people to **d** ___ ___ ___ with change more easily.
   (42 30 30 42) (50 26 31)

15. Computers of the Third Wave will assist the human **m** **i** ___ ___ in much the same way that machines of the Industrial Revolution aided human **m** ___ ___ ___ ___ **l** **e** .
   (38 39) (22 46 11)

16. Cable TV offers people more **f** **r** ___ ___ ___ ___ **m** in choosing what they want to watch, when they want to watch it.
   (15 15 39 17)

17. Pollution has become a serious threat to the health of people and wildlife as well as to the **e** ___ ___ **i** ___ ___ ___ **m** **e** ___ ___ .
   (10 33 23 17 10 10 19)

18. Computers the size of a business card will someday be able to **s** **t** ___ ___ ___ all the information contained in a large library.
   (9 37)

19. Science fiction movies provide an important function. They help people to think and **s** ___ **e** ___ ___ ___ **a** ___ **e** about life in the future.
   (36 25 18 31 19)

20. It is believed that scientists are on the **v** ___ ___ **g** ___ of making many scientific breakthroughs. Some of these **d** ___ ___ **c** **o** ___ **e** ___ ___ **e** ___ will help people to live longer and healthier lives. It's only a **m** ___ **t** **t** ___ ___ of time.
   (24 24) (30 28 44 30 28) (32 34)

Word Forms: Future Words

The English language has changed tremendously during the course of the last four centuries. It is said that if William Shakespeare (1564–1616), perhaps the greatest writer the English Language has ever known, were alive, he would not be able to understand more than half the English words used today in daily conversation. After all, how could Shakespeare understand such words as automobile, telephone, refrigerator, and camera. These miracles of technology did not exist during his lifetime. (There were no dictionaries either, for that matter.) New words had to be created as each new invention appeared. Many of the names for these inventions were formed by combining various prefixes, roots, and suffixes from older languages such as Latin and Greek. As new and more advanced technology is developed, it's inevitable that new and exotic words will have to be thought up to name the inventions and ideas of the future.

Directions: *Study this list of roots and affixes. Then, using the list as a guide, try to identify the different parts and the meaning of the boldface word in the sentences that follow. Of course, the boldface words are not yet part of the English language. But who knows! Perhaps someday they will be.*

Root or Affix	Meaning	Examples
ante	before	anterior, anteroom
anti	against	antinuclear, antisocial
astro, stellar	star	astronaut, stellar
auto	self	automation, autograph
bio	life	biology, biography
chron	time	chronology, synchronize
inter	between	interfere, intermediate
meter	measure	thermometer, speedometer
ology	the study of	psychology, sociology
patho	feeling	sympathy, telepathy
phono	sound	phonograph, telephone
polis	city	metropolis, cosmopolitan
port	carry	portable, transportation
post	after	postgraduate, posttest
pseudo	false	pseudonym, pseudointellectual
re, retro	back	revert, retrospect
sub	below, under	subway, submarine
tele	far away	television, teleconference
trans	across	transfer, transcontinental

1. Many people claim that living in a **suboceanopolis** is a wonderful experience.

   sub: under, polis: city—city under the ocean

2. The trip from New York to California by **telesubmobile** takes only an hour.

   ____

3. People who take space vacations for more than several weeks usually need to have **antestellar and poststellar** checkups.

   ____

4. Although I love to be **transchronoported** to other centuries for a vacation, I still prefer daily life in the twenty-second century.

___

5. When visiting other countries, people find it very convenient to take an **autotranslator** with them.

___

6. Many university students are required to take courses in both **futurology** and **retrospaciology**.

___

7. **Pathometers** help people to know what kind of drug to take each morning.

___

8. Our family is planning to visit a **pseudobiopolis** next weekend.

___

9. Citizens of the planet Xylon knew that a spaceship from another galaxy was approaching when they consulted an **interstellar phonometer**.

___

Class Activity: *Use the roots and affixes listed in this exercise to make up your own "future words."*

The Immortal Bard

ISAAC ASIMOV (1920–)

Isaac Asimov was born in the Soviet Union in 1920. When he was three years old, his parents hid him in their baggage and emigrated to the United States. He grew up in Brooklyn, New York, and later attended Columbia University, where he received a Ph.D. in chemistry in 1948.

When he was eleven he began writing short stories. Seven years later he submitted his first story to a publisher and it was rejected. Today, he is the author of more than two hundred and sixty books as well as hundreds of magazine articles on subjects ranging from serious scientific issues to science fiction. Considered one of the finest and most imaginative science fiction writers at work today, his books include I, Robot *and the popular four-volume* Foundation *series.*

In the short story "The Immortal Bard," Asimov brings William Shakespeare, the great sixteenth-century English playwright, back to life in the twentieth century. While the situation may seem implausible and humorous, it does raise some profound and provocative questions.

"Oh, yes," said Dr. Phineas Welch, "I can bring back the spirits of the illustrious[1] dead."

Scott Robertson, the school's young English instructor, adjusted his glasses and looked to right and left to see if they were overheard. "Really, Dr. Welch?"

"I mean it. And not just the spirits. I bring back the bodies, too."

[1]**illustrious:** famous

"I wouldn't have said it was possible," said Robertson primly.[2]

"Why not? A simple matter of temporal transference."

"You mean time travel? But that's quite-uh-unusual."

"Not if you know how."

"Well, how, Dr. Welch?"

"Think I'm going to tell you?" asked the physicist gravely.[3] He said, "I brought quite a few back. Archimedes, Newton, Galileo. Poor fellows."

"Didn't they like it here? I should think they'd have been fascinated by our modern science," said Robertson. He was beginning to enjoy the conversation.

"Oh, they were. They were. Especially Archimedes. I thought he'd go mad[4] with joy at first after I explained a little of it in some Greek I'd boned up on[5], but no-no-"

"What was wrong?"

"Just a different culture. They couldn't get used to our way of life. They got terribly lonely and frightened. I had to send them back."

"That's too bad."

"Yes. Great minds, but not flexible minds. Not universal. So I tried Shakespeare."

"What?" yelled[6] Robertson. This was getting closer to home.

"Don't yell, my boy," said Welch. "It's bad manners."

"Did you say you brought back Shakespeare?"

"I did. I needed someone with a universal mind; someone who knows people well enough to be able to live with them centuries away from his own time. Shakespeare was the man. I've got his signature. As a memento[7], you know."

"On you?" asked Robertson, eyes bugging[8].

"Right here." Welch fumbled[9] in one vest pocket after another. "Ah, here it is."

A little piece of pasteboard was passed to the instructor. On one side it said "L. Klein & Sons, Wholesale Hardware. On the other side, in scraggly[10] script, was written, "Will Shakesper."

A wild surmise[11] filled Robertson. "What did he look like?"

"Not like his pictures. Bald and an ugly mustache. He spoke in a thick brogue.[12] Of course, I did my best to please him with our times. I told him we thought highly of his plays and still put them on the boards[13]. In fact, I said we thought they were the greatest pieces of literature in the English language, maybe in any language."

"Good, good," said Robertson breathlessly.

"I said people had written volumes of commentaries on his plays. Naturally he wanted to see one and I got one for him from the library."

"And?"

"Oh, he was fascinated. Of course, he had trouble with the current idioms and references to events since 1600, but I helped out. Poor fellow, I don't think he ever expected such treatment. He kept saying, 'God ha' mercy! What cannot be racked from words in five centuries? One would wring, methinks, a flood from a damp clout!"

"He wouldn't say that."

[2]**primly:** formally
[3]**gravely:** seriously
[4]**mad:** crazy
[5]**boned up on:** reviewed
[6]**yelled:** shouted
[7]**memento:** souvenir
[8]**bugging:** opening wide with amazement
[9]**fumbled:** searched in a clumsy, awkward manner
[10]**scraggly:** in poor condition
[11]**surmise:** speculation; guess
[12]**brogue:** accent
[13]**boards:** stage

"Why not? He wrote his plays as quickly as he could. He said he had to on account of the deadlines. He wrote Hamlet in less than six months. The plot was an old one. He just polished[14] it *up.*"

"That's all they do to a telescope mirror. Just polish it up," said the English instructor indignantly.

The physicist disregarded[15] him. "I told the immortal bard that we even gave college courses in Shakespeare."

"I give one."

"I know. I enrolled him in your evening extension course. I never saw a man so eager[16] to find out what posterity thought of him as poor Bill was. He worked hard at it."

"You enrolled[17] William Shakespeare in my course?" mumbled Robertson. Even as a fantasy, the thought staggered[18] him. And was it a fantasy? He was beginning to recall a bald man with a queer[19] way of talking. . .

"Not under his real name, of course," said Dr. Welch. "Never mind what he went under. It was a mistake, that's all. A big mistake. Poor fellow."

"Why was it a mistake? What happened?"

"I had to send him back to 1600," roared Welch indignantly. "How much humiliation do you think a man can stand?"

"What humiliation are you talking about?"

"Why, you poor simpleton[20], you flunked[21] him."

QUESTIONS

1. What incredible thing was Dr. Phineas Welch able to do?
2. Which famous people did Dr. Welch "bring back" first? Why did Dr. Welch decide to "bring back" Shakespeare?
3. What was Shakespeare's reaction when he learned how modern society regarded his plays?
4. What happened to Shakespeare during his stay in the twentieth century?
5. What important point is the author, Isaac Asimov, trying to make in this story?

[14]**polished up:** improved; revised
[15]**disregarded:** ignored
[16]**eager:** anxious; impatient
[17]**enrolled:** registered
[18]**staggered:** astounded; overwhelmed
[19]**queer:** strange; peculiar
[20]**simpleton:** fool; idiot
[21]**flunked:** failed

Back to the Dump

RUSSELL BAKER (1925-   )

Russell Baker was born in Loudoun County, Virginia. Upon his graduation from Johns Hopkins University in 1947, he began his career as a journalist with The Baltimore Sun. *In 1954 he joined* The New York Times *Washington news bureau, where he covered the White House, Congress, and national politics. His* Observer *column has appeared in* The New York Times *since 1962. His* Sunday Observer *appears regularly in* The New York Times Magazine. *His columns have been published in various collections, the most recent of which is* So This Is Depravity. *In 1979 he was awarded the Pulitzer Prize for Distinguished Commentary. His autobiography,* Growing Up, *earned him a Pulitzer Prize in 1983.*

Mr. Baker's unusual blend of humor and concern for the state of the world has won him a loyal following. The column "Back to the Dump" first appeared in The New York Times Magazine *of February 27, 1983.*

When I was a boy everybody urged me to get plenty of sunshine, so I got plenty of sunshine for a long time. One day while I was absorbing July sun as fast as I could, a doctor asked what I thought I was doing.

"Getting plenty of sunshine," I said.

"Are you mad?[1]" he replied.

No, I was not mad, just slow to catch up with life's revisions. Getting plenty of sunshine had been declared dangerous while I was out to lunch. I revised my store of knowledge. Now I get only small droppers of sunshine extracted from the half hour just before sunset.

When I was old enough to notice that girls were pleasantly different from boys, my mother told me the facts of life. "You must always treat a woman like a lady," she said. So for a long time I went through life treating women like ladies.

One day while I was helping a woman into her coat, another woman asked me what I thought I was doing.

"Treating a woman like a lady," I said.

"Are you mad?" she replied.

No, I was not mad, but my interrogator was furious. I had been out to lunch during one of life's revisions and missed the announcement that it was swinish[2] to treat a woman like a lady. I discarded another piece of my childhood education. Now I treat women like ticking bombs.

When I was 17 and for many years afterward, I admired Franklin and Eleanor Roosevelt as the ideal couple. One evening I had an encounter with a ticking bomb, and contemplated behaving like a fool, but rejected the impulse because we weren't married.

"What do you think you're doing?" she asked as I fled.[3] I told her that someday I wanted to be half of a couple as ideal as Franklin and Eleanor Roosevelt.

"Are you mad?" she replied.

No, not mad. I had been out to lunch during another of life's revisions and, so, had missed the disclosure[4] that Eleanor didn't get along well with Franklin and that Franklin fooled around[5] when she was out of town. Another part of my youthful education went to the dump, but too late. By then, age had brought its inevitable energy crisis and I had begun to prefer napping to behaving like a fool.

Perhaps it was not age that defeated me, though. Maybe it was fatigue caused by the constant trips to the dump to discard everything I'd learned in the first half of my life. Life seemed to be an educator's practical joke in which you spent the first half learning and the second half learning that everything you learned in the first half was wrong.

The trips to the dump became more and more frequent. There I lugged[6] the old precept[7] that a hearty breakfast of bacon and eggs was good for me.

[1]**mad:** crazy

[2]**swinish:** like a swine (pig); vulgar; crude

[3]**fled:** ran away

[4]**disclosure:** revelation

[5]**fooled around:** went out with other women

[6]**lugged:** carried (something heavy)

[7]**precept:** rule of moral conduct

I also hauled away the old lesson that it was racist to refer to people of African ancestry as "black." One windy night, I hoisted up[8] the cherished teaching that every American had a duty[9] to drive a two-ton, eight-cylinder automobile with room enough inside for a steamer trunk and the whole darn family, and staggered[10] off to the dump. That was a heavy night's work and left me bent in spine and spirit.

At about this time, movie actors began running for President, astronauts began flying around the planet to get from one desert to another, people began renting one-bedroom apartments for $2,000 a month. Out to the dump went important fragments[11] of my education which had made me believe that movie actors existed to be browbeaten[12] by Congressional investigators, that if you've seen one cactus[13] you've seen them all, and that $2,000 a month ought to buy you a controlling interest in the Gritti Palace Hotel.

No wonder I was tired. And then, a terrible fear seized me. If everything I'd learned in life's first half had to go to the dump, wasn't it inevitable that everything I was learning in the second half would also have to go?

A crushing thought. I'm not getting any younger. I've had the stamina[14] so far to heave[15] out everything I learned in youth, but if everything I've learned since has to go in the next 25 years I'll be too feeble[16] for the job.

I'm sitting here right now wondering what present certainties might have to be junked[17] before the century is out. My conviction that President Reagan is a nice guy, for instance. Will some whippersnapper[18] someday say, "If you hadn't been out to lunch again, old-timer, you'd have read the recent book reporting that Reagan had to be dosed[19] on jolly[20] pills to control his passion for kicking orphans"?

And there's my present fear that the nuclear weapons race could kill us all. Some people already say I wouldn't have that fear if the Russians hadn't manipulated[21] my brain. I think that's silly right now. Considering all the other people I know are manipulating my brain, I don't see how the Russians could get a crack[22] at it. But you never know. Someday I might have to learn that I wasn't really afraid of nuclear war at all, but only under the sway[23] of Moscow Svengalis[24].

It wouldn't surprise me. Live long enough and you'll eventually be wrong about everything.

[8]**hoisted up:** raised
[9]**duty:** responsibility
[10]**staggered:** walked unsteadily
[11]**fragments:** pieces; parts
[12]**browbeaten:** intimidated by a threatening look
[13]**cactus:** a desert plant
[14]**stamina:** endurance; strength
[15]**heave:** throw
[16]**feeble:** weak
[17]**junked:** thrown in the garbage
[18]**whippersnapper:** young, impertinent person
[19]**dosed:** medicated
[20]**jolly:** happy
[21]**manipulated:** controlled; played with
[22]**crack:** chance
[23]**sway:** influence
[24]**Svengali:** a person who has a strong power or influence over other people

QUESTIONS

1. What is meant by the title "Back to the Dump"? What main point is the author, Russell Baker, trying to make here?
2. What different examples or illustrations does he use to support his point of view?
3. What certainties does the author still hold today? Do you think he really expects his present beliefs to be proven wrong? What reason do you think he has for using these examples?
4. What beliefs or ideas did you once have that you were forced to revise because you later learned they were false?

APPENDIX

References and Recommended Readings

The books listed here were of great assistance to us in the writing of the articles that appeared in this text. If you wish to explore these topics further, we recommend these works as a starting point.

CHAPTERS 1 AND 2

The Feminine Mystique, BETTY FRIEDAN (Dell Publishing Company, 1977).

Megatrends: Ten New Directions That Are Transforming Our Lives, JOHN NAISBITT (Warner Books, 1982).

Sisterhood Is Powerful: An Anthology of Writings from the Women's Liberation Movement, edited by ROBIN MORGAN (Random House, 1970).

The Sisterhood of Man, KATHLEEN NEWLAND (Worldwatch Institute, 1979).

CHAPTER 3

Body Language, JULIUS FAST (Pocket Books, 1971).

The Silent Language, EDWARD T. HALL (Doubleday, 1980).

CHAPTERS 4 AND 5

I Have a Dream, by the editors of Time/Life Books (Time/Life Books, 1968).

Black Boy, RICHARD WRIGHT (Harper and Row, 1945).

Black Like Me, JOHN HOWARD GRIFFIN (Signet Books).

Meet Mr. Martin Luther King, Jr., JAMES T. KAY (Random House, 1969).

Roots, ALEX HALEY (Dell, 1977).

Stride Toward Freedom: The Montgomery Story, MARTIN LUTHER KING, JR. (Harper and Row, 1958).

Why We Can't Wait, MARTIN LUTHER KING, JR. (Signet Books, 1964).

Let the Trumpet Sound, STEPHEN P. OATES (Harper and Row, 1982).

CHAPTER 6

Anne Sullivan Macy, NELLA BRADDY (Doubleday, Duran and Company, 1940).

Helen and Teacher: The Story of Helen Keller and Anne Sullivan Macy, JOSEPH P. LASH (Delacorte Press/Seymour Lawrence, 1980).

The Story of My Life, HELEN KELLER (Airmont Publishing Company, 1965).

CHAPTER 7

Aerobics, KENNETH H. COOPER (M. Evans & Company, 1968).

Aerobics for Women, MILDRED COOPER and KENNETH H. COOPER (M. Evans & Company, 1972).

The Aerobic Way, KENNETH H. COOPER (Bantam Books, 1978).

The New Aerobics, KENNETH H. COOPER (M. Evans & Company, 1970).

The Complete Book of Running, JAMES F. FIXX (Random House, 1977).

CHAPTER 8

Passages, GAIL SHEEHY (Dutton, 1974, 1976).

Pathfinders, GAIL SHEEHY (William Morrow & Company, 1981).

The Seasons of a Man's Life, DANIEL J. LEVINSON (Ballantine Books, 1978).

CHAPTER 9

Adventures in Immortality, GEORGE GALLUP, SR. (McGraw-Hill, 1982).

Journeys Out of the Body, ROBERT A. MONROE (Doubleday, 1971).

Life After Life, RAYMOND A. MOODY, JR. (Bantam Books, 1975).

CHAPTERS 10 AND 11

Encounters with the Future: A Forecast of Life into the 21st Century, MARVIN CETRON and THOMAS O'TOOLE (McGraw-Hill, 1982).

Future Shock, ALVIN TOFFLER (Random House, 1970).

Megatrends: Ten New Directions That Are Transforming Our Lives, JOHN NAISBITT (Warner Books, 1982).

Omni Future Almanac, edited by ROBERT WEIL (World Almanac Publications, 1983).

The Third Wave, ALVIN TOFFLER (William Morrow, 1980).

2081: A Hopeful View of the Human Future, GERARD K. O'NEILL (Simon & Schuster/Touchstone, 1981).

Disbelief and Misadventure Explained

In the story *Getting the Point* the security guard was asked if he knew where the bathroom is. The guard responded by pursing his lips (putting his lips together and moving them in an outward direction). For some Hispanics, particularly Puerto Ricans and Dominicans, the lips are often used in this way to indicate a particular direction. For North Americans, however, a similar movement of the lips means that a person is thinking seriously about something. Jim, the North American, thought the guard was thinking about where the bathroom was. To Jim, that seemed ridiculous; Jim thought the guard should know where the bathroom was since the guard worked in the building. The guard, however, thought that he had clearly indicated the direction of the bathroom by using his lips. That's why he thought Jim was "up to no good" when Jim just stood there. Of course, Jim stood there because he was waiting for a clearer response to his question, and that's why he walked away thinking that the guard was not a very helpful person.

In the story *An American in Paris* Nancy was in Paris for the first time, obviously unfamiliar with the local customs. In France, as in many other countries, women often hold hands or link arms while walking together in the streets. Mothers and daughters or two female friends will frequently express their affection and friendship in public in this way. In the United States, on the other hand, people generally engage in such close physical contact only if they have an intimate or sexual relationship with each other. Upon seeing two women touching each other in public, Nancy assumed that they were lovers. Being from a small town, Nancy was shocked and surprised. She thought these Frenchwomen were homosexual, when in fact they were simply women walking together in a friendly way that had nothing to do with homosexual behavior.

In the story *The Shadow of Your Smile* Mr. Simon, the teacher, wanted to speak with Wei Hsiao, a student, because of Wei Hsiao's poor work in class. When Mr. Simon, unhappy with his student's work, spoke to Wei Hsiao, Wei Hsiao smiled at him. For a North American, a smile is usually a sign that you're happy or pleased about something. As Mr. Simon continued to talk, Wei Hsiao continued to smile. Mr. Simon thought that by smiling, Wei Hsiao was not taking him seriously. As a result, Mr. Simon lost his patience, got angry, and finally left the room. To many Asians, however, a smile can also be an expression of embarrassment. By smiling, Wei Hsiao was showing Mr. Simon that he was embarrassed and truly sorry for his bad work in class. That's why, as Mr. Simon got angrier and his voice rose, Wei Hsiao continued smiling, even after the teacher had left the classroom.

Answers to Vocabulary Development Puzzles

Chapter	
3	Communication is a lot more fun when you use your body.
5	I have a dream that the brotherhood of man will become a reality in this day.—DR. MARTIN LUTHER KING, JR.
9	The most beautiful thing we can experience is the mysterious. It is the source of all true art and science.—ALBERT EINSTEIN
10	Those who cannot remember the past are condemned to repeat it.—GEORGE SANTAYANA
11	We should all be concerned about the future because we will have to spend the rest of our lives there.—CHARLES FRANKLIN KETTERING

Review of Prefixes

Prefix	Meaning	Examples
un	not	unstable, unusual, unprepared
il	not	illegal, illiterate, illogical
ir	not	irresponsible, irregular, irrational
in	not	insecure, inequality, ineffective
im	not	improper, imperfect, imbalance
non	not	nonviolent, noncompulsory, nonprofit
dis	not	dislike, disagree, disadvantage
mis	wrong	misconduct, misuse, misunderstand
re	again	reelect, rediscover, reinvent
pre	before	prehistoric, preview, prerecorded
en	give, make	endanger, encourage, entitle, enact
en	in, inside	enclose, engrave, entrance
in	in, inside	internal, insert, invest
anti	against, opposite	antiwar, antigovernment, antilabor
contra	against, opposite	contradict, contraception
inter	between	interstate, international, interrupt
multi	many	multi-national, multiply, multitude
ex	out, outside	exclude, extract, exit
extra	out, outside	extraordinary, extraterrestrial
co	together with	co-worker, cooperate, co-author
col	together with	collaborator, colleague
com	together with	community, complement, composition
con	together with	concur, conspire, connection

Review of Suffixes

Suffixes that Form Nouns		Examples
from verbs:	ion	expression, protection, education
	sion	decision, division, conclusion
	ation	information, expectation, exploitation
	ment	fulfillment, government, improvement
	al	removal, survival, arrival
	ance	performance, acceptance, resistance
	ence	difference, existence, preference
	ing	suffering, understanding, meeting
	y	discovery, delivery, mastery
	er	leader, speaker, worker
	or	translator, governor, operator
	ure	failure, exposure, pressure
from adjectives:	ity	inferiority, humanity, equality
	th	warmth, strength, width
	ness	happiness, weakness, awareness
others:	ist	activist, terrorist, feminist
	ism	activism, terrorism, feminism

Suffixes that Form Verbs		
from nouns or adjectives:	ate	validate, originate, activate
	ify	glorify, clarify, solidify
	ize	terrorize, memorize, humanize
	en	shorten, darken, threaten

Suffixes that Form Adjectives		
from nouns:	ly	friendly, orderly, manly
	ful	powerful, skillful, helpful
	less	powerless, homeless, defenseless
	al	natural, agricultural, traditional
	y	healthy, dirty, wealthy
	ous	dangerous, cancerous, courageous
	ic	historic, artistic, athletic
	like	ladylike, warlike, childlike
from verbs:	ed	stimulated, challenged, excited
	ing	stimulating, challenging, exciting
	ive	protective, supportive, cooperative
	able	imaginable, understandable, bearable
	ant	ignorant, hesitant
	ent	insistent, dependent, different

Suffixes that Form Adverbs		
from adjectives:	ly	protectively, understandably, naturally